EXAMINING RELIGIONS

Christianity

Joe Jenkins

Heinemann

Heinemann Educational Publishers
Halley Court, Jordan Hill, Oxford OX2 8EJ
A Division of Reed Educational & Professional Publishing Ltd

OXFORD MELBOURNE AUCKLAND
JOHANNESBURG BLANTYRE GABORONE
IBADAN PORTSMOUTH (NH) USA CHICAGO

© Joe Jenkins 1989, 1995

First published 1989

Revised edition published 1995

02 01 00
10 9 8 7

British Library Cataloguing in Publication Data
A catalogue record for this book is available from the British
Library

ISBN 0 435 30320 1
Designed and typeset by Gecko Ltd, Bicester, Oxon
Illustrated by Barry Rowe and Gill Bishop
Printed and bound in Spain by Mateu Cromo

Acknowledgements

This book is written in memory of my father.

The author would like to thank the following individuals and
organizations for their help, guidance and inspiration in the
writing of this book. Mary Brown; Alistair Christie; Dr W. Owen
Cole; Samuel Copley; William Dalrymphle; Ray Davey and all
working for peace in Northern Ireland; Liz Eddington; Father
Michael Evans; Professor John Ferguson; Matthew Fox; Kate
Furphy; Georgie for keeping me moving; Anna Grear; my Mum
and brother Jim; Father McGhee of St Joseph's Church, Colwyn
Bay; Jennifer Johnson; Reverend Richard Kirker; Barry Miles;
Aileen Milne; Reverend John Huntington of the United Reformed
Church; Dr Melissa Raphael; Reverend Richard Roberts of the
Church of Wales; David Skidmore of the Church of England; The
Keepers of Trillo's Chapel, Llandrillo-yn-Rhos; Mags Robertson;
Dr Peter Toon; Archbishop Desmond Tutu; Sue Vickerman; Sue
Walton; and all Religious Studies teachers everywhere.

The publishers would like to thank the following for permission to
reproduce copyright material.
Amnesty International for the extracts on pp. 133 and 147,
reproduced by permission of Amnesty International British
Section, 99 Rosebery Avenue, London EC1R 4RE; the Baptist
Church for the statement on p. 149; CARE (Christian Action
Research and Education) for the quotation by Anna Grear on
p. 137; Cassell plc for the extracts from *The Catechism of the Catholic
Church*, 1994, published by Geoffrey Chapman, on pp. 48, 139; the
Catholic Media Office for the extract from *All People Together* on
p. 140; the Central Board of Finance of the Church of England for
the extract from *The Alternative Service Book* on p. 91, for the extract
from an unpublished paper by the Board for Social Responsibility,
quoted in *Abortion and the Church*, Church House Publishing, 1993,
on p. 142, and for the extracts from *Human Fertilization and
Embryology*, 1984, by the Board for Social Responsibility on p. 145
(pupils should not write to Board for Social Responsibility for
further information, additional material from the BSR is available
to *teaching staff only*); the Christian Education Movement for the
extract from *The Ecumenical Movement* by Dr Lorna Brockett on
p. 47; Darton Longman and Todd for the extract from *The Capacity
to Love*, by Jack Dominian on p. 121; the Estate of Martin Luther

King, Jr., for the quotations on pp. 5, 32, 35, 38; Faber and Faber
for the extract from *The Last Temptation*, 1975, by Nikos
Kazantzakis, reproduced by permission of the publishers, on
p. 27; Matthew Fox for the extracts from *The Coming of the Cosmic
Christ*, published by HarperCollins Inc., San Francisco, 1988, and
Original Blessing, published by Bear & Company, Santa Fe, on
pp. 5, 101, 106, 154; HarperCollins Publishers Ltd for the extract
from *Christianity and the World Religions*, 1987, by Hans Küng on
p. 47, for the quotation by Bishop Simon Barrington-Ward, taken
from *Anglican Worship Today*, 1980, on p. 77, for the quotation by
Archbishop Desmond Tutu, taken from *Hope and Suffering*, 1983,
on p. 78, and for the extracts from the *Revised Standard Version* of
the Bible used throughout the book; Longman Group Ltd for the
extracts from the *Longman Dictionary of Contemporary English* on
pp. 53, 74 and 136; Macmillan Publishing Ltd for the extract from
If the War Goes On by Herman Hesse on p. 67; the Methodist
Conference for the quotations on pp. 115, 129, 139, 154, used by
permission of the Methodist Publishing House; Henri Nouwen
for the quotation on p. 107; Orion Publishing Group for the
extract from *The Gnostic Gospels* by Elaine Pagels, reproduced by
permission of the publishers, Weidenfeld and Nicolson, on p. 43;
© Oxford University Press and Cambridge University Press for
extracts from the *New English Bible* used throughout the book;
Penguin Books Ltd for the extracts from *Belonging to the Universe*
by Fritjof Capra on pp. 41, 153; Dr Melissa Raphael, Religious
Studies Department, Cheltenham and Gloucester College of
Higher Education, for the quotation on pp. 70–1; Resurgence for
the quotation by Brother David on p. 75, first published in
Resurgence magazine; Routledge for the extract from *Waiting for
God* by Simone Weil translated by Emma Cranford on p. 30 and
the extract from *A New Model of the Universe* by Peter Ouspensky
on p. 83; the Salvation Army for the quotation on p. 130; Father
Gregory Wirdnam for the quotation on pp. 50–1; John Wood for
the extract on p. 112; the World Council of Churches for the
extracts from *One World* magazine on pp. 56, 57; the Yearly
Meeting of the Religious Society of Friends in Britain (Quakers)
for the quotation by Meg Maslin, © 1995, from *Quaker Faith and
Practice*, on p. 135 and for the quotation by Pat Saunders, © 1960,
from *Christian Faith and Practice*, on p. 155.

The publishers would like to thank the following for permission to
reproduce photographs.
Art Gallery of Western Australia, Perth/Bridgeman Art Library p. 96;
Val Baker/Andes Press Agency p. 72; Bridgeman Art Library pp. 16,
18, 23, 25, 26, 28, 39, 71, 82, 100, 109; British Museum/Bridgeman Art
Library p. 13; Camera Press p. 35 (right); J. Allan Cash p. 58; Werner
Dieterich/Image Bank p. 22; S. K. Dutt/Camera Press p. 35 (left);
Glasgow Museums p. 99; Robin Hanbury-Tenison/Survival
International p. 128; David Hoffman p. 134; Hutchison Library pp.
11, 57, 80 (left), 83 (Tony Souter), 110 (Patricia Goycoolea); Keble
College, Oxford/Bridgeman Art Library p. 6; Keith Ellis Collection
pp. 54, 84, 98; Lightmotif-Paoluzzo p. 66; Murdo MacLeod p. 126;
Danny McKenzie at New Generation Art p. 7; Magnum Photos pp.
68 (S. Meiselas), 90 (Henri Cartier-Bresson), 146, 150 (H. Gruyaert),
154 (Sebastiao Salgado); Museum of Modern Art, New
York/Bridgeman Art Library p. 32; National Gallery p. 74; Network
pp. 60 (Paul Lowe), 64 (Tony Pupkewitz/Rapho), 78 (Mike
Goldwater), 149 (Jenny Matthews); Bury Peerless p. 104; Popperfoto
pp. 35 (centre), 62; Carlos Reyes/Andes Press Agency pp. 103, 106;
Carlos Reyes-Manzo/Andes Press Agency pp. 65, 80 (right), 108, 113;
Science Photo Library pp. 5 (Tony Hallas), 143 (Hank Morgan); Tate
Gallery p. 30 (John Webb); The de Morgan Foundation/Bridgemann
Art Library p. 122; The Society of Friends p. 86; Mark
Wadlow/Russia & Republics Photo Library p. 50.

Cover photograph by: Carlos Reyes/Andes Press Agency (top right
and bottom right); Hutchison Library (left).

The publishers have made every effort to trace copyright holders.
However, if any material has been incorrectly acknowledged, we
would be pleased to correct this at the earliest opportunity.

CONTENTS

We live in an unimaginably huge universe. I find myself in this place at this particular time. How did the earth and the universe come into being? Who am I? What is my life all about? Why am I here? Where am I going? Is there any purpose or meaning to life?

Human beings have always asked questions about the universe, about the world and about themselves. Throughout human history there have appeared great teachers who have helped people to try to answer these and other questions about life. These teachers have included Abraham, Moses, Confucius, Lao-Tzu, the Buddha, Jesus Christ, Muhammad, Guru Nanak and many others. From theirs and other teachings, the great religions of the world have developed – Judaism, Confucianism, Taoism, Buddhism, Christianity, Islam, Sikhism and Hinduism. These teachings and religions have inspired countless people to find meaning and purpose in their lives and continue to do so today.

From the dawn of human history women and men have felt that the world that we see, hear, taste, touch and experience is not the only reality. People have believed, and continue to believe, that as well as the visible world – the physical, external world – there is a deeper, hidden world that we can't see. This is the internal invisible world – the spiritual world.

THE SEARCH

The modern Western world has often been called 'secular'. This basically means that this part of the world is no longer 'religious'. However, on a deeper level, because we are human we still ask basic questions about our existence. We are all still searching for meaning in our lives. Whatever happens to the outer (external) world we still feel a deep need to explore and understand our inner (internal) world. The questions that religions ask, and the answers they try to give, help people to explore and understand the external and internal worlds.

THIS BOOK

This book has been written to help you understand the Christian religion. Every part of the world has been influenced by various religions and spiritual beliefs. In certain parts of the world, including our own, Christianity has had and continues to have a major influence on the way we think, on our history and on our culture.

This book does not suggest in any way that Christianity is the only religion that matters. Of course, for millions of people both here and abroad, some of the other great religions are of profound importance.

In the past, Christianity was influenced by the religion of Judaism. At present, for example in Africa, it is influenced by African tribal religions. In Britain today there are many people who follow other religions, helping to create what is known as a 'multi-faith' society. This results in a rich and diverse society, with a variety of music, literature, food, dress, beliefs, customs and so on.

Often, when people don't understand something they tend to 'stereotype' it. This means they fix an idea of something or someone into a mould which they are not prepared to change. They then insist that this mould is the only possible one. People often stereotype religions as well as stereotyping the followers of religions.

This book aims to begin to break down some of these stereotypes. Stereotyping can lead to dangerous prejudices. It is usually the result of ignorance. If we don't know about something, we tend to stereotype it, and then pretend that we do know. However, each human life is too precious, too mysterious and too important to be stereotyped, and the same is also true of religions.

Because religions are concerned with the external and internal aspects of life, they tend to raise many questions about our own existence. This book aims to make you think for yourself about your own life and your relationship to the world. It aims to make you ask some questions about life. The book does not intend to force any particular beliefs or views on you. It is designed to help you to understand Christian beliefs about life and how these beliefs affect people's lives, and also to help you to think for yourself.

REFLECTIONS

'When I see the glories of the cosmos I can't help but believe that there is a Divine Hand behind it all.'

(Albert Einstein, 1879–1955 – scientist)

'Nature is the art of God.'

(Teilhard de Chardin, 1881–1955 – scientist and priest)

Something should remind us once more that the great things in his universe are things that we never see. You walk out at night and look up at the beautiful stars as they bedeck the heavens like swinging lanterns of eternity, and you think you can see all. Oh, no. You can never see the law of gravitation that holds them there.'

(Dr Martin Luther King, 1929–69)

KEY QUESTIONS

Do you ever feel that there is 'something more to life'? Does the world ever seem so beautiful that you feel there is 'something more to life'? Are there times when you are so full of joy and happiness that you feel there is 'something more to life'? Are there times when you have felt such pain and unhappiness that this has taken you deep within yourself and you have begun to feel that there is 'something more to life'? Or has this pain made you think that life is meaningless? Are there times, when you hear a piece of music or see a painting or photograph, that you feel deeply moved and can't explain in words what you feel? Are there times when you suddenly become aware of the miracle and beauty of nature and feel that there must be some sort of meaning and purpose in life?

THINKING POINTS

- *'It is then the greatest of all lessons to know oneself. For if one knows himself he will know God, and knowing God, he will be made like God.'*

  (Clement of Alexandria, c.150–215 – early Christian)

- *'Though we are God's sons and daughters, we do not realize it yet.'*

  (Meister Eckhart c.1260–1328 – monk and mystic)

- *'I may have in myself the secret and meaning of the earth, the golden sun, the light, the foam-flecked sea.'*

  (Richard Jefferies 1848–87 – Wiltshire writer)

- *'The universe loves us every day the sun rises, and the creator loves us through creation.'*

  (Matthew Fox – priest, theologian and educator)

FOR DISCUSSION

▶ After reading this unit discuss in groups of three or four some of the main ideas that have arisen.

2 JESUS

INTRODUCTION

This section looks at Jesus whose life inspired the Christian religion. We can give only the briefest sketches here and you should read one of the first four books in the New Testament (the **Gospels** of Matthew, Mark, Luke and John) to get an overall picture of his life.

JESUS CHRIST

'Jesus Christ' was not Jesus' proper name. **Christ** was a title, the Greek word for **Messiah** (the anointed one or chosen one). 'Jesus Christ' means 'Jesus the Messiah'. Jesus' real name would have been something like Jesus Bar Joseph (Jesus, son of Joseph). Jesus meant 'God is saviour'.

Background

Jesus was born in Bethlehem in Judea in about 4 BCE. According to the Gospels of Matthew and Luke, Jesus was born to a virgin, named Mary (see unit 12). He was brought up in Galilee in the north. He was a Jew by birth and by religion. During his lifetime, the Jewish people were ruled over by the Romans. The atmosphere in this part of the world was tense and electric. The Jewish people longed for the coming of the Messiah, a messenger from God who would bring with him an era of peace. There were many ideas about the Messiah, but most people hoped he would be a king-like figure who would defeat the Romans. Others believed that his coming would bring with it a final battle that would shake the earth, and that God would re-create everything. Some other Jews, known as the **zealots** were freedom-fighters actively involved in terrorist activities against the Romans. Others, known as the **Essenes**, withdrew to the desert to pray, study and wait for the coming of the Messiah. There were many holy men too, baptizing people in preparation for the coming of the Messiah.

His Ministry

One such holy man, called John the Baptist, baptized Jesus in the River Jordan. The four Gospels all mention a religious experience that Jesus had at this time:

'As soon as Jesus came up out of the water, he saw heaven opening and the Spirit coming down on him like a dove. And a voice came from heaven, "You are my own dear Son. I am pleased with you".'

(Mark 1:10–11)

After this, his preaching ministry began. The Gospels present many stories and sayings about Jesus' ministry. He collected twelve **disciples** (followers of a teacher) around him. News soon spread about his remarkable work. As well as teaching, Jesus healed the sick, performed miracles, raised the dead and cured the mentally ill (exorcisms). However, he was not the sort of Messia the Jews had expected. He was a man of peace and not a mighty warrior. He spoke out against injustice and he taught a message of love, forgiveness and peace, encouraging people to look inside themselve at their own motivation. He attracted huge crowds but his teachings and lifestyle did not always please the authorities. He kept company with people who were regarded as being social outcasts.

Finally, Jesus was arrested, tried and brutally executed in Jerusalem. However, this was not the en

An artist's impression of Jesus 'The Light of the World'

of the story. All the Gospels report that after three days, Jesus miraculously and mysteriously rose from the dead (the **resurrection** – see units 5, 7 and 49). The followers of Jesus saw him after he'd risen from the dead and they also witnessed his **ascension**, when he went up into heaven (see unit 51).

DID JESUS EXIST?

As with any historical person, there is evidence to show that Jesus did exist. Tacitus, a Roman historian who lived at the end of the first century CE, mentions the early Christians (followers of Jesus Christ) and Josephus, a Jewish historian who also lived in the first century CE, wrote about Jesus. Pliny and Suetonius, both Roman writers, referred to Jesus early in the second century CE. The Talmud, a collection of sayings by Jewish rabbis, also mentions him.

Most Christians believe that the Gospels present a rounded picture of the life, death and teachings of Jesus. However, there has been much debate as to how reliable these accounts are. Some scholars have argued that some of the material in the Gospels reflects the views of the early **Church** and not necessarily those of Jesus. What is certain though is that the Gospels were written approximately 30 to 80 years after his death, which suggests that much of what is in them is accurate.

BASIC CHRISTIAN IDEAS ABOUT JESUS

Generally, all Christians believe that Jesus actually existed and lived an earthly life as depicted in the Gospels. They also believe that:

- Jesus was a great teacher, who by his example, and through his words and deeds, has shown them a way of life and a set of values. He taught that a person must be *pure in heart* and it is not enough just to *pretend* to be a good person.
- Jesus revealed through his life, death and resurrection the supreme loving power of God.

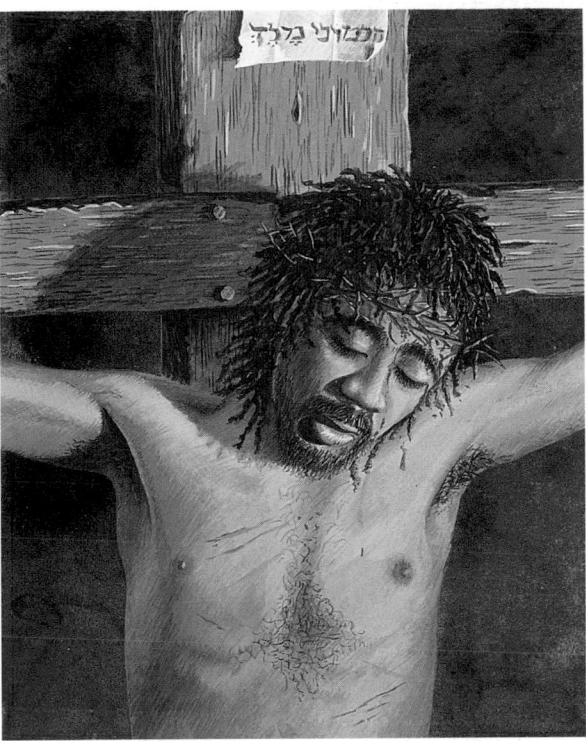

An artist's impression of Jesus on the cross

Christians believe that '*In the beginning was the Word, and the Word was with God, and the Word was God*' (John 1:1) and that '*... the Word was made flesh, and dwelt among us*' (John 1:14). The 'Word' refers to the Divine Creative Presence that existed in the beginning and is identified with the man Jesus.

- Jesus' words and deeds are still as alive today as they were 2000 years ago. Indeed, many Christians feel that Jesus is *alive now* as an actual living presence in their lives.
- Jesus' **incarnation** was the act by which God became a human person, in Jesus Christ (see unit 7). For Christians the incarnation was not only an act of love, but an act of **salvation**. They believe that Jesus Christ, by uniting humanity and God in his own person, re-opened for humanity, the possibility of returning to God. In his own person, Jesus Christ showed what the true 'likeness of God' is.

THINGS TO DO

▶ Read one of the Gospels. After you've finished write down some thoughts you have about the man called Jesus the Christ. Compare your notes with those of another member of your class.

FOR YOUR FOLDERS

▶ Explain in your own words some Christian ideas about Jesus.

3 THE BIBLE

INTRODUCTION

The **Bible** is the holy book of Christians. It is also known as **scripture** or the scriptures. For Christians the Bible is a guide to their worship, beliefs, practices and values. The word Bible comes from a Greek word *biblia*, which means 'the books'. The Bible is not really one book; it is more like a library. It is the world's most translated book. John Wycliffe (1329–84) translated the Bible into English in the fourteenth century. The first approved translation was the 'Great Bible' in 1539. Before this, Bibles were in Latin in Britain. There are modern translations too, including the *New English Bible*, *Good News Bible*, *Revised Standard Version* and the *Jerusalem Bible*. They all try to use modern English so that it is easier to understand. Some of these different translations are used throughout this book.

Christians have often disagreed about how many books there are in the Bible. All accept the 39 books of the Jewish Scriptures (mostly written in Hebrew, with a few sections in Aramaic). These scriptures are known to Christians as the Old Testament (written between the 12th and the 2nd centuries BCE). When the scriptures were translated into Greek, about 250 BCE, other books known as the **Apocrypha** (a Greek word meaning 'hidden things') were introduced. This version, known as the **Septuagint**, was inherited by the Christian Church (the Christian Community). During the Reformation (see unit 21) some Christians rejected the Apocrypha, while other churches kept it. Another 27 books were added by Christians. These were written about Jesus and became known as the New Testament. So the Christian Bible is a library consisting of either 66 books, or if the thirteen books of the Apocrypha are added, 79 books.

The two parts of the Bible are called **testaments** (special agreements), because both Jews and Christians believe that God has made a special agreement with humankind, also known as a **covenant**. In the Old Testament God promises to guide the Jews and reveal his laws to them. In the New Testament, Christians believe that God has shown his love for the world by sending them a Messenger – his only Son, Jesus Christ.

The word **canon** is used to describe a collection of books which have the authority of a religious community. 'Canon' is a Greek word which meant 'a measuring rod', and it came to mean a list of books accepted as genuine. The canon of the Bible means the correct list of books that are in it.

THE OLD TESTAMENT – THE JEWISH SCRIPTURES

The part of the Jewish Scriptures which Christians call the Old Testament is very important to both Jews and Christians. The New Testament writers often used the Old Testament writings to show that the history of the people in the Old Testament was a preparation for the coming of Jesus. From the Christian point of view, the Jewish Scriptures prophesy (foretell) the coming of Jesus, the Messiah. Most English versions have 39 separate books including five law books, twelve history books, five poetry books and seventeen prophetic books containing symbolic writings.

THE NEW TESTAMENT

The New Testament contains 27 different books. There are five 'history' books (though these contain teachings as well as history), 21 letters of the early Christians and one prophetic book, called the *Book of Revelation*.

Four of the 'history' books are the Gospels (a word meaning 'Good News'). These tell the story of the teaching of Jesus. They are called *Matthew*, *Mark*, *Luke* and *John*, named after the people thought to have written them. The first three are similar in style and use material that is common to all three. Because of this they are often called the *Synoptic Gospels*. There has been much debate about when they were written, but most 'scholars' (experts) today agree that they were written between 60 and 110 CE, with Mark's Gospel being written first. The Gospels spend little time describing the childhood of Jesus and are mainly concerned with the last few years of his life when he became a public teacher. They concentrate particularly on the last week of his life – **Holy Week** (see unit 48). Each Gospel has its own special message. While there are some differences in style and content, most Christians accept them all as contributing to a greater understanding of the meaning of Jesus' life.

The fifth 'history' book, The *Acts of the Apostles* (**apostle** means 'follower' or 'one who is sent') is about the birth of the Church (see unit 51). This book concentrates mainly on the lives of Peter, one of Jesus' disciples, and Paul, an early Christian who wrote about the emerging Church.

The 21 letters or **epistles** (meaning letters) were written by the early Christian leaders. They were written to the Churches giving advice, guidance and encouragement. They help Christians today understand the beliefs and concerns of the early Church.

The prophetic book is called the *Book of Revelation* (sometimes called the *Apocalypse*). It was written towards the end of the first century CE and is full of visions, symbols and strange events. Its theme is that good will eventually win over evil, and that Christ will return to earth in victory. It is written in a powerfully poetic style. Different Christians interpret it in different ways. Some see it as being poetry with symbolic meaning whilst others take it literally.

THE BIBLE IN CHRISTIAN LIFE AND WORSHIP

The Bible is used in many different ways by Christians. To a Christian the Bible is no ordinary book – it is sacred, holy and inspired.

'All Scripture is inspired by God, and is useful for teaching the truth, rebuking the error, correcting faults, and giving instruction for right living.' (2 Timothy 3:16, *Revised Standard Version*)

Christians believe that the Bible is in some way the Word of God, which can teach, inspire and guide them in their everyday lives.

In Christian worship, lessons from the Bible are read, and the **congregation** (those who are present; the audience) listens. The Bible is read every Sunday in every Christian place of worship throughout the world. Usually the congregation will hear two short readings during the service, one from the Old Testament and one from the New Testament. Many churches use a lectionary, which is a set of readings operating over the whole year. Each Sunday different passages are selected for reading. This ensures that people who go to church will be able to have a wide selection of readings. In churches, the Bible is usually kept on a **lectern**, which is a stand, often in the shape of an eagle. During most services the leader of the Church will give a **sermon** (a talk or message), quoting from the Bible but explaining what the reading might mean. The Bible may also be studied in small groups, which meet in church or someone's home. The minister, or a member of the congregation, will read out some passages and the people will think about the words, meditate on them or discuss the meaning. Bible studies may be applied to the problems of everyday living. These may be personal problems or social problems like racism or war. By doing this, Christians try to come to a deeper understanding of their faith and the way it can be applied to their lives and to the modern world. To Christians, therefore, the Bible contains guidelines and teachings that are *relevant* to modern life.

The Bible is also used for personal study. Some Christians may set aside a few minutes every day for prayer and study (see units 52 and 53). They may open the Bible at random, or study a particular section, or use the Bible reading notes written by Christian leaders, which will guide them through passages.

Some Christians might use collections of various prayers, Psalms and readings, called the **daily offices** of morning and evening prayer (see units 37 and 42). A particular passage may be read through slowly, several times, so that its meaning can be understood. After doing this for a period of time, they will try to think about the deeper meaning of the words and then perhaps say a prayer. This is an example of the use of the Bible in meditation.

4 THINKING ABOUT THE BIBLE

This unit looks at some key questions about the authority, inspiration and interpretation of the Bible, and what these mean for Christians.

Key question 1: *How can Christians believe in a collection of books as old as the Bible?*
Often people ask: 'Is the Bible reliable? How do we know that it has not just been made up?' There are a number of ways in which most Christians would try to answer these sorts of questions.

First, all the world religions have their own sacred scriptures. These scriptures have appeared at various stages of history and in different parts of the world. Although they've appeared at different times and at different places, they have remarkable similarities. They all teach that the world and the universe were created, that the universe is not meaningless and that it has a purpose. They also teach that human beings too have a purpose. We all have a divine spark within us and our individual purpose is part of a cosmic purpose. This purpose is explained in the Bible and in all sacred literature.

Secondly, research by modern historians, archaeologists and scientists, who have studied the texts of the Bible and the period of history in which the books were written, show that they are historical documents. The places and dates mentioned in the Bible actually agree with other historical evidence. For example, non-Christian historians of the time of Jesus, such as Tacitus, a Roman historian and Josephus, a Jewish historian, both refer to Jesus. The Bible is one of the world's oldest collection of books. We don't question other historical documents, so Christians believe that we should not dismiss the Bible either.

Thirdly, many of the writings in the Bible have for 2000 years, influenced the world. These teachings are full of wisdom and have been, and still are, *true in themselves*. Without them the history of the world would probably have been even bloodier and more cruel than it has been. It's no good saying, 'I don't believe in the Bible,' because its teachings about how human beings should treat each other and the world around them, are as true today as they've always been.

Key question 2: *What does it mean to say the Bible is the inspired word of God?*
Although Christians will use other books in their worship and their faith, the Bible has special authority for them. They believe the Bible consists of God's revelation – the truths and purposes God has revealed for humankind through the written word. It is the inspired word of God. However, the expression, 'inspired word of God' means different things to different Christians. Because of this, different Christians interpret the Bible in different ways.

The fundamentalist view

Some Christians think that the Bible is the *direct word of God*, passed down through the writers. They believe the Bible is free from all error because it contains not the words of human beings, but the Word of God. Everything in the Bible is true and the Bible is the actual Word of God, literally word for word.

The conservative view

Some Christians think that the Word of God came to the writers directly from God, but that the writers' own personalities and writing styles were included. The Bible is therefore *the Word of God, interpreted by the human mind.*

The liberal view

Some Christians think that the Bible writers were inspired to write. However, the writers, being human, were capable of making mistakes. Also they were influenced by the ideas and world views of their own time. They had insight into human life that others did not have and they were able to put this into words. The Bible therefore *contains within it the word of God, but it is not directly the Word itself.*

The psychological view

Some Christians think that, like all sacred literature, the Bible contains an outer and an inner meaning. It contains a higher meaning than just the literal words, and aims to make a person think for themselves and lift their understanding about their purpose on earth. The Bible comes from the higher mind. It contains great knowledge about what it means to be human. It can be read literally, but *on a deeper level, it can also speak to each reader about what we are, and what we possibly can become.*

Christians, therefore, do not all agree on how the Bible can be interpreted. These different viewpoints will obviously affect their beliefs about their religion and the purpose of human life. For instance, fundamentalists who think the Bible is to be read literally will believe that God made the world in six days and therefore reject theories about the evolution of life. Conservatives will see the six-day creation story as a poem, which explains why the world was created, but not how. Liberals and those who hold a psychological view see the story as

So, if and when Christians need an answer to a particular question, they will look to one, two or perhaps all three of these sources. For example, many Roman Catholic Christians (see unit 23) believe that the Church has the right to decide the correct interpretation of the Bible. For them, the authority of the Church may be stressed more than the authority of the Bible. For some Protestant Christians (see unit 26), on the other hand, final authority comes from the Bible rather than the Church.

Christians believe that the Bible is relevant today

having great symbolic meanings which explain, at a deeper level, the mysterious workings of creation (see unit 5).

Key question 3: *How can a book that was written so long ago have any meaning for people today?*
Today there are many issues and problems in the world that are modern ones. For instance, the writers of the Bible knew nothing about nuclear weapons, surrogate motherhood, pollution, test-tube babies, etc. (See Part 5 of this book for an explanation of these issues.) Very generally, Christians would say that the *essential teachings* of the Bible are relevant to people today. Human nature does not change. The teachings in the Bible are eternal. These teachings about love, mercy, forgiveness, justice, etc. are just as relevant today as they were 2000 years ago.

Key question 4: *How much authority does the Bible have among Christians?*
Generally, Christians believe that final authority for their beliefs and practices comes from three sources:

- the Bible
  the Church
  individual conscience.

5 CENTRAL CHRISTIAN BELIEFS

THE APOSTLES' CREED

'I believe in God
the Father Almighty,
Maker of Heaven and earth,
And in Jesus Christ
His only Son our Lord,
who was conceived by the Holy Ghost,
Born of the Virgin Mary,
Suffered under Pontius Pilate,
Was crucified, dead and buried;
He descended into hell:
The third day he rose again from the dead;
He ascended into heaven,
And sitteth on the right hand of God the Father
Almighty,
From thence he shall come to judge the quick and
the dead.
I believe in the Holy Ghost;
The Holy Catholic Church;
The Communion of Saints;
The forgiveness of sins;
The resurrection of the body;
And the life everlasting.'

If we look at the Apostle's Creed, which was formulated around 450 CE, we begin to see some of the central beliefs of the Christian religion.

In this unit we shall look at some of the main ideas concerning belief in God, the Holy Spirit and Jesus. In later units we will explore these beliefs in more depth.

GOD

Christians believe in one God who revealed him/herself to the world as Father, Son and Holy Spirit. These are not three different gods, but rather different sorts of activity of God. The term **Trinity** (see unit 8) is used to cover the activities of Father, Son and Holy Spirit.

Seven centuries ago an English writer whose name is still not known wrote a classic book to which he or she gave the name *The Cloud of Unknowing*. In this book the writer said that however much people seem to know about God, this God must always remain unknown to us, or at least unknown to the thinking part of us (the 'intellect'). When it comes to the emotional part of us, and love, the writer said it is then a different matter:

'He may well be loved, but He may not be thought of. He may be reached and held close by means of love, but by means of thought, never.'

(The Cloud of Unknowing)

However, to Christians there are some ideas about God that help them to begin to understand God, and certain characteristics have been attributed (given) to God.

Traditionally these characteristics are that God is: one; the creator; the uncaused cause; omnipotent (all powerful); omnipresent (present everywhere); omniscient (all knowing); eternal and unchanging; benevolent (all loving); holy; perfect; willing to reveal principle truths to humankind; a personal God.

THE HOLY SPIRIT

The Greek word which is translated 'spirit' can also mean 'wind' or 'breath'. In the Apostles' Creed the Holy Spirit is called the Holy Ghost. For Christians the Holy Spirit is an invisible force or power that makes them aware of powers beyond themselves. It is so powerful and so moving that it can change their lives and give them guidance and inner strength. Christian tradition has pointed to the Holy Spirit as:

- *giving* – inspiration, guidance, comfort, special gifts

- *revealing* – God's truths, especially through the life of Jesus

- *being* – creative, and a source of great holiness, power and love

- *active* – through God's creation and in the lives of all humankind.

JESUS CHRIST

At the centre of Christian belief is Jesus the Christ. Throughout Christian history the idea that God became incarnate (he took on the form of a human being) in Jesus, has affected worship, theology (the study of religion), practice and belief. The idea that God became flesh has been developed into rich ritual in the Orthodox (see unit 24) and Roman Catholic (see unit 23) traditions and into a profound reverence for holy scripture in the Protestant tradition (see unit 25). Despite some slight differences all the main Christian Churches agree that Jesus Christ represents God's presence on earth.

Each Christian generation has tended to picture

Jesus according to its own interests and tastes. To a peasant age, Jesus could be a simple tradesman. A soldier in the Middle Ages may see Jesus as the commander of his regiment, evoking total loyalty and bravery. A contemplative nun might picture Jesus as her spiritual husband, the lover burning her deepest soul. Aspects of Jesus' life, his preaching, healing and teaching have offered artists and ordinary people limitless scope for their imagination. The portrait of his life in the New Testament has been full enough to show that Jesus was completely human, yet able to take the divinity of God into human concerns. But it has also allowed readers to develop a Jesus who they can let into their own hearts.

At the heart of the Christian faith is Jesus' death and resurrection. Christians believe that the Son of God's death for human beings shows the immensity of God's love.

By rising from death, Christians believe Jesus has restored the life which human beings deeply long for. The mystery of the resurrection is at the very heart of Christian faith.

Christians believe that Jesus' death shows the immensity of God's love

THINKING POINT

- *'He is the image of the invisible God, the first-born of all creation; for in him all things were created, in heaven and earth, visible and invisible, whether thrones or dominians or principalities or authorities – all things were created through him and for him. He is before all things and in him all things hold together. He is the first-born from the dead, that is in everything he might be pre-eminent. For in him all the fullness of God was pleased to dwell and through him to reconcile to himself all things, whether on earth or in heaven, making peace by his death on the cross.'*

(Colossians 1:15–20)

FOR YOUR FOLDERS

▶ Look back at the characteristics Christians attribute to God. In your own words try to explain what each of these words means.

▶ What do you think the author of *The Cloud of Unknowing* meant by the words 'but He may not be thought of'?

▶ Explain in your own words what Christians believe about the Holy Spirit and about Jesus Christ.

▶ The passage from Colossians has been called a 'Hymn to the Cosmic Christ'. Find out the meaning of the word 'cosmic'. What do you think the idea of the 'Cosmic Christ' might mean.

SPIRIT

In the past many Christians who were uneducated had a very simple idea of God. They thought 'he' was like a very wise, kind, bearded old man, in a long flowing cloak, who lived somewhere up beyond the clouds. 'He' sat on his golden throne and watched everything that was happening on earth.

However, few Christians today believe in this picture of God. In John's Gospel, Jesus says, 'God is a spirit' (John 4:24). 'Spirit' means something very different from a man or a woman. It is more like a presence, a force, or invisible energy. Christians believe that through prayer, meditation, contemplation and worship they can communicate with this force.

Other names for God might include *Holy One*, *Ultimate Reality*, *The Absolute*. Although Christians have tried to explain what God is like, they all agree that this Power that brought everything into existence is *mysterious*.

CREATOR

Christians believe that the universe was created. For something to be created, there must be a *creator*. In the past, when people read the Bible literally, they thought that God made everything in six days. Today some **fundamentalist** Christians (see unit 3) still believe this. Most Christians however take the account of the creation symbolically (see unit 5), and they interpret it to mean that the universe came about because of the mystery of the Holy One, and not just by chance. In fact, they would argue, it makes more sense to believe in a created universe, than not to believe in one. The wonders and beauty of nature, the complexity of life on earth, the order that can be seen in the smallest atom, all point to the probability of order, design and purpose. The universe does not seem meaningless. Rather, the mysterious planets, stars and suns, the earth, the variety and complexity of life, all point to a meaningful universe. Modern science, too, is discovering that everything on earth is interconnected; and astronomy shows us that the earth is connected to the solar system and its sun, which in turn are connected to the Milky Way. Modern science and religion both point to a universe brimming over with meaning (see unit 19). A leading nuclear physicist, Sir James Jeans, once remarked that in his opinion, as a scientist, the universe looks like 'a Great Thought'.

So most Christians today would argue that the idea of a creative God makes more sense than to say everything just 'happened to get here by some sort of strange accident or coincidence'. One of the greatest scientists of modern times, Albert Einstein, believed in a created world and was amazed at its order. He was so sure that the world was created, he once said, 'What I want to know is *how* God created this world.'

THE GROUND OF OUR BEING

Some Christians believe that God is present in all things and all things are present in God (Pantheism). God is not separate or something 'out there'. God is therefore of a *different order of being*. One of the greatest theologians (somebody who studies ideas about God) of the twentieth century, Paul Tillich (1886–1965), coined the phrase 'the ground of our being' to describe God. By this he meant that God is to be found deep within all and everything as the source of our life and our very being. This source of all life must be infinite (without limit) and eternal (without beginning or end). Human beings are not infinite or eternal. We live and die. This means we have limits. Christians argue therefore that the finite mind (us) can never fully understand the infinite mind (the source). So God is a mystery, like a huge boundless ocean that stretches into the distance.

THINKING POINT

- *'God is creating the entire universe fully and totally in this present now. Everything God created six thousand years ago – and even previous to that as God made the world – God creates now all at once. Everything which God created millions of years ago and everything which will be created by God after millions of years – if the world endures till then – God is creating all that in the innermost and deepest realms of the soul.*

  Everything of the past and everything of the present and everything of the future God creates in the innermost realms of the soul.'

  (Meister Eckhart)

FOR YOUR FOLDERS

▶ What words do Christians use to define God? What are the meanings of these words?

▶ Read the Creation story in Genesis 1. Why do most modern Christians believe that God did not make the world in six days? What is the creation story all about? Is it possible for a Christian to believe the theory of evolution?

▶ Why might Christians argue that it is more ridiculous not to believe in God than to believe in God?

▶ What ideas does modern science have that point to the existence of a creator God?

▶ What do Christians mean when they say that God is 'the ground of our being?'

▶ Why is God a mystery for Christians?

▶ After reading this unit, write an essay on Christian ideas about God.

REFLECTIONS

'We are at fault as long as we see God in what is outside us.'

(Meister Eckhart)

'God is not only fatherly. God is also mother who lifts her loved child from the ground to her knee.'

(Mechtild of Magdeburg 1210–80 – Dominican nun)

'So God created man in his own image.'

(Genesis 1:27)

'God is beauty.'

(St Francis of Assisi 1181–1225)

'God is love.'

(1 John 4:16)

'Pigs eat acorns, but neither consider the sun that gave them life, nor the influence of the heavens by which they were nourished, nor the very root of the tree from whence they came.'

(Thomas Traherne, c. 1636–74 – cleric and poet)

'The image of God is found essentially and personally in all humankind. Each possesses it whole, entire and undivided, and all together not more than one alone. In this way we are all one, ultimately united in our eternal image, which is the image of God and the source in us all of our life.'

(Jan van Ruysbroeck, 1293–1381 – founder of a group of contemplatives who lived in a forest)

7 JESUS CHRIST

At the heart of the Christian religion is the figure of Jesus Christ. In the Apostles' Creed (see page 12), it states, 'I believe in Jesus Christ, his only Son, our Lord.' For Christians Jesus is God's son. But what does this mean?

THE SON OF GOD

As we saw in unit 6, God is not understood as being a person. The word 'son' is used in a different way. It is a *metaphor*, which means it stands for something that should not be taken word for word. For Christians, the expression 'only son' means that Jesus was a very holy person, a man full of Godliness who showed God's love to the world.

To try to get a better understanding of the expression 'the Son of God', it is helpful to explore how it is used in the New Testament.

In John 10:30, Jesus says, 'I and my Father are One,' and in Matthew 11:27, 'No one knows the Son except the Father, and no one knows the Father except the Son.' Biblical scholars suggest that Jesus himself, in his earthly life, was aware that in his own actions and sufferings, God's work was being done. However, this awareness is not self-centred – it was a mission and a task that Jesus knew he had to fulfil. Philippians 2:6 says:

'Though he was in the form of God, he did not count equality with God a thing to be grasped, but emptied himself, taking the form of a servant, being born in the likeness of man ... he humbled himself and became obedient unto death, even death on a cross.'

Note the main ideas here: he 'emptied himself', 'took the form of a servant', 'humbled himself', 'became obedient unto death'. All these expressions indicate the basic theme in the phrase 'Son of God' in the New Testament. God comes down into the world, in human form, prepared to sacrifice himself for the sake of his creation. The key words are *obedience, suffering, self-sacrifice*. The Son of God came down to the earth, with all its pain and suffering, to show humankind its true destiny and purpose.

In Paul's writings there is the idea of reconciliation (to restore, to bring to agreement, to settle, harmonize). Paul writes that God sent his Son, 'that *we* might receive adoption as sons'. The goal of reconciliation is that all human beings should become 'sons', by which Paul means free human beings, no longer slaves.

Freedom is the ultimate purpose of sending God's Son. The purpose of his journey down into earth is to free human beings from their present state. For Christians there is little doubt that in the mission of the Son of God, what is at stake is the destiny of humanity.

Christians believe that God became human in Jesus Christ

THE LORDSHIP OF JESUS

Another key phrase in the Apostles' Creed: is 'Our Lord'. The word used for Lord is *kyrios*. The word is often used in both the Old and New Testaments. For Christians, 'Lord' does not refer to an earthly king, bristling with power. The true Lord for them is the man from Nazareth, Jesus, a *servant* of humanity. Christians believe not in the love of power, but the power of love.

The word **incarnation** means 'in the body'. Christians believe that God became man in Jesus Christ. God became human flesh and blood, in order to show the world his purpose. They believe that God and humankind were joined together in the life of Jesus, and that Jesus was, in a mysterious way, God become man. Thomas Aquinas (1225–74), a Christian thinker, explained the incarnation as accomplishing the following: 'God became human and humans became God and Sharers in the divine nature'.

THE CROSS

The story of the **crucifixion** (death on a cross) and the resurrection of Jesus lie at the heart of Christian faith and practice (see Mark 15 and 16). The cross is the most important symbol in the Christian religion. The cross is understood and interpreted by modern Christians in a number of ways.

First, the cross shows that God came down into the darkness of the world. He went through and overcame the experience of a brutal death. He has shown that good is stronger than evil, light more powerful than darkness.

Second, the cross shows that God is involved in the world. He is involved in the struggles of everyday life and is not a distant, uncaring God.

Third, God became flesh and blood to show people the way forward. He gave people the choice to listen to his message. The people didn't listen and nailed him to a cross.

Fourth, the symbol of the cross can represent the intersection of passing time (the horizontal line), by the eternal (the vertical line). This point of intersection represents the here and now, and as such, the cross can be used as a tool for prayer and contemplation.

There are other, more traditional, views about Jesus' death on the cross. In ancient times the ritual of sacrifice was popular. Blood was thought to contain a life-force. By shedding his own blood on the cross, God, through Christ, forgave and purified the human race. This idea is known as **atonement** (making amends). Jesus' death is described by some Christians as a sacrifice, because he gave up his own life out of love for God's creation.

THINKING POINT

- *'The divine person who assumed our nature suffered death on the cross, a death which shook the earth, opened heaven and pleased God. From the first day of creation to the last night there has never been, nor will there be, so exalted and magnificent an act.'*

  (Dante, 1265–1321 – Italian poet)

FOR YOUR FOLDERS

▶ Explain the meaning of the following words: metaphor; obedience; suffering; self-sacrifice; reconciliation; *kyrios*; emptying oneself; servant; incarnation; the Word; sacrifice; atonement.

▶ What ideas about the Son of God are found in the New Testament?

▶ Who do Christians believe the 'Son of God' was? What was his mission?

▶ What sort of Lord do Christians think Jesus is?

▶ Explain the idea of the incarnation.

▶ Why is the symbol of the cross so important for Christians? What does the cross mean for different Christians?

▶ Write a short essay exploring the key beliefs that Christians have about Jesus Christ.

8 THE TRINITY

INTRODUCTION

When St Patrick (c. 385–461 CE) was trying to explain Christian beliefs to his converts, the natives of Ireland, it is said he picked a shamrock. The shamrock has leaves that are in three parts – if you pull the pieces apart you no longer have a leaf, yet every bit of it is the same stuff as the whole leaf. In this legend, St Patrick was trying to explain the Christian idea of the **Trinity**. Belief in God as Trinity is fundamental for Christians. The way they understand the relationship between God, Jesus Christ and the Holy Spirit rests on the idea of the Trinity.

WHAT IS THE TRINITY?

Christians believe that God is involved in the world, and in a personal way with individuals. Christians speak of God as 'Father, Son and Holy Spirit'. This idea is called the Trinity (from 'tri', meaning three and 'unity', or 'three in one'). To help us think how three things can be one, they suggest we think of a triangle, with three sides but one shape.

The doctrine is not actually spelt out in the Bible although there are passages showing a threefold pattern; like this one describing the baptism of Jesus:

> *'And straightway coming up out of the water, he saw the heavens opened, and the* Spirit *like a dove descending upon him. And there came a* voice *from heaven, saying, Thou art my beloved* Son, *in whom I am well pleased.'*

(Mark 1:10–11)

Matthew's Gospel finishes with Jesus saying to his disciples:

> *'Go ye therefore and teach all nations, baptizing them in the name of the Father, and of the Son, and of the Holy Ghost, teaching them to observe all things whatsoever I have commanded you: and lo, I am with you always, even unto the end of the world.'*

(Matthew 28:19–20)

In the second book of Corinthians, St Paul finishes his letter with the following words, known as the Grace:

> *'May the grace of the Lord Jesus Christ and the love of God, and the fellowship of the Holy Spirit be with you all.'*

(2 Corinthians 13:14)

Christians speak of God as Father, Son and Holy Spirit

It was against this biblical background that the leaders of the early Church formulated the early creeds. In it, they stressed that although the three parts of the Trinity work in *different* ways, they are all working *together*.

- The Creator Father is God.
- The Son is the Saviour or **Redeemer** and gives new life.
- The Holy Spirit is the Sanctifier, the One who makes holy.

These three, the Creator, Redeemer and the Sanctifier are not to be taken as three gods, but one God working in three ways. The Christian religion, like the Jewish faith, is **monotheistic** (it believes in only One God). In the Old Testament are the words: 'Israel, remember this! The Lord – and the Lord alone – is our God!' (Deuteronomy 6:4).

The Trinity is monotheistic too. When the Creeds were being written, people began to speak about three 'persons' in God – Father, Son and Holy Spirit. Some modern Christians think of three minds, spirits or energies, which are all part of the same God – and exist in harmony – God the Father loving the Son, and the Holy Spirit as the force that unites them. But Christians believe in one God, not three. In the light of this basic belief, some Christians think it easier to speak in terms of three *roles* in God, not three individual people. In other words, God has three ways of being God. He is in himself, Father, Son and Spirit, one God. The doctrine of the Trinity is intended to strengthen (not weaken) ideas about the oneness of God. It refers to God's inner richness, not dividing him into parts, but describing the nature of his oneness as a living and full unity. These three ways of being God, whether they are seen as being persons or roles, are eternal (everlasting).

- God the Father is the Creator, the cosmic energy behind the universe.
- The Son is God, incarnated in Jesus Christ, working to redeem the world.
- The Holy Spirit is the presence of God living within the world, bringing people to new life.

The Doctrine of the Trinity has been called the summing up of the Gospel – the *Law of Three*. The words Father, Son and Holy Spirit refer to one and the same God, but Christians cannot say who God is without referring to Jesus Christ, and to the Holy Spirit. The Trinity is further discussed in unit 51.

THE HOLY SPIRIT

A theologian once remarked that the Bible is the 'Book of the Holy Spirit'. In the Old Testament one word used for spirit is *ruah*, which means *'breath'*. It is seen as the life-giving breath of God. Without this breath there can be no life. Another word used is *lebab*, standing for the deepest sense which the self has of itself (*self-awareness*, consciousness).

In the New Testament, it is the Holy Spirit which comes to humanity and delivers humankind from death, decay and destruction. The Holy Spirit brings with it freedom, faith, goodness, joy and peace. The work of Jesus makes possible the birth of the Holy Spirit within human beings. It is life-giving. The idea of the Holy Spirit is intended to show how God is working in the world. It is part of God's creative power which continues to work in the world.

Who is the Holy Spirit? For Christians, the Holy Spirit is a mystery, 'a compassionate outpouring of the Creator and the Son' (Mechtild of Magdeburg).

In John 14–16, Jesus speaks of the Spirit as the **paraclete** (in the Greek) that he would send in his place on earth. This has been translated as meaning helper or comforter.

CREATION SPIRITUALITY

A newly discovered movement within Christianity, often called 'Creation Spirituality', views the Trinity as God the Creator, Jesus the Liberator and the Holy Spirit as Sanctifier. It teaches that the creator of the earth, and not only Jesus, needs to be revered. The creator is the one who fills the universe everywhere with beauty and power, light and darkness in an ongoing act of creation.

Jesus the Liberator is the divine child who lives in us all. He is the Cosmic Christ who frees people by his teachings. The Holy Spirit is the Spirit of Wisdom which existed before all things. In biblical literature this mind, energy or force, brings order from chaos and lies at the heart of the creative process. The 'Spirit of God moved upon the face of the waters' (Genesis 1:2).

FOR YOUR FOLDERS

▶ Explain the meaning of the following words: Tri-unity; sanctifier; monotheistic; self-giving; *ruah*; *lebab*; self-awareness; paraclete.

▶ What does the word 'Trinity' mean?

▶ What roles do each of the persons of God have according to Christians?

▶ What difficulties might arise for Christians if people misunderstand the Doctrine of the Trinity?

▶ Explain in a paragraph what you think the Doctrine of the Trinity means.

▶ Briefly try to explain what Creation Spirituality is about.

▶ Why do Christians believe that the Holy Spirit is so important in explaining and understanding Christian belief?

9 SALVATION

SIN

For most Christians, **sin** means turning away from God and putting yourself first. It refers to being self-centred and therefore careless about the feelings of others. In the Gospels, the Greek word translated as sin is *harmartia*, which means *missing the mark*, like a spear thrown at an object and failing to hit it. From this meaning comes the idea of someone failing in their purpose, erring or doing wrong.

Everyone has a side to themselves that they've acquired from imitating others in life. This is not our true self. Whatever we do from this side of ourselves, i.e. the false side, is not really what we want to do. It is pretence. Every time we act from our false side we are missing the mark, not being true to our real selves.

Sin is not just a list of 'dos and don'ts'. In the Gospels a sin is not an individual's action, but the inner attitude of a person who does it, and the effect it has on other people. It means to go against the will of God.

THE FALL

The Old Testament book of *Genesis* contains the story of Adam and Eve (Genesis 2–3). Although Christians interpret this story in different ways (see unit 4) many see it as being symbolic of the meaning of sin. Adam and Eve are put in a beautiful garden where they have many different kinds of trees to eat from, including the Tree of Life. They are told that under no circumstances may they eat from one tree, the Tree of Knowledge of Good and Evil. The serpent, who represents evil, however, tempts them to eat from the forbidden tree. Something strange happens to them, and they are changed inside and start to scheme. God casts them out of the Garden of Eden to the world outside. In the outside world things are tough and difficult. This is known as the **Fall**, i.e. the fall into disobedience and sin.

The Tree of Life may stand for the path of truth, life and goodness. The Tree of Knowledge may stand for falsity. Adam and Eve disobey God, they turn away from God and become self-centred. They care only for their own desires and subsequently things begin to go terribly wrong.

HUMAN NATURE

Christian Churches have traditionally taught the idea of **original sin**. There are many ways of interpreting this doctrine. In the past it was thought that all human beings had a sort of 'moral stain' in them, passed down from generation to generation.

People were born with a streak of badness (wickedness, evil) in them. Some Christians still believe that all human beings are born with some sort of moral flaw or defect in them.

Many modern Christians, though, have a different interpretation. They believe that the story of Adam and Eve and the Fall has another meaning. It tries to show how human beings are all faced with a choice between good and evil, knowledge or ignorance. They believe that human beings are born pure and stainless. However, as they grow they begin to absorb all the things of the world. Many of these things have a negative influence: anger, pride, selfishness, lust, jealousy and greed. All these negative emotions already exist in the world and we absorb them as we grow. In time, they become part of us. We become conditioned and our personalities are made up by the influences of the world around us. From the purity of childhood we fall into a state of sleep when our lives become dominated by negative emotions, imaginings, attachments and self love.

Venial and mortal sin

Roman Catholic Christians (see unit 23) think there are two different types of sin. *Venial* sins are less serious sins, like telling a lie. Some Christians will confess these privately to God in prayer. *Mortal* sins are considered more serious (e.g. murder).

SALVATION

Christian Churches believe that sin is a disobedience of God's standards. Sin leads to a breakdown in the relationship between the person who has committed the sin, and the person or people who have been sinned against. **Salvation** can mean *wholeness* or *health*. For Christians it means turning to God and being open to God. Christians feel that a healing relationship begins as the relationship is restored. Salvation is about becoming a complete human being, at peace with oneself, with others and with God. Christians believe that God comes to people's assistance (sometimes called **grace** which can be defined as undeserved love), so they can be freed from sinful self-centredness into a new and fuller life. Salvation is therefore something that can be given to people, by the will and work of God. However, salvation does not just happen. Most Christians believe that it is a life-long struggle in which people work to turn away from love of oneself, to love of one's neighbour and love of God. Grace is given to those who *sincerely* ask for it and who are prepared and willing to let go of their selfish desires.

Christians sometimes look to their **conscience** as a guide. *Conscience is a state in which a person really feels what they are truly like.* This can be a painful experience, but one that can possibly make a person more determined to seek for truth in their life.

Some Christians feel that this process begins with the act of **baptism** (see unit 55). Some think it is a symbolic act, when the original sin that has been 'inherited from Adam' is washed away. Most Christians believe that baptism is only the beginning of the process and people need to seek truth all through their lives.

Other Christians feel that baptism alone is not enough. They feel that a person needs to have a personal conversion experience. They believe that this happens when a person comes to accept that Jesus died for them personally. They feel they must give up their lives to Jesus. Many believe that they will have everlasting life because Jesus died for their sins. Again, this process is seen as being life-long, whereby people will struggle to form a living relationship with Jesus every day of their lives.

There are some differences of emphasis about salvation within the Churches. The Orthodox and Roman Catholic emphasis is generally that the relationship between God and people only really begins to change when they become part of the Christian community. They can experience God's grace especially in the **sacraments** (see unit 41) and through the **mass** (see unit 43). The Protestant emphasis is on *faith*. The new relationship between God and people does not depend on the rituals of the Church, but rather depends on the person having faith in Jesus Christ.

Although these differences might seem small they have been and still are the cause of controversy.

KEY WORDS

Grace – the undeserving loving help that humanity receives from God.
Redeemed – ('Redemption' is from the Latin for 'brought back'.) Jesus is called 'Redeemer' because Christians believe that through his sacrifice on the cross people are now able to find their way back into full union with God.

FOR YOUR FOLDERS

▶ What does *harmartia* mean?

▶ Explain the meaning of sin.

▶ What is the story of Adam and Eve? How does it help Christians to understand the meaning of sin?

▶ How might the way the story is interpreted affect Christian views about human nature?

▶ What do you understand by 'conscience'?

▶ Explain the Roman Catholic teachings on sin.

▶ Write a paragraph on Christian ideas about salvation.

THINKING POINTS

● *'Ask and it shall be given you: seek, and ye shall find; knock and it shall be opened unto you.'*

(Jesus in Matthew 7:7)

● *'God is ready when you are, and is waiting for you. But what am I to do, you say, and how am I to "lay hold"? Lift up your heart to God with humble love; and mean God himself, and not what you get out of him.'*

(*The Cloud of Unknowing*)

10 THE CHURCH

INTRODUCTION

In the New Testament the word *ekklesia* is used for the **church**. This means literally an assembly of people, a believing community. The people who are part of the Church are attempting to carry on the work of Jesus, in some way, in response to his teaching. Because of this, in the New Testament, the Church is called the *Body of Christ*. This means a group of people trying to follow Jesus Christ on earth with the help and guidance of the Holy Spirit.

THE NICENE CREED

In the Nicene Creed (see unit 21), the Church is described as being one, holy, catholic and apostolic.
One – Christians believe that unity within the Church is essential and it is the will of God that it be one.
Holy – The Church is a sacred representation of God's will on earth. It provides the physical and material presence of Jesus Christ and continues His work in the world.
Catholic – This refers to the worldwide (or universal) community of Christians. This includes all the different Churches around the world (see units 22–26).
Apostolic – This means that the Church is based on the teachings of Jesus and the apostles, which were handed down through the New Testament.
Roman Catholics, Anglicans and Orthodox Christians feel that because they can trace their history and authority back to the apostles, they are true to the teachings of the original apostles. These Churches have similar beliefs and practices, especially about baptism and the Eucharist (see units 43 and 55). However, many Free Churches (see unit 25) feel that they have a right to call themselves Apostolic, because they try to follow the teachings of the Bible. They don't think it matters if they haven't got a line of bishops going back to the apostles.

HOUSE CHURCHES

In Britain a fairly new phenomenon has appeared on the Christian scene. These are *House Churches*. Originally, as the name suggests, people would worship in one another's houses. Today, as the movement has grown, the worshippers may meet in halls, old cinemas, rented school buildings, etc. In the last few years purpose-built centres have sprung up.

House Churches originated among many Christians who felt that traditional places of worship

The Church should, ideally, represent the material presence of Christ on Earth

had become too formal, inflexible and unfriendly. They looked for a less formal and more friendly and personal environment.

THE COMMUNION OF SAINTS

Another way that Christians have thought about the Church is as the Communion of Saints. Not all Christians would speak of the Church in this way, but among Roman Catholics, Orthodox and Anglican Christians this view is acceptable. They believe that the Church has been founded by God for all eternity and is the community of all Christian people. The end of mortal life, they would argue, does not make any difference to a person's status as a Christian. So the Communion of Saints includes all Christians, living and departed. It is the fellowship of all Christians alive and dead. Obviously, for Christians living today, many of these people would not be known personally to them. However, they believe that because of their shared faith they are all in communion.

In the New Testament, saints are simply people who are made holy. That is, they are **sanctified** (made holy) by the Holy Spirit, who continues the work of Jesus Christ. Taken this way, 'saints' simply means 'Christians'. There is another meaning to the word, though. Although all Christians are sanctified in Christ, some people are seen as being especially holy. They have lived lives very close to God and have set fine examples for others to follow.

Roman Catholic, Orthodox and some Anglican Christians believe that they can ask the saints in heaven to pray for them. The saints are thought to be closer to God and therefore their prayers have special power. In the past some Christians have dedicated a new church building to a particular saint, in the expectation that they will have the help of her or his prayers. Some Christians as well adopt, either as individuals or as groups, a particular saint as their patron.

Saints first began to be honoured when they were **martyred** (died willingly for their beliefs) in the Roman Empire. Many of the people mentioned by name in the New Testament automatically became saints as they lived their lives close to Jesus.

CANONIZATION

The Roman Catholic Church goes through a long and complicated process before they pronounce people saints. This is called **canonization** (which means formal admission to the list of saints). The Church authorities study every aspect of the dead person's life in great detail, before deciding whether to make that person a saint. The **Pope**, who is the leader of the Roman Catholic Church, will make the final decision. However, as not everyone who has lived a good saintly life is known to the authorities, all these unknown people are honoured in the Feast of All Saints on 1 November.

In the Orthodox Church, saints are pronounced by local councils of bishops. The Anglican Church honours the saints that were established before the Church split with Rome during the Reformation (see unit 21). It does not name any new saints, although unofficially many people are honoured as saints.

Protestant Christians generally do not agree with the idea of saints. They feel that a person should pray to Jesus Christ, without having to refer to a saint. They are fearful that people might start treating saints like gods. However, Christians who do accept the saints would argue that they are in no way a substitute for Jesus Christ, and that God can still be approached directly through prayer and contemplation.

Saint Nicholas, a Russian saint

FOR YOUR FOLDERS

▶ Explain the meaning of the following words or phrases: *ekklesia*; Body of Christ; one, holy, catholic and apostolic church; Communion of Saints; saints; martyr; sanctified; canonization.

▶ What are House Churches?

▶ Find out about a local saint who has either lived in your area or is connected in some way. Write a profile about them.

▶ Make a list of some saints that you have heard of.

▶ Explain the different attitudes to the Communion of Saints in the Christian Church.

11 ETERNAL LIFE

INTRODUCTION

In the Apostles' Creed (see unit 5), are the words, 'I believe in ... The resurrection of the body, And the life everlasting'. There are many passages in the Bible about the life of the world to come, or the afterlife. Some of these passages are particularly powerful:

> 'And immediately I was in the Spirit: and behold a seat was put in heaven and one sat on the seat. And he that sat was to look upon like a jasper stone, and a sardine stone. And there was a rainbow about the seat in sight like to an emerald. And about the seat were twenty-four seats. And upon the seats twenty-four elders sitting clothed in white raiment, and had on their heads crowns of gold. And out of the seat proceeded lightnings, and thunderings, and voices, and there were seven lamps of fire.'

(Revelation 4:2–5)

This poetic passage can either be read literally (i.e. heaven is exactly like this), or it can be seen as a symbolic poem, full of deeper meanings. Although some Christians will read it literally, many will see it symbolically.

In the past, many Christians believed that heaven was a place somewhere up above the sky. When somebody died their spirit floated up to this place to be with God. Some Jews believed that the dead were actually raised up in new bodies. Both these viewpoints can be found in different parts of the Bible. However, the writers often stressed that because the afterlife is so mysterious, they couldn't really explain what it was like in words, so they used symbols to try and help explain it.

ST PAUL

St Paul's Epistles seem to combine both these ideas. He wrote about a new body being taken to another dimension, a spiritual place:

> 'This is how it will be when the dead are raised to life. When the body is buried, it is mortal; when raised it will be immortal. When buried, it is ugly and weak; when raised it will be beautiful and strong. When buried, it is a physical body; when raised it will be a spiritual body.'

(Corinthians 15:42–4)

VIEWS ON THE AFTERLIFE

Many Christians believe that all human beings have an immortal soul. This is indestructible and, after the body dies, the soul will continue to survive in another dimension. Very little can be said about this other dimension, but generally Christians believe the soul will live on in a new, spiritual body. Other Christians believe that we do not have an immortal soul and there is nothing that automatically survives death. Some feel that somehow the soul has to be *worked* for in this life, it is not automatically given. Others believe that the afterlife is an act of God, and that somehow, at death, God creates a new life for people.

JUDGEMENT

Like non-Christians, Christians have often been baffled by the seeming injustice of life. What, if anything, becomes of somebody as wicked as Adolf Hitler? What became of his millions of innocent victims? Why do the good sometimes die young? Is there a day of judgement?

In the Bible there are ideas about hell, a place of terror, fire and torture. Some people are raised to eternal life while the damned are thrown into a lake of fire. This doctrine of hell has been used *and abused* by the Church over the ages. Often if somebody disagreed with the Church they would be threatened with the fires of hell. Today, some Christians put fear into the hearts of people by saying that if they disagree with their ideas, or if they don't follow *their* view of Jesus, they will go to hell. These attitudes can lead to guilt, fear, blind acceptance, intolerance, and can actually put people off Christianity.

Many modern Christians feel very uncomfortable about the idea of hell, a place of eternal torture. They argue that if God is a God of love, as he is constantly depicted in the Gospels, how could he reject people in such a cruel way? If this is the case, God would be responsible for running an eternal place of torment, an everlasting torture chamber. Many Christians see the Bible verses about hell as being *symbolic*. Hell is a state of mind not a place. It is being cut off from God. Many Christians feel that people put themselves into a state of hell by their remorse, regrets or guilt over things they have done, or by following selfish desires and never really finding happiness in them. Some other Christians might argue that hell exists but it is not eternal. It is a state in which people who have died struggle with themselves, before being able to go to heaven. They have to come to terms with all

An artist's impression of paradise

the things they've done in life, and everything is *revealed* or shown to them.

The Roman Catholic Church believes in **purgatory**. Purgatory is an intermediate (in between) phase or state, in which people who've not been terribly bad or terribly good have to be prepared for heaven. Today, many Roman Catholics, and some Anglicans, believe that in purgatory people have to be purified from their evil. However, the official teachings of these Churches is still that hell is eternal, even though many thinking Christians feel otherwise, stressing the loving and merciful qualities of God.

In Matthew 25:31–46 Jesus tells the **parable** of the Last Judgement. The parables of Jesus have many meanings. They can be read literally or they can make readers think for themselves and be read symbolically. In this parable in Matthew's Gospel, righteous, good people stand to the right hand side of the Son of Man (Jesus) when he returns to judge the earth. They are sent into heaven. The unrighteous are sent into the 'eternal fire which has been prepared for the Devil and his angels'. This happens after all the inner thoughts, attitudes and motives of the people have been revealed. Those that helped Christ (in other humans) when he was sick, hungry or naked are sent to heaven. Those who closed their hearts and minds to the needs of others are sent into the eternal fire.

This parable can be interpreted in a number of ways. The two most obvious are, the literal way of seeing God as sending some people to hell, or the symbolic interpretation, relating to people's own

consciences. The parable also stresses that salvation is open not just to those who call themselves Christians, but to those who 'did the will of God' by showing concern for their neighbours. Most modern Christians feel that a parable such as this one shows that there is a place in the Kingdom for people from faiths other than the Christian one. Also there is a place for those who did not even believe in God in their lives, but who have carried out his will without even knowing it by developing themselves and helping others.

THE PAROUSIA

Some Christians believe that the Kingdom of God has not yet come to earth. They believe Christ will return. The word for the return of Christ is **parousia**, a Greek word meaning 'the presence'. This sort of Christian belief is called **eschatology** (the study of last things, or, the end of time).

Christians interpret these ideas in different ways. Some believe Christ will return; others feel his return won't be a physical one but rather a spiritual one; some Christians feel it is a symbolic idea about the defeat of good over evil, but they don't know how or when this will take place; and others feel that the spirit of the cosmic Christ is present now.

FOR YOUR FOLDERS

▶ Find out the meaning of the following words and phrases: symbolic; indestructible; revealed; purgatory; parousia; eschatology.

▶ What does it mean to interpret something literally and symbolically?

▶ Explain the different interpretations Christians might give to the Biblical passages quoted and mentioned in this unit.

▶ What ideas do modern Christians have about the afterlife? How are these ideas different from more traditional ideas?

▶ Write an essay on the Christian view of the afterlife. Conclude it by explaining what your views are. Give reasons for your views.

12 MARY – MOTHER OF GOD

For millions of Christians, the Virgin Mary, is a beloved figure. Shrines to the Virgin Mary exist in many parts of the world, especially in Ireland, around the Mediterranean and in South America. Thousands of churches around the world have been named after her. Many Christians, down the ages, have reported seeing visions of Mary, e.g. at Lourdes (see unit 54).

Mary is given a unique place in both the Roman Catholic Church and the Orthodox Churches. She is regarded as being a link between heaven and earth and because she is the mother of Jesus, she has special access to him. Roman Catholic and Orthodox Christians believe that she can and does 'intercede' (speak in favour) with Jesus, on behalf of people who pray to her.

Mary was given the title 'Mother of God' (*Theotokos* in Greek) in 431 CE as a sign of her special role. Roman Catholic and some Orthodox Christians believe that since the Holy Spirit, rather than a man, gave her the seed of creation, she was a virgin. Other Christians, noting that the word used for 'virgin' in the Hebrew language is *Almah*, meaning 'a young woman', think that Mary was not necessarily a virgin.

The Roman Catholic and Orthodox Churches believe that Mary's body was taken up to heaven when she died. This is called the **Assumption**. A feast day is held on 15 August to celebrate this.

THE IMMACULATE CONCEPTION

The Roman Catholic Church teaches that Mary, alone of all human beings since Adam and Eve, was born without sin, and remained free from sin all her life. They believe that no ordinary person could have given birth to Jesus, so Mary must have been free from sin. This is called the **Immaculate Conception**.

Other Christians do not hold this view. They believe Mary was human, not sinless.

MARY IN THE GOSPELS

There is not a great deal about Mary in the Gospels. The Gospels of Matthew and Luke record the birth of Jesus and they stress that Mary was an important person.

Roman Catholic Christians stress that they do not actually worship Mary but honour her highly because of her place in God's plan for the world. Many Protestant Christians, however, feel uncomfortable about Mary's role, and this has led to great controversy in the past. However, today some Protestant Churches are willing to discuss her role and an **Ecumenical** Society of the Virgin Mary now exists.

'The Annunciation', when the Angel Gabriel appeared to Mary; by the painter Botticelli

THINKING POINTS

- *'Mary, ground of all being, greetings! Greetings to you, lovely and loving Mother.'*

  (Hildegarde of Bingen, 1098–1179 – Benedictine nun)

- *'Mary, you birthed to earth your son, you birthed the Son of God from heaven by breathing the spirit of God.'*

  (Mechtild of Magdeburg)

- *'We are all meant to be mothers of God. For God is always needing to be born.'*

  (Meister Eckhart)

FOR DISCUSSION

▶ To many writers and artists throughout the ages, the Virgin Mary has been a figure who has been accorded great respect. In this extract, from his book *The Last Temptation*, Nikos Kazantzakis expresses this respect for her.

'Mary sat on a high stool in the tiny yard of her house. She was spinning. It was still bright outside, the summer light drew slowly away from the face of the earth and did not wish to leave. Mary spun and her mind twirled now this way, now that – together with the spindle. Memory and imagination joined: her life seemed half truth, half fable. The petty round of daily tasks had lasted for years and then suddenly the stunning uninvited peacock – the miracle – had come and covered her tormented existence with its long golden wings.

A brilliantly white dove flew down from the roof opposite, beat its wings for a moment over her head and then alighted with dignity on the pebbles of the yard and began to walk methodically round Mary's feet. It spread its tail-feathers, bent its neck, turned its head

and looked at Mary, its round eye flashing in the evening light like a ruby.
It looked at her – spoke to her. She called the bird in a very tender voice, and the delighted dove took a hop and landed on her joined knees.

Mary placed her hand on the dove which sat upon her knees. Caressing the dove, she struggled to bring the lightning back to mind after thirty years and to untangle its hidden meaning. She closed her eyes. In her palm she felt the dove's tiny warm body and beating heart . . . Suddenly – she did not realize how, she did not know why – dove and lightning were one; she was sure of it; the heartbeats and the thunder – all were God. Now for the first time she was able to make out the words hidden in the thunder, hidden in the dove's cooing: "Hail Mary . . . Hail Mary." Without a doubt, this was what God had cried: "Hail Mary." '

(Nikos Kazantzakis)

13 RELIGIOUS EXPERIENCE

INTRODUCTION

Christians may spend their whole lives without having any remarkable or earth-shattering experiences. They may never see hosts of angels coming down from heaven with golden trumpets or hear mighty voices calling them from the sky. Their lives are spent in a sort of quiet simple faith, believing that God came down to earth and taught people how life should be lived. Sometimes in prayer they may feel that the words come alive, or in deep contemplation feel a peace that is beyond understanding, or experience peace and refreshment through worship. Or they may believe that God is at work when they meet others, or when they're with loved ones, or when they hear stories of tremendous courage or self-sacrifice, or when they see a sunrise.

WAYS OF SEEING

The so-called simple facts of life may be enough to convince Christians that there is more to life than just the physical world. People can experience a powerful sense of awe and wonder at the beauty of nature, and this can reassure them that life has meaning and purpose. The sight of a star shooting across the night sky, a stunningly beautiful sunset, the birth of a child or the complex beauty of an atom under a microscope, can give people a sense of an 'otherness' or holiness.

The English poet William Blake (1757–1827) wrote about this sense of holiness which he said can be found in the smallest of things:

> *'To see a World in a Grain of Sand,*
> *And heaven in a Wild Flower,*
> *Hold Infinity in the palm of your hand*
> *And eternity in an hour.'*

A SENSE OF JOY AND PRESENCE

Sometimes quite unexpectedly, a person may experience a deep 'sense of presence', a great joy, or a powerful feeling of themselves as being at one with everything around them. In this extract a 15-year-old boy speaks about his experience:

> *'The thing happened one summer afternoon, on the school cricket field, while I was sitting on the grass, waiting my turn to bat. I was thinking about nothing in particular, just enjoying the pleasures of midsummer idleness. Suddenly and without warning, something invisible seemed to be drawn across the sky, changing the world about me into a kind of tent of concentrated and enhanced significance. What had been merely an outside became an inside. The outside world was somehow changed into something which was experienced as "mine", but on a level where the word has no meaning: for "I" was no longer the familiar self.'*

For Christians there are other experiences that convince them of an 'otherness', a God, an Ultimate Reality, the Holy One.

CURED BY FAITH

The Gospels have many stories about healing miracles. Often Jesus told people who had been cured that their **faith** had cured them. Today, some people in the medical profession have found that if a person believes hard enough that they are going to get well, they might do so. There is a growing realization too, that the state of the body and the state of the mind are closely related.

Some Christians today practise the art of healing, and services of healing are held. There are reports of people actually being healed because of their faith. Of

Blake's 'Jacob's Ladder', illustrating other dimensions of reality

course nobody really knows what happens – whether God actually intervenes, or if faith unlocks certain self-healing powers within the person themself.

VISIONS

Throughout the history of the Christian Church, right up to the present day, there have been cases of visions. The first case recorded in the New Testament is when the risen Christ appeared to his disciples. The most dramatic case in the New Testament is the case of Saul (later to become St Paul), who had up to this point been persecuting the early Christians:

> '. . . suddenly a light from the sky flashed all around him. He fell to the ground and heard a voice saying, "Saul, Saul, why do you persecute me?" "Tell me, Lord," he said, "who you are." The voice answered, "I am Jesus whom you are persecuting."'
>
> (Acts 9:3–5)

One of the most famous visions involved a 14-year-old French girl, Bernadette Soubirous. She is believed to have seen the Virgin Mary on numerous occasions in a cave on a bank of a river in France. The site became famous as Lourdes, which now attracts millions of Christians every year who come to pray and to be healed. There are other places around the world which have become shrines, after people believe they have experienced visions there (see unit 54).

Christians may interpret visions differently. Some think that people do see an actual spiritual form that briefly appears in the world. Other Christians may argue that these people see something in their minds, yet this doesn't mean they're not true. *The creative mind might be in touch with a deeper reality than it normally sees.* The psychologist Carl Gustav Jung (1875–1961) called this deeper reality the *collective unconscious* – a level of reality deep within the mind that is common to us all. We don't normally touch this reality, but when we do, we can experience through dreams or visions *another dimension of reality.*

PENTECOSTAL WORSHIP

Pentecostal Christians are part of the Charismatic Movement (see unit 25). They believe that God gives them the gifts of healing and prophecy that St Paul mentions in 1 Corinthians 12:4–11.

BEING SAVED

Some people may unexpectedly have a conversion experience, where they feel that God has come into their lives. They may feel challenged to make a decision to 'accept Jesus into their lives'. They feel that they have a new life and have a sense of being loved and forgiven. Some people make an instant decision to 'give their lives to Christ' and accept him as their 'Saviour'. They talk about 'being saved' and about 'being born again'. These conversion experiences can have a powerful effect on the way these people think and feel about their lives. Often they become very enthusiastic about their experience and want everyone to share it. Some other Christians do not agree with these converts. They may even become impatient with them, especially if the converts argue that others are not really Christians if they haven't shared the same experience as themselves, or if the converts tell them that only those who have accepted Jesus go to heaven and the rest go to hell. These ideas can frighten some people and put others off religion for life. Many Christians feel that these sorts of ideas are dangerous.

FOR YOUR FOLDERS

▶ What do you think the expression a 'quiet simple faith' means?

▶ In what situations might people experience a sense of the Holy One?

▶ What does it mean to be 'cured by faith'? What are your views on this?

▶ Explain what you think visions are. What do different Christians say about them?

▶ What do you understand by the phrase 'the collective unconscious'?

▶ Although many Christians do not have earth-shattering experiences, what benefits might they feel from prayer and worship?

▶ Describe what happens to people who call themselves 'saved'. What are the dangers of these beliefs according to some Christians?

This unit looks at a strand of religious life that has had a great influence on human thought.

Throughout the ages, in all parts of the world and in all religious traditions, people have had experiences that have changed their lives. Sometimes these experiences are described as *mystical*. Mysticism has inspired religious thought, music, poetry, art and architecture. So what is mysticism?

One suggested meaning is *'a break through the world of time and history into one of eternity and timelessness.'* In medieval times this 'breakthrough' was related to a particular type of insight or knowledge about God, and was sometimes called **contemplation**. It was used to describe a rare and advanced form of spiritual experience not found among ordinary religious people. Medieval theologians (people who study ideas about God) called it a 'stretching out of the soul into God through the urge of love'.

More simply, mysticism could be described as an awareness of *beyond*, or an awareness which is interwoven with the material world yet is not part of it. It is an awareness of the *unseen, over and above the seen*.

However it is defined, the remarkable thing about all mystical experiences, whenever and wherever people have had them, is their similarity. The experiences of a Buddhist mystic over 2000 years ago in Tibet are similar to the experience of a medieval mystic in Germany 500 years ago, or a modern twentieth-century mystic. Although living at different times, in different places and from different religious traditions, their experiences are similar.

Mystical experience may happen to anyone, sometimes quite unexpectedly, but when it occurs it is clearly recognizable. It may happen once in a lifetime: but when it does happen it brings illumination and may change a whole life.

'Suddenly it happened, and, as everybody knows, it cannot be described in words. The Bible phrase, "I saw the heavens open," seems as good as any if not taken literally. I remember saying to myself, in awe and rapture, "So it's like this; now I know what Heaven is like, now I know what they mean in church." The words of the 23rd Psalm came into my head and I began repeating them: "He maketh me to lie down in green pastures; He leadeth me beside the still waters." Soon it faded and I was alone in the meadow with the baby and the brook and the sweet-smelling lime trees. But though it passed and only the earthly beauty remained, I was filled with great gladness. I had seen the "far distances".'

(A girl of 9 – recounted in later life)

'It was during one of those recitations that, as I told you, Christ himself came down and took possession of me . . . in this sudden possession of me by Christ, neither my senses nor my imagination had any part; I only felt in the midst of my suffering the presence of a love, like that which one can read in the smile of a beloved face . . . '

(Simone Weil, 1909–43 – French thinker)

The world as we see it with our senses is only a part of reality

FOR DISCUSSION

▶ The following ideas have arisen from the experiences and reflections of mystics. Some of these ideas are at the heart of Christian belief, although not all Christians would agree with them. Read them carefully and discuss them in groups of about six.

● The world as we see it with our senses is only a part of reality. There is much that we don't know about the universe and ourselves and the meaning of everything.

● The world of matter and the world of thought arise from a Divine Source. The words 'God', 'The Absolute', 'The Holy One', 'Ultimate Reality', can never give us a sense of the true power of this Source.

● Humans are capable of finding knowledge about this Divine Source. This knowledge does not necessarily come from the mind alone, but from feelings and intuition too. Even scientific discovery has been based on intuition and the same can be the case with spiritual discovery.

● We are not who we think we are. We have a self, an ego, an awareness of ourselves that we carry round with us, but we also have another self – our true self. This true self is within us and is not usually obvious. It can be called spirit, soul, eternal self, the inner person, the divine spark of which we normally know very little. However, anyone who really wishes to discover this spirit, eternal self, inner person, etc., and is prepared to make the necessary effort can do so. Indeed, by doing so they can discover the Divine Source, which, according to mystics is of a similar or like nature. As Jesus said, 'For, behold, the Kingdom of God is within you' (Luke 17:21).

● We need to ask, 'Why am I here?' Our lives are relatively short, and seemingly insignificant when we look at the immensity of the universe. If we just follow the ego part of ourself what is left for us when we die? All our pleasures, our savings, our possessions, our careers, will come to nothing. If we can truly see this and fully understand it, we will come to realize that the chief purpose of our existence is to seek, discover and identify with our true selves. This, according to mystics, will show us Truth and not just the bits of truth which our limited knowledge shows us, the way we are at present.

● All human beings have a Divine spark within them. This spark of Divinity comes from God, The Holy One. All human beings have the ability to reconnect with this Divinity. The mystics through the ages show us that this is possible – yet we are asleep to our true destinies and to our cosmic possibilities. Our destiny is not in time or history but is one of eternal life, eternity and timelessness.

REFLECTION

'To know, to understand is not enough; the deep spirit of humankind craves for something more, for something which has been given many names, salvation, redemption, eternal life, the Kingdom of Heaven, union with God. A lonely being, contained in the brief span between birth and death, as a physical entity, only an insignificant bundle of atoms in a vast, frightening, impersonal universe, soon to return to dust and be known no more. Yet he feels that he is more than this. He is aware of a 'spark' within him, of himself as an image, perhaps more than an image of divinity, of an undivided Unity from which he is separated and to which he longs to return. He may forget for a time that he is a King's son, forget the Pearl he was sent down to Egypt to find, forget the Glorious Robe which once he wore in his Father's Kingdom, and be sunk in sleep. But the divine light is there within him and cannot for ever be quenched.'

(F. C. Happold – modern writer)

You have probably already experienced both physical and mental suffering in your life. Suffering is part of life – no human being can escape it. Different people respond differently to others' suffering. Some typical responses might include: 'It's nothing to do with me'; 'I must try to help'; 'It's their own fault anyway'; 'It is through suffering that we learn to grow as human beings'. Many people are driven to ask the questions 'Why is there so much suffering in the world?', 'Why if there is a God does he allow such suffering?'.

THE PROBLEM OF EVIL

For **theists** (people who believe in God) the problem of suffering and evil poses some serious questions. Why does God allow evil? Why doesn't God do something about it? If God is all-powerful he must be able to prevent evil. If God is all-loving he must be willing to prevent evil. But if God is both able and willing to prevent evil, then why does evil exist?

Christians believe that much suffering is caused by selfcentredness and ignorance

Traditionally Christian thinkers have said that there are two types of suffering:

- moral – caused by human sin, ignorance and selfishness
- natural – caused by natural phenomena like earthquakes, disease, floods, etc.

Some Christian responses to the problem of evil might include the following.

- A traditional Christian response to suffering is to say that after death all the suffering of this world will be forgotten in the joy of a new life.

- Suffering is caused by selfishness and selfcentredness. This selfishness is sin (see unit 9). Sin is part of human nature and affects everyone. Sin does not mean simply doing something wrong, it is a whole attitude that leads people away from God.

- Human beings have free will: they are free to choose between good and evil, knowledge and ignorance. It is not God that causes suffering but rather human attitudes to life.

- Suffering is part of life. It is only through suffering that people learn to grow into better people. In a world without suffering there would be nothing to struggle for or against, nothing to strive for. 'Suffering is part of your training' (Hebrews 12:7).

- Jesus Christ, the Son of God, was tortured to death. Yet Christians believe that he rose from the dead. Out of the darkness and death came light and hope.

- Suffering is part of life. It is a challenge and because it is energy, it can be transformed into something positive.

- Suffering is built into the birth process of the universe. By suffering we can recognize the pain of others.

THINKING POINT

- *'We must learn that to expect God to do everything while we do nothing is not faith but superstition.'*

(Dr Martin Luther King)

REFLECTIONS

'Human suffering, the sum total of suffering poured out at each moment over the whole earth, is like an immeasurable ocean. But what makes up this immensity? Is it blackness, emptiness, barren wastes? No, indeed: it is potential energy . . . If all the sick people in the world were simultaneously to turn their sufferings into a simple shared longing for the speedy completion of the Kingdom of God through the conquering and organizing of the earth, what a vast leap towards God the world would thereby make!'

(Teilhard de Chardin)

'Dearest Lord, may I see you today and every day in the person of your sick, and, whilst nursing them, minister unto you. Though you hide yourself behind the unattractive disguise of the irritable, the exacting, the unreasonable, may I still recognize you, and say, "Jesus, my patient, how sweet it is to serve you."'

(Opening words of the Daily Prayer, used at Mother Teresa's orphanage in Calcutta)

'The world itself is no problem, but we are a problem to ourselves because we are alienated from ourselves.'

(Thomas Merton, 1915–68 – a Trappist monk who worked for peace and justice in the modern world)

'One of my guards came to me one day and asked, "Do you remember those first six months?" I remembered only too well! They had been horrible, cruel, and this man was the worst. "Now," he said, "Abouna, dear Father, do you forgive me?" I looked at him. "Saeed," I said, "I hated. I need your forgiveness." At that moment I was free.'

(Father Lawrence Jenco – hostage in Beirut)

'Who is this whose ignorant words cloud my design in darkness? Brace yourself and stand up like a man; I will ask questions and you will answer. Where were you when I laid the earth's foundations? Tell me, if you know and understand.'

(Job 38:1–4)

FOR YOUR FOLDERS

▶ What sorts of things make you personally suffer? Are there any ways of escaping this suffering do you think?

▶ Can you believe in God even though there is so much suffering in the world? Give reasons for your answer. Discuss them with a friend.

▶ Look at the reflections. Write down what you think they say about suffering.

▶ Write an essay on the Problem of Evil.

▶ Explain what you think Martin Luther King's words mean.

'Greater love has no man than this, that a man lay down his life for his friends.'

(John 15:13)

Throughout history people have sometimes felt so strongly about something that they are prepared to dedicate their whole lives to their beliefs, and sometimes even willing to die for their beliefs.

Sometimes these beliefs may mean that they do things that are not acceptable to others. However, when people act on beliefs that do no harm to others and are part of an attempt to make the world a more peaceful, just and fair place then these people deserve our respect.

People who are willing to die for their beliefs are usually called **martyrs**. They believe that some force or ideal far greater than their own lives calls them to make a sacrifice of themselves.

THE HIDDEN MULTITUDE

Of course there have been tens of thousands of courageous men and women who have not become known, whose faith has inspired their lives and the lives of others. This prayer, by a poet unknown, was found scribbled on a piece of wrapping paper near the body of a dead child at Ravensbruk concentration camp, one of the Nazi death camps of World War II.

A prisoner's prayer

'O, Lord,
remember not only the men and women of good will
but also those of evil will.
But do not remember all the suffering
they have inflicted upon us;
remember the fruits we have borne
thanks to this suffering –
our comradeship, our loyalty, our humility,
our courage, our generosity,
the greatness of heart
which has grown out of all this;
and when they come to the judgement,
let all the fruits that we have borne
be their forgiveness.'

OSCAR ROMERO

Oscar Romero was Archbishop in El Salvador where the government has consistently violated human rights. Most of the people live in desperate poverty, and in order to keep power the government has brutally and cruelly crushed any opposition. Despite many threats against his life, Romero spoke out against the government in his sermons. In 1980 he was gunned down by four masked men while he celebrated mass in his cathedral. His last words were, *'May Christ's sacrifice give us the courage to offer our own bodies for justice and peace'*.

MOTHER TERESA OF CALCUTTA

For over fifty years, this nun has dedicated her life to helping the destitute and dying people of Calcutta. Her Christian faith has inspired her to live in the slums and share her life with the poor. She says, *'What these people need even more than food and shelter is to be wanted. They understand that even if they only have a few hours left to live, they are loved. Make us worthy Lord, to serve those throughout the world who live and die poor and hungry.'*

MAXIMILIAN KOLBE

Maximilian Kolbe was a Polish Catholic priest who was arrested and taken to Auschwitz, one of the Nazi death camps, in 1941. Auschwitz was a living hell – thousands of people died every day from beatings, torture, disease, starvation or in the gas chambers. Priests were especially ill-treated and on one occasion Father Kolbe was stripped naked and whipped fifty times. One day the guards picked out a man to be tortured to death. Father Kolbe stood and said, 'Take me instead'. He was stripped and thrown into a stinking hole where he starved to death. His heroism echoed through the camp. In 1982 he was made a saint. He once said, *'My aim in life is to serve others'*.

MARTIN LUTHER KING

Dr Martin Luther King was an American Baptist minister. He was dedicated to trying to change the way that black people were treated in America. They earned half as much as white people; many were not allowed to vote; they were not allowed into

Mother Teresa

Martin Luther King

The death of Oscar Romero

certain public places that were reserved for whites only. Despite many death threats he organized campaigns, boycotts, marches and other forms of peaceful protest to bring justice for the black people of America. In 1965 equal voting rights were given to the black people. In 1968, when he was only 39, he was assassinated. His life and his vision of a peaceful and fairer world have become an inspiration for oppressed people all over the world. In a speech he once said, '*I have a dream that one day all God's children, blacks, whites, Jews, Gentiles, Protestants and Catholics, will be able to join hands and sing in the words of the black people's old song, Free at last, free at last, thank God Almighty, we are free at last*'.

FOR YOUR FOLDERS

▶ Oscar Romero spoke of 'Christ's sacrifice'. What was Christ's sacrifice? How do you think Christ's sacrifice has inspired Christians to struggle against injustice and oppression?

▶ Write an essay, using the prisoner's prayer and the profiles in this unit, on 'Service and sacrifice in the twentieth century'.

We live in what is often called the 'technological age'. Modern science and technology have enabled human beings to do the most remarkable things, such as space exploration, the transplantation of human organs, satellite links and global communication, the invention of microchips and complex computer systems, world travel in a matter of hours, the splitting of the atom and the creation of nuclear weapons. As far as scientific and technological knowledge goes, human evolution has certainly been remarkable.

We live in a world that is full of conflict and human misery. Two-thirds of the world's people go hungry; wars and violence rage all over the world; pollution threatens to make the planet earth uninhabitable; our psychiatric hospitals are full of sad and confused individuals; people are cruel to each other in thoughts, words and deeds. As far as knowledge about ourselves and the way we treat others goes, human beings have a lot to learn.

We live in a world in which, especially in the technologically advanced West, we like to think that we've found the answers to the great mysteries of life. Yet we only have to pick up a newspaper or watch the news on television, or experience conflict and pain in our own lives, our homes and our communities to realize that we have a lot to learn.

Yet, because we are human, we still search for the answers to questions that have always puzzled humanity. How can we develop as individuals? How can we learn to get on with others? How can we find peace of mind within ourselves? How should we try to live in this huge, confusing world of ours?

An important part of all sacred writings from all religious traditions is concerned with questions like these. Christians look to the teachings of Jesus Christ as laid out in the Gospels to give them guidance as to how they should live. Christians, and many non-Christians too, believe that Jesus Christ represents the finest example of an ideal person. All the qualities that make up the ideal person are to be found in the way he lived, his attitude towards others and his devotion to God.

Jesus' teachings are challenging. They require self-sacrifice and service. In fact they are so challenging and so demanding that few people in the world today or in the past have been able to follow them completely. In the Gospels the teachings set an *ideal – something people should try to aim for*. If we look at the following teachings, for example, we find that this ideal requires that people have to change the way they think and act.

'Ye have heard how it is said thou shalt love thine neighbour, and hate thine enemy. But I say unto you, love your enemies. Bless them that curse you. Do good to them that hate you.'

(Matthew 5:44–5)

'Ye shall therefore be perfect, even as your father which is in heaven is perfect.'

(Matthew 5:48)

'And thou shalt love the Lord thy God with all thy heart, and with all thy soul, and with all thy mind, and with all thy strength. This is the first commandment. And the second is like unto this. Thou shalt love thy neighbour as thyself. There is none other commandment greater than these.'

(Mark 12:30–1)

'Therefore whatsoever ye would that men should do to you, even so do ye to them.'

(Matthew 7:12)

'Ye have heard how it is said, an eye for an eye: a tooth for a tooth. But I say to you, that ye resist not wrong but whosoever give thee a blow on thy right cheek, turn to him the other.'

(Matthew 5:38–9)

'The Kingdom of God cometh not with waiting for. Neither shall men say: Lo here, lo there. For behold, the Kingdom of God is with you.'

(Luke 17:20–1)

'Judge not, that ye be not judged. For as ye judge, so shall ye be judged.'

(Matthew 7:1)

'Go and sell all that thou hast, and give to the poor, and thou shalt have treasure in heaven and come and follow me, and take up thy cross.'

(Mark 10:21)

'For God sent not his son into the world, to condemn the world: but that the world through him might be saved.'

(John 3:17)

'I am the light of the world. He that followeth me shall not walk in darkness: but shall have the light of life.'

(John 8:12)

'This is my commandment, that ye love together as I have loved you. Greater love than this hath no man, than that a man bestow his life for his friends. Ye are my friends, if ye do whatsoever I command you.'

(John 15:12–14)

There can be little doubt that few people live out these teachings in their daily lives. In the Gospels Jesus Christ teaches that people need to change from within themselves. This idea is often referred to in the Gospels as 'being reborn'. The teachings in the Gospels are basically about humanity rising above the violence which characterizes our present existence, and working towards developing and evolving as human beings. They teach that humanity is capable of undergoing a definite inner development and evolution. This inner evolution requires that people become more understanding and aware of themselves, of others, of the world and of God.

Christians believe that if people worked towards the ideal that Jesus Christ sets in the Gospels, then the world, with all its conflict and violence can begin to change for the better.

FOR YOUR FOLDERS

▶ *'As far as knowledge about ourselves and the way we treat others goes, human beings have a lot to learn.'* What do you think this statement means? Can you think of examples from the world today that back up this statement?

▶ Why do you think Jesus Christ's teachings are often said to be challenging?

▶ Read the quotes from the Gospels again. In a world of violence, revenge, anger, selfishness, pride, poverty and injustice, what might happen to this world if people really began to be 'reborn' and were able to apply these teachings to their daily lives?

CLASS READING

▶ Jesus opens his Sermon on the Mount with the **Beatitudes** (nine blessings). This extract is taken from Matthew 5:1–12, from the *Authorized Version* of the Bible. One pupil could volunteer to read the Beatitudes to the class.

'And seeing the multitudes, he went up into a mountain: and when he was set, his disciples came unto him and he opened his mouth, and taught them, saying,
Blessed are the poor in spirit: for theirs is the kingdom of heaven.
Blessed are they that mourn: for they shall be comforted.
Blessed are the meek: for they shall inherit the earth.
Blessed are they which do hunger and thirst after righteousness: for they shall be filled.
Blessed are the merciful: for they shall obtain mercy.
Blessed are the pure in heart: for they shall see God.
Blessed are the peacemakers: for they shall be called the children of God.
Blessed are they which are persecuted for righteousness' sake: for theirs is the kingdom of heaven.
Blessed are ye, when men shall revile you, and persecute you, and shall say all manner of evil against you falsely, for my sake.
Rejoice, and be exceeding glad: for great is your reward in heaven: for so persecuted they the prophets which were before you.'

(Matthew 5:1–12)

REFLECTIONS

'For God so loved the world that he gave His only begotten Son...'

(John 3:16)

'A new commandment I give unto you, That ye love one another as I have loved you; that ye also love one another.'

(John 13:34)

'Christ cannot appear in anyone save as love, a love which shows itself in life. For this we must die to ourselves: this is the experience of the cross.'

(William Law, 1686–1761 – writer)

'There are three words for "love" in the Greek New Testament; one is the word "eros". Eros is a sort of romantic love. There is and can always be something beautiful about eros. Some of the most beautiful love in all the world has been expressed this way.

Then the Greek language talks about "philos", which is another word for love – a kind of intimate love between friends. This is the kind of love you have for those people that you get along with well, and those whom you like on this level you love because you are loved.

Then the Greek language has another word for love, and that is the word "agape". Agape is more than romantic love, it is more than friendship. Agape is understanding, creative, redemptive goodwill towards all people. Agape is an overflowing love that seeks nothing in return. Theologians would say that it is the love of God operating in the human heart. When you rise to love on this level, you love all men not because you like them, not because their ways appeal to you, but you love them because God loves them. This is what Jesus meant when he said, "Love your enemies". And I'm happy that he didn't say, "Like your enemies", because there are some people that I find it very difficult to like. Liking is an affectionate emotion, and I can't like anyone who would bomb my home. I can't like anyone who would exploit me. I can't like anyone who would trample over me with injustices. I can't like them. But Jesus reminds us that love is greater than liking. Love is understanding, creative, redemptive goodwill towards all people.'

(Dr Martin Luther King)

'Love is patient; love is kind and envies no one. Love is never boastful nor conceited, nor rude; never selfish, not quick to take offence. Love keeps no score of wrongs; does not gloat over other men's sins, but delights in the truth. There is nothing love cannot face; there is no limit to its faith, its hope, and its endurance. Love will never come to an end.'

(St Paul, 1 Corinthians 13:4–8)

'We have just enough religion to make us hate, but not enough to make us love one another.'

(Jonathan Swift)

'It is in the love of Jesus that you have your help. The nature of love is that it shares everything. Love Jesus and everything he has is yours. Because he is God, he is maker and giver of time. Because he is Man, he has given true heed to time.'

(The Cloud of Unknowing)

'Even as love crowns you so shall he crucify you. Even as he is for your growth so is he for your pruning.'

(Kahlil Gibran, 1883–1931 – Lebanese Maronite Christian, poet and artist)

'In the centre of the shopping district, I was suddenly overwhelmed by the feeling that I loved all those people, that they were mine and I theirs, that we could not be alien to one another even though we were total strangers. It was like waking from a dream of separateness, of self-isolation in a special world. The sense of liberation from an illusory difference was such a relief and such a joy to me that I almost laughed out loud ... It is a glorious destiny to be a member of the human race, though it is a race dedicated to many absurdities and one which makes many terrible mistakes: yet, with all that, God Himself gloried in becoming a member of the human race. A member of the human race! To think that such a commonplace feeling should suddenly seem like news that one holds the winning ticket in a cosmic sweepstake ... There is no way of telling people that they are all walking around shining like the sun ... There are no strangers ... If only we could see each other (as we really are) all the time. There would be no more war, no more hatred, no more cruelty, no more greed ... I suppose the big problem is that we would fall down and worship each other ... the gate of heaven is everywhere.'

(Thomas Merton – Trappist monk)

FOR YOUR FOLDERS

In this unit there are reflections on the meaning of Christian love. After reading these reflections answer the following questions and then discuss your ideas about love with a friend.

▶ Explain 'eros', 'philos' and 'agape'.

▶ Which different types of love do they refer to?

▶ What is love according to St Paul?

▶ In St John's Gospel what is Jesus' new commandment?

▶ Explain what you think Dr Martin Luther King, Jonathan Swift, Kahlil Gibran, William Law and Thomas Merton mean by love.

▶ 'Love will never come to an end.' What do you think St Paul meant?

'And God so loved the world that he gave his only begotten Son.'
(John 3:16)

19 CHRISTIANITY AND SCIENCE

INTRODUCTION

Two of the most powerful and important activities throughout human history have been religion and science. They have affected human history probably more than any other activities. Both activities, religion and science, ask questions about the universe in which we live. Scientists ask the question *how?* How did this happen? How did this begin? How can we explain this? Religions ask the question *why?* Why did this happen? Why did this begin? Why am I here?

Over the last 300 years or so, science has had a powerful effect on the way we look at life. Before this, religion was the most powerful human activity. During the past century, because of the rise of modern science, many people have thought that science has explained everything, and Christian ideas are no longer important. More and more people in the West have turned away from religion, believing that science has given humankind all the answers. However, many scientists would disagree with this. They know that science is a process. Scientific ideas are always changing. Scientific laws change as new discoveries are made. For example, the theory of relativity developed by Albert Einstein in the twentieth century threw new light on Isaac Newton's discoveries of the seventeenth century, yet now Einstein's theory has been replaced by the General Theory of Relativity. Religious truths do not change in the same way, and this has often led to conflict between the Christian Churches and science.

CONFLICTS

The universe is enormous. By 'the universe' we mean every physical thing that exists, all matter distributed among and between all the galaxies, all forms of energy, all non-material things such as black holes and gravity waves, and all of space. Scientists who study the universe, like astrophysicists, cosmologists and astronomers, estimate that there are 100 billion galaxies, each with 100 billion stars. In the past the Church taught that the world was at the centre of the universe and that everything revolved around it. When Galileo Galilei (1564–1642) proved that the world revolved around the sun the Pope had him thrown into prison. The Church saw science as being a threat to its teachings. This attitude lasted right up to the middle of the present century.

In 1869, when *On the Origin of Species* by Charles Darwin (1809–82) was published, many Christians felt outraged. They took his theory of natural selection – commonly called evolution – as a threat

to their view of creation, as expressed in Genesis 1–2. Over the next few decades both Christians and non-Christians misinterpreted Darwin's theory. However, Darwin himself remained a firm believer in the existence of a creator God. He once wrote:

'No man can stand in the tropic forests without feeling that they are temples filled with various productions of the God of nature, and that there is more in man than the breath of his body.'

THE THREE-DECKER UNIVERSE

Among many people today, there is the view that science has in some way 'disproved' Christianity. However, the reality is different. What modern science *has* done is seriously question the very traditional, medieval Christian picture of the universe. This simplistic view of the universe looked something like this:

God is a wise old man living 'up there' somewhere in heaven. Below 'his' world, which 'he' created in six days, burn the everlasting fires of hell. The world and its human inhabitants have a very special place in God's affections, and the whole universe revolves around us.

This medieval view is sometimes called the 'three-decker universe' (i.e. heaven, earth, hell). It is easy to understand why some Christians who hold these views have felt threatened by the discoveries of the likes of Galileo and Darwin.

THE CREATION MYTH

One of the chief problems between scientific and Christian thinking has been the interpretation of Genesis. Fundamentalist Christians, who believe that the Bible is true, word for word, have felt they must reject evolutionary theories because they don't fit in with their own literal interpretation of the Creation Story in Genesis. Many Christians today, however, have a very different view. They accept evolutionary theories yet also accept the Creation Story in the Book of Genesis. They believe that the Creation Story, written down over 2400 years ago, is a creation *myth*. The myth had been known for many hundreds of years before it was written down. It had been passed by word of mouth from one generation to another. It was written down by the ancient Hebrews. A myth is not a false story, it can be a true story. *A myth contains the nearest approach to absolute truth that can be stated in words.* Sometimes it is not always easy to explain something in words. It is certainly not easy explaining something as huge and mysterious as the beginning of the universe in words. By using metaphorical language, people get over this problem. A metaphor is like picture language. For example, if somebody asks you, 'What is life?' you might answer, 'It's a journey without a map.'

A very important metaphor in the Creation Myth is the word 'day'. The Hebrew word for *day* is *iom. Iom* has nothing to do with a period of time, like 24 hours. When the ancient Hebrews used the word *iom* it did not refer to a time but to a process (a stream of events that continue to happen). So when they wrote that things were created in a day, they meant that creation takes place over a long period of time *as an ongoing process*. Many Christians believe therefore that the Creation Myth, written 2300 years before Darwin's time, was speaking of an evolutionary process.

ORIGINS OF THE UNIVERSE

Some people still argue that the universe did not have a beginning, but that it has always existed. This is sometimes called the 'Steady State theory'. However, today most astronomers believe that the universe came into being about 18 billion years ago in a gigantic explosion. This is called the 'Big Bang theory'. They also think that the universe is expanding. The temperature at the Big Bang was estimated to be a million billion degrees celsius and the effects of this massive explosion can still be seen in the universe today. Many Christians feel that the Big Bang theory confirms their belief that the universe was created out of nothing. Christians *and* scientists realize that we are talking here about a great mystery. Many questions are raised. When did time begin? What *is* time? Was there a Creator? Where was the Creator? Can the Creator act outside of time? Who made the Creator? Some Christians say that God is self-existing, the *First Cause*, dependent on nothing – whereas everything existing is dependent on God.

RESOLUTIONS

Exciting new discoveries in nuclear physics suggest to many people that the ancient religions contain truths which modern scientists are only just beginning to discover. With the help of the most sophisticated technology, modern physicists have been able to probe more and more deeply into nature. In search of the ultimate building blocks, they discovered atoms, nuclei, electrons, protons and neutrons and many other subatomic particles in the sub-microscopic world. In this tiniest of worlds, remarkable discoveries have been made. The universe is experienced as a dynamic web of inseparable energy patterns. *Everything is connected.* Everything is vibrating with energy. Many modern physicists are beginning to feel that their discoveries of harmonious inter-relationships between all things are similar in nature to the findings of the mystics of religion (see unit 14). These amazing discoveries suggest that the universe is a living whole in which everything has meaning and purpose. Fritjof Capra, a modern physicist, writes:

'Penetrating into even deeper realms of matter, the physicist has become aware of the essential unity of all things and events. More than that, he has also learnt that he himself and his consciousness are an integral part of this unity. Thus the mystic and the physicist arrive at the same conclusion; one starting from the inner realm, the other from the outer world.'

Dom Bede Griffiths (1908–93), a Christian monk, wrote:

'God and the world are not two. There is no God over there, and a world over here. This is an illusion. This universe is a web of interdependent relationships, and we are all parts of this inter-related universe. The whole is in every part, and nothing happens in any part of the universe which doesn't affect the whole ... It's a marvellous vision when you think about it.'

FOR YOUR FOLDERS

▶ What are the differences and similarities between religious and scientific activities?

▶ Write paragraphs on the following: conflicts; the three-decker universe; the Creation Myth; origins of the universe; resolutions.

▶ How do you think it is possible for a scientist to be a Christian?

PENTECOST

The fifth book in the New Testament is called the *Acts of the Apostles*, and was written during the latter part of the first century CE by Luke. His book is the chief source of information about the beginnings of the Christian Church. The following passage is taken from Acts 2 and is an account of what happened to Jesus' disciples during the Jewish festival of Pentecost, fifty days after Jesus' death:

> *'When Pentecost day came round, they had all met in one room, when suddenly they heard what sounded like a powerful wind from heaven, the noise of which filled the entire house in which they were sitting; and something appeared to them that seemed like tongues of fire... they were all filled with the Holy Spirit, and began to speak foreign languages as the Spirit gave them the gift of speech.'*

(Acts 2:1–4)

Christians do not agree on the exact meaning of Luke's story. Some believe that the events did really happen as described, that is, that the disciples actually heard the sound of a great wind and saw tongues of fire in the air. Other Christians think that Luke used wind and fire as symbols of the power and excitement with which the disciples were inspired. However, Luke's message is that the first Christians believed that in founding their Church they were acting under God's inspiration. Luke says that on the morning of Pentecost there were about 120 disciples of Jesus in Jersulam, but by evening their numbers had increased to over 3000. Luke's message is clear – only fifty days after the death of Jesus, his message could inspire large numbers of people to be his disciples and from that time on the religion of Christianity was a force to be reckoned with in the ancient world.

PETER AND PAUL

During the first two centuries CE Christianity began to spread across the known world. Two of the most important figures during this period were Peter, a disciple of Jesus, and Saul of Tarsus, a Jew who later called himself Paul.

Jesus had said to Peter:

> *'You are Peter, the Rock; and on this rock I will build my church.'*

(Matthew 16:18

These words prove to some Christians that Peter wa meant to be the leader of the early Church. This passage in Matthew's Gospel is especially important to Roman Catholic Christians, who regard their leader, called the Pope, as being the successor of Peter (see unit 22).

As the Christian religion began to spread, opposition to it grew and many Christians were killed by its opponents. One such opponent, Saul of Tarsus, took part in this 'persecution' (inflicting suffering on others). However, one day he experienced an event that changed his life. Whilst walking on a road he was blinded by a vision and he heard a voice say, 'Saul, Saul, why do you persecute me?' After this he became convinced of the truth of the Christian faith and set out on long journeys all over the ancient world telling people about Christianity. On his journeys Saul (who changed his name to Paul), wrote many letters, called **Epistles**, which are to be found in the New Testament. In the Epistles, Paul does not recount the life of Jesus, but tries to explain what the early Christians felt was the enormous significance of Jesus' life for the world. After many adventures he arrived in Rome, the capital city of the ancient world, and was beheaded by the Romans in 67 CE. The Romans believed that their emperor was God, not some Jewish teacher whom they had crucified years before.

WORSHIP

In the early years Christians met in houses or in the open air to worship. There were no actual churches built for the first 300 years due to the persecution and poverty of Christians. During this period the Christians thought that Jesus would come again and that the end of the world was very near, so there seemed little point in building places of worship. However, as the years passed, leaders of the Church called bishops, were appointed to look after the areas where there were large groups of Christians.

It was not until the third century CE that the Roman emperors began to tolerate Christianity. The Emperor himself, called Constantine, became a Christian and built a new city called Constantinople Churches were built and Christianity became the new religion of the Roman Empire.

AUTHORITY

By 200 CE Christianity had become established as an institution, headed by bishops, priests and deacons. The early church leadership consisted of a small band of people who taught that their authority came through the Apostles (who had seen the Risen Christ), Peter, and hence from Christ. According to this view, nobody could ever claim to equal their authority – much less challenge it. This was the official view. Any potential leader could only derive their authority from the Apostles. This has been the teaching of the Roman Catholic Church for 2000 years. In other words only the Church leadership has access to the truth of Christianity.

Another group called the Gnostics (from the Greek *gnosis*, meaning knowledge) rejected this view. The Resurrection, they insisted, was not an unique event in the past, but rather symbolized how Christ's presence could be experienced in the present.

GNOSTICISM

In 1945 an astonishing discovery was made near Nag Hammadi in the Egyptian desert. An Arab peasant found 52 papyrus texts buried in an earthenware jar. They included gospels dating from around the same time as the four Gospels were written. Texts such as the Gospels of Thomas, the Gospel of Philip and the Gospel of Mary, show that some Gnostic Christians challenged priestly authority and instead believed *in the presence of the Divine within the human,* that the way to salvation was through self-knowledge and that God was both male and female. Some of the writings, like the Gospel of Mary, suggest that whoever 'sees the Lord' through inner vision can claim that their authority equals that of the Apostles and their successors, the bishops, priests and deacons. The Gnostic teachings were (and some people would argue still are) a potential threat to the institutionalized church.

FOR YOUR FOLDERS

▶ Why do you think that Christians regard Pentecost as being the 'birthday of the Church'?

▶ Why do you think that the early Christians were persecuted? Can you think of groups of people who are persecuted in the world today?

▶ Read Acts 27. This chapter gives an idea of the adventures and difficulties Paul experienced during his journeys. Why do you think the Christian Church regards Paul's journeys as being very important in the history of Christianity?

▶ Explain the Christian Church's teaching on authority.

▶ What have been the consequences of this teaching for 2000 years?

▶ How was this authority questioned by the Gnostics? Who were the Gnostics?

▶ Why according to Elaine Pagels (see thinking point) was the discovery of Nag Hammadi so significant?

▶ What questions about institutionalized Christianity do you think the writings raise?

THINKING POINT

● *'When Muhammed Ali (the Egyptian peasant) smashed that jar filled with papyrus on the cliff near Nag Hammadi and was disappointed not to find gold, he could not have imagined the implications of his accidental find. Had they been discovered 1000 years earlier, the Gnostic texts almost certainly would have been burned for their heresy. But they remained hidden until the twentieth century ... Today we read them with different eyes, not merely as "madness and blasphemy" but as Christians in the first centuries experienced them – a powerful alternative to what we know as orthodox Christian tradition.'*

(Elaine Pagels – modern theologian)

C. 70 CE COUNCIL IN JERUSALEM

The disciples of Jesus were mainly Jewish. The apostle Paul (see unit 20) wanted the early Church to accept Gentiles (non-Jews) into it. After much debate, Gentile converts were recognized as being part of the Church.

325 CE THE COUNCIL OF NICAEA

Arguments about who Jesus was began very early in the history of Christianity. The study of religion is called **theology**, and Christian theologians soon began to disagree about certain **doctrines** (teachings). Questions like: 'Is Jesus truly God?' 'Was Jesus merely a man?' 'Is he both?' were discussed. The first Christian emperor, *Constantine*, called together the first **ecumenical** (worldwide) council of the Christian Church in Nicaea, to discuss these and other questions. The assembled bishops issued a statement about Christian belief (called a **creed**): the Nicene Creed. However, the debates and discussions continued.

381 CE THE FIRST COUNCIL OF CONSTANTINOPLE

The Nicene Creed was reaffirmed and the Council spoke also of the Holy Spirit as equal to the other two persons, 'worshipped and glorified together with the Father and the Son'. The Church in Constantinople was also given 'seniority of honour', after Rome.

451 CE THE COUNCIL OF CHALCEDON

The Council affirmed that Christ 'perfect in Godhead and perfect in humanity' is made known in two natures. Christians in Egypt, Syria and elsewhere rejected this. They were willing to accept that Christ is *from two natures* but not that he is *in two natures*. They separated from Constantinople (known as the Great Schism) and in time the Coptic and Syrian Orthodox Churches were born.

C. 432 CE ST PATRICK (C. 385–C. 461)

St Patrick, a missionary bishop, went to Ireland and established an organized Church.

C. 540 CE THE FIRST MONASTERY

In Monte Cassino in Italy, an Italian Christian called *Benedict* formed a community of men who totally dedicated themselves and their lives to God. Benedict wrote a list of rules by which all his monks had to live (see unit 35).

563 CE COLUMBA

A Celtic monk, *Columba*, started a monastery on the Isle of Iona off the west coast of Scotland. Iona became a centre for the spread of Christianity throughout Britain (see unit 27).

787 CE SECOND COUNCIL OF NICAEA

The Council fully accepted the use of icons in Orthodox worship of God.

988 CE ESTABLISHMENT OF THE CHURCH OF RUSSIA

Vladmir, Prince of Kiev (956–1015) was baptized by missionaries.

1054 CE THE GREAT SCHISM

The word 'schism' means 'tear' in Greek. Over the centuries two main centres of power had developed within Christianity. One was in Rome and the other in Constantinople. After much argument between the *Pope* (the head of the Church in Rome) and the *Patriarch* (the head of the Church in Constantinople) the two centres were torn apart and separated. From this time on, there were two great Christian Churches in the world: the **Catholic** (universal) Church which is based in Rome; and the **Orthodox** (right-thinking) Church which is based in Constantinople.

1095 CE FIRST CRUSADE BEGINS

Christians and Muslims engage in a long and bloody war. The Christian idea of a '**just war**' emerges (see unit 74).

1187 CE JERUSALEM, THE HOLY CITY, IS CAPTURED BY THE TURKS

1233 CE THE INQUISITION

The history of Christianity has often been marred by terrible brutality and bloodshed. *Pope Gregory IX* set up an **Inquisition** (a tribunal or court) to search out and destroy people who were regarded as being 'heretics' (people who did not follow the teachings of the Roman Catholic Church). The Inquisition was cruel, violent and terrifying. Christian theologians went to great lengths to justify using terrible methods of torture to force confessions from so-called heretics. They said it was better for a heretic to suffer pain on earth rather than suffer eternal torture in hell. People found guilty of heresy were handed over to the state and burnt at the stake.

1517 CE THE REFORMATION

During the Middle Ages the Church had enormous power. Many people began to think that the Church was abusing this power. In 1517 a German priest called *Martin Luther* nailed a document on a church door condemning many of the practices of the Church. This was the start of a wave of Church reform which swept through Europe. Many people believed, like Luther, that the Church had lost sight of the true message of Jesus Christ and had become too concerned with wealth and the material world. Luther's act was the beginning of a widespread movement which split the western world. His protest marked the beginning of the formation of the Protestant Churches which began to pull away from the power of Rome.

1526 CE WILLIAM TYNDALE (1492–1536) COMPLETES HIS TRANSLATION OF THE NEW TESTAMENT FROM GREEK INTO ENGLISH

1534 CE KING HENRY VIII BECOMES SUPREME HEAD OF THE CHURCH IN ENGLAND

King Henry VIII and *Pope Leo X* came into dispute because the Pope refused to let the King have a divorce. Henry declared himself Head of the Church in England to replace the Pope. After Henry's death, his break with Rome heralded the **Reformation** in England.

1545 CE THE COUNCIL OF TRENT

The Roman Catholic Church formulated doctrines to protect itself against the growing Reformation. For a hundred years Europe was torn by wars and persecution which often had religious causes.

1611 CE KING JAMES BIBLE (AUTHORIZED VERSION) PUBLISHED

1620 CE THE MAYFLOWER SAILS FROM EUROPE TAKING TO AMERICA ITS FIRST CHRISTIANS

1854 CE POPE PIUS IX ESTABLISHES THE IMMACULATE CONCEPTION OF THE VIRGIN MARY AS AN ARTICLE OF THE ROMAN CATHOLIC FAITH

1859 CE 'ON THE ORIGIN OF SPECIES' BY CHARLES DARWIN PUBLISHED

See unit 19.

1934 CE CREATION OF THE CONFESSING CHURCH

Protestant Christians create the Confessing Church and stand up to the horrors of Hitler's Nazis.

1948 CE FOUNDATION OF THE WORLD COUNCIL OF CHURCHES

See unit 27.

1962–5 CE THE SECOND VATICAN COUNCIL

See unit 23.

1994 CE WOMEN PRIESTS ARE FULLY ORDAINED BY THE CHURCH OF ENGLAND

KEY WORDS

theology	Catholic
doctrines	Orthodox
ecumenical	Inquisition
creed	Reformation
Great Schism	just war

FOR YOUR FOLDERS

▶ Write a sentence about each key word and phrase in this unit and each of the important people in italics.

It is estimated that there are over 20,000 distinct **denominations** (branches) in the modern Christian world. All these denominations belong to much larger groups or 'families'. Unit 21 described how the Church became split into three families. The diagram below illustrates what happened. The chart shows the major differences between these families. The next few units look at these families in more detail.

The Families of Christianity

Christianity developed three major traditions, which arose from particular historical events. To understand them today, it helps to know how each tradition began.

500

From early centuries, the Church had Eastern (Greek-speaking) tradition – based in Alexandria, Antioch, Constaninople – and Western (Latin-speaking) tradition, based in Rome.

1054 The Great Schism: East and West separate

Byzantine Church survived the victories of Islam.Today there are strong Eastern Orthodox Churches in Greece, Russia, Romania and elsewhere.

1000

Strong medieval Church, but with many abuses.

1517 Luther's 95 Theses: the Reformation begins

1500

Counter-Reformation, Council of Trent.

Lutherans, Reformed Churches, Anabaptists and Anglicans made up the Protestant tradition. Protestants have had a tendency to divide. Baptists, Methodists, Quakers, Pentecostals and other groups bring their particular emphasis.

	CATHOLICISM	PROTESTANTISM	ORTHODOXY
	The Roman Catholic Church	The Reformed or Protestant Churches and Groups	The Orthodox Churches
What are they?	All Christians who acknowledge and accept the authority of the Pope (the Bishop of Rome) (see unit 23). There are Catholic groups which are non-Roman, e.g. the Maronites of Lebanon.	All Christian groups who base their beliefs and practices on the Reformation. They include Baptists, United Reformed Church, Methodists, Quakers, Lutherans, Congregationalists, the Pentecostal Church, Salvation Army, etc. (see unit 25).	A group of national or regional churches sometimes called 'eastern' Orthodox which originally accepted the leadership of the Patriarch of Constantinople. There are fifteen Orthodox Churches, including the Russian, Greek and Rumanian Orthodox Churches.
How are they organized?	The Pope is the Head and under him are cardinals, archbishops, priests. There are no separate branches but the Church does have 'orders' of monks and nuns.	Each denomination has its own local, national (and sometimes international) organization. Most belong to the World Council of Churches (see unit 27).	Each Church is self-governing and independent and run by its own Patriarch. Under him there are bishops and priests. They have monks and nuns but they do not have separate 'orders'.
What things do they emphasize?	• The authority of the Pope; • To be the one true Church; • The seven sacraments (see unit 41) of which the Mass is the central point.	• The importance of the Bible, not the traditions of any Church; • The authority of the Bible does not require the Church to interpret it.	• They have the 'true' faith, beliefs and practices handed down by Jesus Christ to his Apostles (see unit 24).

The division of Christianity has led to much conflict, bloodshed and persecution in Christian history. Indeed, in many ways it has been a history of death and division which has gone against the teachings of Jesus Christ. For instance, in Croatia during World War II the fascist government sponsored the forced conversion of the local Serbian Orthodox population to Catholicism. About 350,000 people who refused to submit were slaughtered. Northern Ireland over recent years is an example of how the Christian religion has been abused by some Protestant and Roman Catholic Christians, leading to terrible bloodshed and human tragedy.

THE ECUMENICAL MOVEMENT

However, over the last few decades a movement known as the **Ecumenical** Movement has arisen, aiming to bring unity. The Ecumenical Movement was started to help in missionary work. Divisions among Christians hindered the Churches' efforts to spread the Gospel. This doesn't mean that the Movement is trying to make all Christians 'the same' (which would destroy what is distinctive in each Christian tradition), but it does call on Christians to co-operate in worship and service as far as their conscience allows, and to try and understand each other.

THE WORLD COUNCIL OF CHURCHES

An organization that has had a great influence on the ecumenical movement is the World Council of Churches (WCC) (see unit 27). This was founded in Amsterdam in 1948. With representatives from the Orthodox and Protestant Churches it spearheads and promotes united Christian action throughout the world. As well as dealing with religious themes it also looks at current world problems, such as racism, the arms trade, human rights and world poverty. Critics of the WCC have accused it of being too much concerned with political issues rather than with the Gospel, but for many Christians today, working for peace and justice is seen as part of their faith. The WCC claims to represent over 400 million Christians. It does not claim to be a 'super-Church', but rather a fellowship of Churches. The Roman Catholic Church is not a member of the WCC although some Catholic representatives have taken part in some activities.

THE PAN-ORTHODOX CONFERENCE

This was set up by the Orthodox Church in 1961 and its main aim is to enter into friendly discussions – aimed at promoting unity – with all non-Orthodox Christians.

COMMUNITIES

The effects of the Ecumenical Movement can also be seen in certain communities which are trying to promote a more ecumenical approach. These include communities at Corrymeela (see unit 29), Taizé and Iona (see unit 28).

TALKING POINTS

● *'A cynic might say that the Churches are coming together to fight for survival, at a time when their influence and numbers are declining. But it is also the case that many exciting and creative things are happening at all levels of the Church.'*

(Dr Lorna Brockett)

● *'The ecumenical dialogue is today anything but the speciality of a few starry-eyed peaceniks. For the first time in history it has now taken on the character of an urgent desire for world peace. It can help to make our earth more liveable, by making it more peaceful and reconciled.'*

(Hans Küng, *Christianity and the World Religions*, Collins 1987)

FOR YOUR FOLDERS

▶ Write a sentence about the following words and phrases: ecumenical; unity; WCC.

▶ *'Church attendances falling.'* How could some people argue that the Ecumenical Movement grew because of fears about the survival of the Church?

▶ What problems does the Ecumenical Movement still face?

The Roman Catholic Church believes itself, historically and in its teachings, to be in continuity with the first disciples. The Church holds that God's teachings have been safeguarded and made authentic by the authority of the Church. This authority is exercised especially by the bishops of the local churches, who are still in harmony with the Bishop of Rome (the Pope). Roman Catholics believe that the Pope is the successor of Peter, the disciple (see unit 20). The Pope has special authority and many Roman Catholics believe that he is **infallible** (without error) when he speaks to, and in the name of, the Church, on questions of faith or morals.

The **Catechism** of the Roman Catholic Church (extracts below) gives a summary of some of the beliefs and teachings of the Church.

'Christ Jesus "gave himself for us to redeem us from all iniquity and to purify for himself a people of his own" (Titus 2:14).

"You are a chosen race, a royal priesthood, a holy nation, God's own people" (1 Peter 2:9).

One enters into the People of God by faith and Baptism. "All men are called to belong to the new People of God" so that, in Christ, "men may form one family and one People of God".

The Church is the Body of Christ. Through the Spirit and his action in the sacraments, above all the Eucharist, Christ, who once was dead and is now risen, establishes the community of believers as his own Body.

In the unity of this Body, there is a diversity of members and functions. All members are linked to one another, especially to those who are suffering, to the poor and persecuted.

The Church is this Body of which Christ is the head: she lives from him, in him and for him; he lives with her and in her.

The Church is the Bride of Christ: he loved her and handed himself over for her. He has purified her by his blood and made her the fruitful mother of all God's children.

The Church is the Temple of the Holy Spirit. The Spirit is the soul, as it were, of the Mystical Body, the source of its life, of its unity in diversity, and of the riches of its gifts and charisms.

Hence the universal Church is seen to be "a people brought into unity from the unity of the Father, the Son and the Holy Spirit".'

(Catechism of the Catholic Church, 1994)

THE SECOND VATICAN COUNCIL

For many years the Roman Catholic Church altered very little in its organization, its beliefs and its attitude towards the other Christian Churches. However, in recent times, while still insisting on the truth of its traditional teachings, the Roman Catholic Church has begun to change its outlook on the world. These changes were set in motion by a 76-year-old Italian Pope called Angelo Roncalli, who in 1958 became Pope John XXIII.

In 1962 Pope John XXIII called a Council of Roman Catholic Churchmen from all over the world to meet at the Vatican. This assembly of 2600 bishops, cardinals, abbots and heads of religious orders was called the Second Vatican Council. The First Vatican Council had been in 1869. The aim of the Second Vatican Council was to try to bring the Church up to date and make it more aware of the issues facing people in the twentieth century. Before the Council, Pope John XXIII had set up the Vatican Secretariat for promoting Christian unity – a committee that looked at the relationship between the Roman Catholic Church and other churches.

When John XXIII died in 1963 his successor Pope Paul VI continued the work of the Council.

WHY WAS THE SECOND VATICAN COUNCIL SO IMPORTANT?

- For the first time the Roman Catholic Church began to acknowledge and listen to the other Christian Churches. A greater atmosphere of tolerance and trust was created. Religious intolerance and the religious persecutions of the past were condemned.

- Before the Council, worship was carried out in Latin. Millions of people never really understood what was being said. After the Council, worship was in the vernacular (i.e. the actual language of the people).

- There was less Church censorship of reading material and teachers in schools had more freedom.

- The Church described itself as 'the pilgrim people of God'. This was a new emphasis underlining the importance of every believer, and seeing the followers of Jesus Christ as being 'on the way together'.

- The problems facing the human race were looked at seriously. The Council called for the abolition of nuclear weapons; an end to the arms trade; a fairer distribution of the world's resources; a renewed struggle against racism; a greater understanding of the communist world.

- A more tolerant attitude was adopted towards other world religions.

However, many of the Church's teachings remained the same:

- Papal infallibility was confirmed.

- Beliefs about the Virgin Mary (see unit 12) remained the same.

- Artificial forms of contraception were condemned (see unit 57).

- Abortion was 'an evil that poisoned society' (see unit 70).

TALKING POINTS FROM THE COUNCIL

- 'We must not remain indifferent to those communities whose citizens suffer from poverty, misery and hunger.'

- 'The arms race should cease... nuclear weapons should be banned.'

- 'Virginity must be regarded as a gift from God.'

- 'From the moment of conception life must be guarded with the greatest care. '

- 'All who are baptized have a right to be honoured as Christians.'

FOR YOUR FOLDERS

▶ Write a letter to a friend who knows nothing about the Roman Catholic Church explaining something about it.

▶ What changes did the Second Vatican Council bring about?

▶ Which teachings remained the same?

▶ What is papal infallibility? Why might some non-Catholics see this as causing problems for Church unity?

▶ Why do you think the Second Vatican Council is seen by many as being so important?

▶ Imagine you are a newspaper reporter at the Council. Write an article about what you consider to be the most important aspects of the Council. The article should be about 100 words long.

FURTHER READING

For more information on the Roman Catholic Church see *Roman Catholic Christianity*, by Clare Richards, Heinemann Educational 1995.

In this unit Father Gregory Wirdnam of the British Orthodox Church explains his Orthodox faith.

'The Orthodox faith is built upon the two foundations of holy scripture and holy tradition. We believe in the teachings of Jesus Christ as revealed in the Gospels and through the witness of the apostles, beginning with the letters of Paul and Peter, which have been transmitted to us through the Church and continue even now through the grace of the Holy Spirit. Our belief is encapsulated in the Niceno-Constantinopolitan creed which we recite at each celebration of the Divine Liturgy and in the decrees of the Holy Ecumenical Councils. We believe in the Holy Trinity – God the Father, the creator of all things, God the Son, who became man, died for our sins and rose again from the dead, and God the Holy Ghost, the Spirit of Truth who fills all things. Our Lord and Saviour Jesus Christ is both God and human, born of the blessed Virgin Mary, the **Theotokos** *or Mother of God.*

At one time, all Christians were part of the one holy, **Catholic** *(worldwide), Apostolic Church, but in the eleventh century the Western Churches broke away from the Eastern ones and were further divided at the time of the Protestant Reformation. Orthodox Christians can be found in all parts of the world, often among communities with a common ethnic background. The Byzantine Orthodox – mainly Russian and Greek – are probably most familiar to Western Christians, but there are also the Oriental Orthodox from Syria, Ethiopia, Armenia, Southern India and the Coptic Church in Egypt. Byzantine and Oriental Orthodox share a common faith and tradition.*

Being an Orthodox Christian involves much more than simply attending church regularly, although that is fundamental to the faith. Believing in Our Lord Jesus Christ means making a change in one's life and behaviour, turning away from the impermanent things of this world and trying to become more like Christ each day in word and deed, advancing from glory to glory, like the holy men and women, the saints, have done. This spiritual struggle is hard. It could never be sustained by humankind alone but only when God and humanity work together. Not only

An Orthodox church in Russia

human beings but the whole of God's creation must be **transfigured** *by the light of God's love working through us, for everything created by God is good – especially human beings who were formed in his image and likeness. Evil entered into the world through humankind's disobedience when we fell from God's grace and is personified in the devil. Evil must be resisted wherever it is found – especially in our own hearts. The image of God in humankind has been defaced by sin and must be restored to its original likeness.*

Difficult questions and moral decisions must be answered according to one's own conscience through prayer, through the teachings of Our Lord and with the guidance of the Church. It is essential that all these are consulted because human beings are prone to error by their very nature. Spiritual warfare requires unceasing vigilance.

To help and assist us, Our Lord left us the Holy Sacraments, especially the Holy **Eucharist** *when we share in his body and blood [see units 41 and 43]. This is the heart of the Divine* **Liturgy** *– the most important service for Orthodox Christians. In addition, there are the* sacraments of **Baptism** *(the washing away of sin);* **Chrismation** *(receiving the Holy Spirit through anointing with holy oil);* **Ordination** *(the setting apart of bishops, priests and deacons by the laying on of hands);* **Marriage** *(the sanctification of the union between man and woman);* **Confession** *(receiving forgiveness of sins committed after Baptism); and* **Holy Unction** *(anointing a sick person with holy oil).* [See units 41 and 55–7.] *On each of these occasions we believe that God is present and gives his grace and blessing upon us. For a short time in each celebration of the Liturgy we are lifted up to heaven in the presence of God and his holy angels.*

This sense of mystery is a very strong element in Orthodox belief and worship. God cannot be understood through human reason, which is limited, or through the senses, which are liable to error, but he can be understood through our spiritual understanding, which can glimpse beyond what appears on the surface. Through prayer and stillness we can gradually come closer to God, whose Son shared our humanity. Many Orthodox Christians use the beautiful 'Jesus Prayer' ('Oh Lord Jesus Christ, Son of God, have mercy on me, a sinner') as a means of focusing their whole being on God. This wonderful prayer originated in monasteries, which have always been storehouses of Orthodox spirituality and fountains of wisdom. They continue to witness to the strength of faith in all parts of the world.

In our struggles to be more like Christ we continue to have successes and failures. Christ is our ultimate goal but we will only reach him and achieve salvation at his second coming. For us, salvation cannot be achieved in a moment. It is a process that begins at Baptism and continues throughout our lives. Even the faithful departed, continue to be prayed for in the Orthodox tradition and the saints who have gone before us watch over us, for in the eyes of God we are all one family. The **icons** *that adorn our churches remind us of this and we venerate the holy men and women they represent.*

In the name of the Father and the Son and the Holy Ghost. Amen.'

TALKING POINTS

- *'We know that our life is temporary, and we had better live with Christ and offer ourselves, and have true life in him... The pressures of life have brought us that really deep life of close relation with God.'*

  (Pope Shenouda III – leader of the Egyptian Coptic Church)

- *'The object of our search is the fire of grace which enters into the heart... When the spark of God Himself – grace – appears in the heart, it is the prayer of Jesus which quickens it and fans it into flame... The essential thing is to hold oneself ready before God, calling out to Him from the depths of one's heart... God is concerned with the heart.'*

  (Bishop Theophanes)

- *'An icon or a cross does not exist simply to direct our imagination during our prayers. It is a material centre in which there rests an energy, a divine force, which unites itself to human art.'*

  (Vladimir Lossky)

FOR YOUR FOLDERS

▶ Briefly outline the major beliefs of Orthodox Christians.

▶ Explain the following words and phrases: Theotokos; Catholic; icons; transfigured; the Jesus Prayer.

▶ What do you think Father Gregory means by the 'spiritual struggle'?

▶ How are Christians assisted in this struggle according to the Orthodox faith?

▶ What part does prayer play in the faith?

▶ Explain in your own words the Orthodox view on salvation.

Unit 21 describes how the Protestant Churches grew from the Reformation in the sixteenth century. This unit looks at some of the main characteristics of the largest Protestant Churches.

THE LUTHERAN CHURCH

The Lutheran Church is found mainly in the German-speaking countries, Scandinavia and North America. There are about 70 million Lutherans in the world today, and they trace their origins back to the teachings of the German monk, Martin Luther (1483–1546). They stress Luther's ideas, especially the idea of 'justification by **faith**', which Luther defined as 'having true faith that Christ is your saviour, then at once you will have a gracious God'. In their worship they emphasize preaching, the sacraments, Bible readings and **hymn** singing, and they have women **priests**.

THE REFORMED CHURCHES

After the Roman Catholic Church, the Reformed Churches are the most widely spread throughout the world. Beginning in the sixteenth century with Martin Luther and the Swiss reformers, Zwingli and John Calvin (1509–64), the Reformed Movement spread in all directions across Europe. In the next century it grew in many other parts of the world. The main reason it spread so far and so wide was the huge division it experienced within itself. However, despite these divisions, all the Reformed Churches have some common characteristics. They all place a strong emphasis on the importance of the Bible, on God's sovereignty, his justification and sanctification of the believer, and Jesus' headship of the Church. The most obvious similarity is in the way the Churches are run. There are three types of leader at the local level: the minister, the elder and the deacon. Because the elder or **presbyter** is the main figure, many Reformed Churches in English-speaking countries call themselves 'Presbyterian'. Congregational Churches also belong to the Reformed family.

Scotland has a strong Reformed Church tradition. The national church is the Presbyterian Church of Scotland. In some of the smaller Presbyterian Churches traces of the Puritan tradition, with its emphasis on preaching and Sunday observance, is strong. Wales, Northern Ireland and the Irish Republic each have their own Presbyterian Church, while in England the Presbyterian and Congregational Churches united in 1972 to form the **United Reformed Church** (see unit 42).

THE FREE CHURCHES

From the English-speaking churches of the seventeenth and eighteenth centuries came a number of churches now known as the Free Churches or Non-conformist Churches. The best known include the Baptists, the Methodists, the Pentecostal Churches, the Salvation Army and the Society of Friends (sometimes known as 'Quakers').

The Baptists

There are some 32 million Baptists worldwide. The main characteristics of the Baptist Churches are:

● **'the priesthood of believers'** – all members fully participate in every aspect of the life of the Church.

● **'believers' baptism'** – only people who are able to understand and accept the Christian faith, and who can explain their own personal decision to follow Jesus Christ, are baptized (see unit 55).

The Methodists

The founders of Methodism were two eighteenth-century Anglican clergymen, John Wesley (1703–91) and Charles Wesley (1707–88). Methodists keep their worship simple. It is made up of hymn singing, prayers, Bible readings and a sermon. Except for Holy Communion, Methodists rarely use a service book. Hymn singing plays an important part in Methodism. The Wesleys, who wrote some of the finest hymns in the Christian religion, wanted to 'inject some life into services'. The first words in the Methodist hymn book state, 'Methodism was born in song'.

The Pentecostal Churches

The Pentecostal Church puts great emphasis on the day of Pentecost, when the first Christians experienced the living power of the Holy Spirit (see unit 20). The distinctive doctrine of the Pentecostalists is their belief in the 'baptism of the Holy Spirit', an individual experience of God said to enrich and empower the Christian life. Many believe that glossolating (speaking in tongues) is the initial physical evidence of an encounter with God. The Pentecostal Churches are active in sending missionaries around the world and they lay great stress on **evangelism** (spreading the message) and mission. There are many branches of the Pentecostal Church including Wesleyan Pentecostalists, Baptistic Pentecostalists, Oneness Pentecostalists and Pentecostal Apostolics. Around the world, there are also Indigenous Pentecostals who usually reflect features of their own culture or founder, or both (e.g. the snake-handling Pentecostals in the Appalachian mountains of North America).

The Salvation Army

The Salvation Army was founded by William Booth (1829–1912), a Methodist minister who worked in the slums of Victorian England. The movement is built on military lines. The minister is an 'officer', the members are 'soldiers', and they all wear uniforms. The place where they meet for worship is called a 'Citadel'. The Salvation Army works all over the world among the poor and underprivileged. Music is a very important part of the Army's worship, and every service or open air meeting is filled with the sounds of brass bands, hand clapping and the singing of 'songs' (hymns). There is no set form of worship and the leader of a meeting has almost complete freedom to plan it as he or she wishes.

The Society of Friends ('Quakers')

'Quaker' was the nickname given to the founder of the Society of Friends, George Fox (1624–91), by a judge whom he told to 'quake and fear at the word [of God]'. Quakers' worship is extremely simple and they reject all ceremony. They base their religion on the belief that God speaks directly to the heart of everyone. They have no creed, sacraments, ordained ministry, ordered services or sacred buildings. In their services silence is important, with people speaking if they feel moved to do so (see unit 42).

The Evangelicals

Evangelical Christians are among the fastest growing groups in Christianity today. The word 'evangelical' is defined as 'certain Christian churches which believe in the importance of religious teaching, of faith and of studying the Bible, rather than in ceremonies' (Longman, *Dictionary of Contemporary English*) and 'churches or individuals who present the "good news" with a view to the conversion of hearers to their faith'.

Evangelical Christians stress:

● the Bible as the inspired word of God

● the need for a personal relationship with Jesus Christ through 'conversion' and a 'new birth'

● their commitment to convert others.

The Charismatic movement

In the various Christian denominations, there are sometimes groups and congregations who exhibit an uninhibited joy about their faith . Worshippers often clap their hands, raise their hands or lead the prayers. This movement first emerged in California in the USA in the 1960s and became known as the Charismatic Movement. The word 'charismatic' comes from a Greek word meaning 'gifts', referring to the special powers Christians believe are given by the Holy Spirit. These gifts include healing, prophecy and speaking in tongues (see unit 4).

FOR YOUR FOLDERS

▶ Explain the following words and phrases: Protestant; justification by faith; Presbyter; Free Churches; Citadel; priesthood of all believers; believers' baptism; Quaker; 'Baptism of the Holy Spirit'; glossolating.

▶ Write a few sentences about the main characteristics of the different groups you have looked at in this unit, and about Martin Luther, John Calvin, the Wesleys, William Booth and George Fox.

▶ What reasons can you give for the differences in Protestant Christian worship and belief?

The enthronement of the Archbishop of Canterbury, in 1991

The **Anglican** Church began with the Church of England, but today Anglican Churches are found all over the world. The Church of England separated from the Church of Rome in the sixteenth century for political and doctrinal reasons. The authority of the Pope over the Church of England was rejected. Instead the monarch became Supreme Governor of the Church, appointing archbishops and bishops. The link between Church and State, known as 'establishment', still survives in England. (The 'Established Church' in Scotland is the Presbyterian Church of Scotland.) Through establishment, the Church of England is closely linked with many aspects of life in England. Bishops of the Church can sit in the House of Lords and so take a direct part in the government of the country.

Anglicans are agreed that their Church is part of the 'Catholic' Church (not the Roman Catholic Church, but the holy catholic Church referred to in the Creeds). Not all Anglicans are happy to be called Protestant. In practice some priests and local congregations are closer to the Protestant tradition while others follow a Roman Catholic lead in some of their beliefs and practices.

'At its best ... the Anglican Church ... tries to hold together the more Catholic traditions; the evangelical emphasis on the Bible and personal conversion and openness to new ideas.'

(Donald Coggan, formerly Archbishop of Canterbury)

Because of this diversity, and because Anglicans frequently claim that they have no doctrine of their own but only that of the universal Church, it is difficult to summarize the Anglican position. However, at the Lambeth Conference in 1920, the following four points were emphasized.

- The Holy Scriptures contain everything necessary for salvation.
- The Apostles' Creed and the Nicene Creed express Christian faith.
- The two sacraments of Baptism and the Lord's Supper are celebrated.
- 'The historic episcopate' (i.e. the line of bishops in a carefully maintained succession) is preserved.

Today the Church of England has about 18,000 churches, most with a square tower or lofty spire outside and the long nave leading to the altar inside.

A WORLDWIDE CHURCH

During the eighteenth and nineteenth centuries the Church of England grew rapidly throughout the world, due to expanding British influence through trade and colonization and missionary activity (see units 30 and 75). Although the Anglican family of Churches is not one of the largest it is, after the Roman Catholic Church, possibly the most widespread. The Anglican Churches are mostly found in countries which were once British but are now independent, e.g. the United States, Australia and Canada, but the largest Anglican populations overseas are in Africa. In Africa and South America the Anglican Churches reach well outside the former colonial territories. Almost all these Churches are now independent but recognize the Archbishop of Canterbury as their leader and the focus of their unity. Every ten years the Anglican Churches, represented by their bishops, meet at the Lambeth Conference (named after Lambeth Palace, the Archbishop's London residence). This is the most important 'instrument of unity' between the different Churches.

The Anglican Churches are also united by a shared conviction that worship is at the heart of their life and mission. Until quite recently all Anglicans used a version of *The Book of Common Prayer* – first used in the sixteenth century and in some versions almost unchanged. Today's modern versions allow for more variety, but there are certain central ingredients in common (e.g. hymns, psalms, confessional prayers, sermons) and the outline of the service is familiar all over the world.

THE CHURCH AT WORK

The Church of England is concerned about the type of society we live in. It has many organizations concerned with helping the poor, helpless and underprivileged members of society.

- **The Children's Society** (see unit 64) which runs adoption agencies, schools and nurseries for disabled children, gypsy playgroups, hostels for single parents and their babies, etc. as well as promoting the welfare of deprived children.

- **The Church Army** made up of about 150 'officers' who help the aged, run housing schemes for the homeless, run hostels, work with prisoners, etc.

Prayers, psalms, canticles (short religious songs) and hymns play an important part of Anglican Church services. Here is the *Benedicte Omnia Opera*, one of the most beautiful canticles used in the services:

1   *O all ye works of the Lord, bless ye the Lord:*
        praise him, and magnify him for ever.

2   *O ye angels of the Lord, bless ye the Lord:*
        praise him, and magnify him for ever.

3   *O ye heavens, bless ye the Lord:*
    O ye waters that be above the firmament, bless ye the Lord:
    O all ye powers of the Lord, bless ye the Lord:
        praise him and magnify him for ever.

4   *O ye sun and moon, bless ye the Lord:*
    O ye stars of heaven, bless ye the Lord:
    O ye showers and dew, bless ye the Lord:
        praise him, and magnify him for ever.

5   *O ye winds of God, bless ye the Lord:*
    O ye fire and heat, bless ye the Lord:
    O ye winter and summer, bless ye the Lord:
        praise him, and magnify him for ever.

6   *O ye dews and frosts, bless ye the Lord:*
    O ye frost and cold, bless ye the Lord:
    O ye ice and snow, bless ye the Lord:
        praise him, and magnify him for ever.

7   *O ye nights and days, bless ye the Lord:*
    O ye light and darkness, bless ye the Lord:
    O ye lightnings and clouds, bless ye the Lord:
        praise him, and magnify him for ever.

8   *O let the earth bless the Lord:*
    O ye mountains and hills, bless ye the Lord:
    O all ye green things upon the earth, bless ye the Lord:
        praise him, and magnify him for ever.

9   *O ye wells, bless ye the Lord:*
    O ye seas and floods, bless ye the Lord:
    O ye whales and all that move in the waters, bless ye the Lord:
        praise him, and magnify him for ever.

10   *O all ye fowls of the air, bless ye the Lord:*
    O all ye beasts and cattle, bless ye the Lord:
    O ye children of men, bless ye the Lord:
        praise him, and magnify him for ever.

11   *O let Israel bless the Lord:*
    O ye priests of the Lord, bless ye the Lord:
    O ye servants of the Lord, bless ye the Lord:
        praise him, and magnify him for ever.

12   *O ye spirits and souls of the righteous, bless ye the Lord:*
    O ye holy and humble men of heart, bless ye the Lord:
    O Ananias, Azarias, and Misael, bless ye the Lord:
        praise him, and magnify him for ever.
    Glory be to the Father, and to the Son: and to the Holy Spirit;
    As it was in the beginning, is now, and ever shall be: world without end. Amen.

FOR YOUR FOLDERS

▶ Why is the Church of England often called the 'Established Church'?

▶ Why do you think the Anglican Church has been called 'the middle way'?

▶ Which event and which book have helped keep a sense of unity within the Anglican Church?

▶ In the last few units you have studied the 'three great families'. Write an article about them called 'A family divided yet together'.

The World Council of Churches (WCC) was formed in 1948.

'It is a fellowship of Churches which confess the Lord Jesus Christ as God and Saviour according to the scriptures, and therefore seek to fulfil together their common calling to the glory of the One God, Father, Son and Holy Spirit.'

Apart from the Roman Catholic Church and some Evangelical Churches, all significant Christian Churches now belong to the WCC. Since 1961 the Roman Catholic Church has sent official observers to the general assemblies. These assemblies are attended by thousands of delegates from all over the world. They discuss a wide variety of issues.

The twentieth century has seen remarkable progress towards Christian unity. There have been few Church mergers, but there have been great changes in the attitudes of different Churches to one another. Most Churches recognize that they do not necessarily possess the whole truth and are more willing to learn from others.

The WCC has not been without troubles and controversy. For example, some Christians have argued that the WCC has become too 'political', whereas others believe that part of the Christian mission on earth is to become involved with political and social issues. Generally the WCC has three main areas of work:

- faith and witness – making people aware of the Christian message
- justice and service – helping to promote peace and justice in the world
- communication – promoting tolerance and knowledge globally.

FOR YOUR FOLDERS

Read the reflection opposite and answer the following questions.

▶ Who are the millions who face 'a daily struggle for survival'?

▶ What is the 'Ecumenical Movement'?

▶ What do you think were the major concerns of this Assembly?

▶ What do you think are some of the major beliefs of the WCC?

▶ *'The misery and chaos of the world result from the rejection of God's design for us.'* Comment.

'There is a great divide between North and South, between East and West'

REFLECTION

'We are filled with praise to God for the grace given to us since our last meeting. In many places churches have grown in numbers and depth of commitment. We rejoice in courage and faith shown in adversity. We are humbled by those newly called to be martyrs. The Holy Spirit has poured out these and many other gifts, so that we meet with thanksgiving.

This meeting comes in a succession which began at Amsterdam in 1948 with the commitment to stay together. Since then we have been called to grow together and to struggle together. Here under the theme "Jesus Christ, the Life of the World" we are called to live together...

We hear the cries of millions who face a daily struggle for survival, who are crushed by military power or the propaganda of the powerful. We see the camps of refugees and the tears of all who suffer inhuman loss. We sense the fear of rich groups and nations and the hopelessness of many in the world rich in things who live in great emptiness of spirit. There is a great divide between North and South, between East and West. Our world – God's world – has to choose between "life and death, blessing and curse"...

The misery and chaos of the world result from the rejection of God's design for us. Constantly, in public and private, fellowship is broken, life is mutilated and we live alone. In the life of Jesus we meet the very life of God, face to face. He experienced our life, our birth and childhood, our tiredness, our laughter and tears. He shared food with the hungry, love with the rejected, healing with the sick, forgiveness with the penitent...

The division of the Church at central points of its life, our failure to witness with courage and imagination, our clinging to old prejudice, our share in the injustice of the world – all this tells us that we are disobedient. Yet God's graciousness amazes us, for we are still called to be God's people, the house of living stones built on Christ the foundation. One sign of this grace is the Ecumenical Movement in which no member or Church stands alone.

The Assembly therefore renews its commitment to Church unity. We take slow, stumbling steps on the way to the visible unity of the Church but we are sure the direction is essential to our faithfulness...

We renew our commitment to mission and evangelism. By this we mean that deep identification with others in which we can tell the good news that Jesus Christ, God and Saviour, is the Life of the World. We cannot impose faith by our eloquence. We can nourish it with patience and caring so that the Holy Spirit, God the Evangelist, may give us the words to speak. Our proclamation has to be translated into every language and culture. Whatever our context among people of living faith and no faith, we remember that God's love is for everyone, without exception...

We renew our commitment to justice and peace. Since Jesus Christ healed and challenged the whole of life, so we are called to serve the life of all. We see God's good gift battered by the powers of death. Injustice denies God's gifts of unity, sharing and responsibility. When nations, groups and systems hold the power of deciding other people's lives, they love that power. God's way is to share power, to give it to every person...

The arms race everywhere consumes great resources that are desperately needed to support human life. Those who threaten with military might are dealing in the politics of death. It is a time of crisis for us all. We stand in solidarity across the world to call persistently, in every forum, for a halt to the arms race. The life which is God's good gift must be guarded when national security becomes the excuse for arrogant militarism. The tree of peace has justice for its roots.

Life is given. We receive God's gift with constant thankfulness... We are astounded and surprised that the eternal purpose of God is persistently entrusted to ordinary people. That is the risk God takes. The forces of death are strong. The gift of life in Christ is stronger. We commit ourselves to live that life, with all its risks and joys, and therefore dare to cry, with all the host of heaven, "O death, where is your victory?" Christ is risen. He is risen indeed.'

(*One World*, WCC Magazine)

This unit looks at two Christian communities that are living examples of ecumenism working in the world today.

◇

IONA

Iona is an island off the west coast of Scotland. It was regarded as being a holy place when St Columba went there in 563 CE. The Iona community was founded by the Reverend George Macleod in 1938. Whilst working in the slum areas of Glasgow, Macleod had come to believe that many working people had lost touch with the Church. He wanted to form a community in which everyone from all walks of life could live, work and worship together. After years of hard work Macleod and others rebuilt the abbey on the island and the community grew. Today there are about 150 people. Over 1000 people a year visit the abbey and the youth camp. Members of the community keep half an hour for prayer every morning, give five per cent of their money to the community fund and try to live together by following Christian ideals. The reflection on this page gives an account of a visit made to Iona by a 16-year-old girl.

The abbey of St Columba, Iona

REFLECTION

'Iona struck me almost immediately as being a beautiful and special place. The light is so bright, the sea so wild and the weather so changeable. We were met from our small boat by two community members who took us to the restored abbey. After dinner we introduced ourselves – everyone was so friendly and we were given our little chores for the week.

During the week we had talks and discussions about all sorts of things, especially about world poverty and world peace. We learnt about how the work of Iona goes on in the slums of Glasgow and we felt the commitment of the people living on Iona. After a week there I felt rested both in body and mind. In a strange sort of way I felt that I had experienced a force greater than myself – I call this force God. I had also made friends for life because they had lived and shared this Iona experience with me.'

(Author's interview)

TAIZÉ

'That Christ may grow in me, I must know my own weakness and that of my brothers. For them I will become all things to all, and even give my life, for Christ's sake and the Gospel's.'

(From *The Rule of the Community*)

These words are often spoken by the brothers of Taizé, a Christian community in a small village in France. The brothers, who come from all over the world themselves, work amongst the poor in places like Kenya, New York, Bangladesh and Japan.

The Taizé community was founded by a young student called Roger Schutz in 1940. He felt strongly that there was a need for a new kind of monasticism within the Protestant Church (see unit 35). The members of the Taizé community take the traditional vows of poverty, chastity and obedience. The brothers provide for thousands of visitors every year and have their own printing press, co-operative farm and pottery. Taizé is particularly aware of the needs of young people and every year thousands of them from all over the world camp in the fields around the monastery, taking part in private and public worship, discussions and manual work.

The reflection below gives an account of one person's experience at Taizé.

REFLECTION

'The Church of Reconciliation rose in front of me... inside it was dark, cool and crowded. We sat on the carpeted floor. It was quiet; the brothers in robes knelt or sat in a wide line down the centre of the church. The service began. We sang, listened to Bible readings in several languages, and prayed in even more languages; then a long period of silence and meditation followed. To sit on the floor – shoulder to shoulder – in silence – this was very powerful. I could feel the silence. After this, you could take communion, Roman Catholics on one side of the church, the rest on the other ....

Lying on my bed, events of the day flashed by, as did the week. Talking and listening, caring and sharing, discussing what Christianity had to offer and not only with Christians. What remains in my mind? – the weekly Easter perhaps! The pace quickens, the church is jam-packed on Fridays as the cross is laid flat on the floor, prayers are offered for persecuted Christians and for those who are prisoners of conscience. You may press your head to the cross as a sign to commit all that weighs you down to Christ.

It is sad to leave a place where one has felt at home. I had only really started to understand Taizé. It wasn't just the personality of Brother Roger, nor the brothers, nor the place, nor even all the people I had shared my life with for a week. In some way it was all of them rolled into one. To be part of something living, vital, enthusiastic and emotional is tremendous, for it makes you vital too. Perhaps the vitality in all of us is to be used for the benefits of the community and the world.'

(Author's interview)

FOR YOUR FOLDERS

▶ Write a sentence about Roger Schutz and George Macleod.

▶ What do you think are the aims of the Taizé and Iona communities?

▶ Why did the person at Taizé describe his experience as 'vital and enthusiastic'?

▶ Why do you think many people have lost touch with the Church? Give reasons.

▶ What did the person at Iona experience?

▶ Do you think that young people, whether Christian or not, should have access to places like Iona and Taizé?

▶ Note some of the similarities and differences between the two communities.

In the recent past Northern Ireland has been torn apart by internal division and the religious conflict between Roman Catholics and Protestants is often said to be the root cause of this conflict. Whether this is true or not, in one part of Northern Ireland a religious community is trying in its own way to work for peace.

Corrymeela was founded in 1965 by Ray Davey, a chaplain, and by Christians – Catholics and Protestants – who were aware of the deep divisions within Northern Ireland. The main site is at Ballycastle on the beautiful County Antrim coast.

The main aim of the community, which has 140 members and over 1000 'friends', is **reconciliation**. The Ballycastle centre provides a place where people from different traditions can meet and talk freely. In the course of the year, 8000 people from a wide variety of traditions and backgrounds visit Corrymeela. Each group is in residence for between two days and a week. They include families under stress, like families of prisoners; those bereaved in the violence; single-parent groups; those from areas of tension and social deprivation; school, youth and church groups; the unemployed; the disabled; senior citizens; group conferences on peace work and social, political and religious issues; the victims of violence.

An important part of the work at Corrymeela is about trying to help young people to understand themselves, their relationships and their communities. The community at Corrymeela run what is known as 'seed groups'. This involves about twenty young people between the ages of 18 and 21, meeting every weekend for six months. The

Reverend Douglas Baker, a worker at Corrymeela, explains the ideas of the seed group:

'Jesus uses the way seeds grow as a parable to help his followers understand how God's kingdom grows in the world. It is a powerful message of hope for all who in each generation long for the spread of God's kingdom and through their own lives seek to become tools through whom it is nurtured. The aims we have identified for the "seed groups" are:

- **reflecting** *on all of the experiences and influences which have shaped who we are – on the issues and choices which confront us in terms of who we shall become;*
- **understanding** *ourselves and our relationships with others;*
- **relating** *the Christian faith to our own experience;*
- **building** *bridges of trust, understanding and personal friendship;*
- **encouraging** *the development of ideas for reconciliation.'*

Many Christians pray that the deep divisions within Northern Ireland are at last being healed

KEY IDEAS

'Corrymeela is a *symbol* that Catholics and Protestants can work together in real Christian fellowship.

It is a *channel* through which all sorts of people can work together, using their unique talents to build a new society.

It is a *challenge* not to surrender to apathy or despair but to work courageously for peace and understanding wherever we are.'

(*Corrymeela* leaflet)

REFLECTION 1

Aine went to Corrymeela after her son was murdered.

'I was just having a wee cry in the kitchen. Mostly now I'm all right but sometimes it comes over me round this time – when he'd be comin' in for his supper with his dad. They worked together at the plumbin', see. And you know how a lad likes his food – he'd say, 'Great, Mum! It's onions tonight and you've been cryin'!' People say that I will forget all these details but how can I? It was Corrymeela got me where I am now. I would never have come to myself without it. I never felt at Mass what I felt at those prayers together in Corrymeela. Protestants and Catholics we were, all together, and the Protestants know 'twas theirs killed my son and they prayed special for me – and it worked! I'll never be happy again, see. But I'm not angry no more.'

REFLECTION 2

Dorothy Wilson, a Corrymeela member, is involved in integrated schools for Protestant *and* Catholic children.

'To allow Protestant and Catholic children in Northern Ireland to be educated together without becoming any less Protestant or any less Catholic is vital... There is a long-standing, violent conflict in Northern Ireland, and the two sides in the conflict often know very little about each other. Part of the underlying philosophy of the new schools is the view that, if children went to school together, some of the mutual ignorance might be dissolved.'

REFLECTION 3

Barry is a Catholic and a Nationalist.

'At Corrymeela I met people from the Protestant and Unionist tradition who live in the same town as me and whom I had never talked with before. The discussions were initially very wary. Deep emotions were stirred in me, but soon, very soon, we were sharing our different views and experiences. I was overwhelmed at what came out and how people listened to one another. At the end of the weekend I went along with the others to the short Corrymeela Community service. At the finish we were invited to say the Our Father (the Lord's Prayer). We took hands and during the prayer I began to cry into myself and at the end outwardly. I have never experienced anything like it before. It was also the first time in my life I had ever prayed with Protestants. After that weekend some of us stayed together, and we still meet and organize projects for adults and young people in the town.'

FOR YOUR FOLDERS

▶ Explain the work that is done at Corrymeela.

▶ After reading the reflections, explain why many Christians feel that this work is so important.

▶ Why are 'integrated schools' so important?

▶ Ray Davey once described Corrymeela as 'the place you don't have to whisper'. What do you think he means by these words?

Missionaries often became equated with white colonization

'Jesus drew near and said to them ... "Go then, to all peoples everywhere and make them my disciples".'

(Matthew 28:18–19)

At the heart of the Christian belief is the idea that in Jesus Christ, God made the way of salvation possible for humanity. Many Christians feel they have a duty to share this belief with all people, and there are Christian missionaries at work all over the world today. They believe they have a mission to help people discover Jesus Christ and accept him into their hearts. Christianity is often called a 'missionary religion'.

As with other beliefs and ideas, Christians have different views about mission and the task of the Church:

● The task of the Church is to convert people to the Christian life and make them members of the Church. Only through belief in Jesus Christ can people find salvation.

● The task of the Church is to 'plant' Christian communities in places where none existed before. Local people should control their own churches.

● It is not up to the Church to convert people. God is already at work in the world wherever people are working for peace and justice. People should be left alone to follow their own traditions.

'WHITE SOULS'

During the seventeenth, eighteenth and nineteenth centuries Europe began to colonize the world. With its great wealth and power it began to carve up the world for its own economic and military gain. Alongside this colonial activity came the Christian missionaries who often believed that there were millions of 'unfortunate pagans' who were desperately in need of conversion. As well as bringing their religion, these missionaries brought with them European values and morals, often equating these values with 'godliness'. Increasingly, missionaries became identified with white colonization and all the exploitation that this entailed. White missionaries were often totally ignorant of the richness of the peoples' own cultures, histories and religions. Indeed, many of the attitudes of the missionaries seem to be far from 'Christian'.

> *'Did not Christ come into the world to make the souls if not the bodies of blacks inwardly white? Colonial expansion was a kind of official crusade against the children of darkness... whiteness itself was assumed to be the norm, dark skins deviations from the norm.'*
>
> (Alan Davies, 'The Ideology of Racism')

The hope of spreading Christianity was linked with changing attitudes to race. After Darwin's *On the Origin of Species* was published in 1859, it appeared possible to fit the non-European races into Darwin's theory of the survival of the fittest. If human history, like natural history, was governed by the survival of the fittest, the races of the West, with their advanced technology, had appeared to survive more effectively. Clearly therefore their Christian duty was to extend their leadership throughout the world. There can be little doubt that much missionary work, through ignorance and arrogance about racial and cultural superiority, caused a great deal of suffering.

To their credit many missionaries worked to combat slavery and helped to spread the benefits of Western know-how, like medical services and literacy. By the 1920s many missionaries, particularly in Africa, were beginning to see that their most important task was to help the peoples of Africa prepare for self-government.

A MULTI-FAITH SOCIETY

Over the last few decades in Britain there has been a growth in the number of people who follow religions other than Christianity. The growth of our multi-faith society has made many Christians reconsider their beliefs about missionary activities. Very generally two different approaches to this matter can be found among Christians:

All religions are different paths to salvation. One religion is not 'superior' in any way to another. Therefore the Church's mission is not to try and convert the followers of these other religions. Its mission is to understand others, learn from them,

share ideas about the meaning of life and, by the example of its members, bear witness to the teachings of Jesus Christ..

● Ultimately the only way to God and salvation is through belief in Jesus Christ. Followers of other religions are not wrong but can only go a short way on the path to fully understanding God.

FOR DISCUSSION

▶ Consider what happened when white European Christians landed on the American continent in 1492. At that time there were approximately 80 million inhabitants of the Americas. By 1550 only 10 million remained.

TALKING POINT

● *'We imposed our civilization as a condition of accepting the Gospel. We tried to make you be like us and in so doing we helped to destroy the vision that made you what you were . . . . We ask you to forgive us.'*

(*An Apology to Native Elders from the United Church of Canada,* 15 August 1986)

FOR YOUR FOLDERS

▶ Why do many Christians believe that their religion is a 'missionary' one?

▶ Briefly explain the different views about mission and the task of the Church.

▶ 'Christian missionary activity has in the past been equated with economic exploitation, cultural rape and racism.' Explain what you think this statement means.

▶ What is a 'multi-faith' society? How has it affected the way many Christians see the role of the Churches?

Christianity is a world religion. It has influenced, and has been influenced by, cultures all over the world. This can be clearly seen in the huge continent of Africa. Africa is a continent of great diversity. The conditions, beliefs and practices in Africa are as varied as the continent itself. Christianity is not a new phenomenon in Africa. The Ethiopian Orthodox Church was founded in the fourth century CE and the Coptic Orthodox Church was traditionally founded by St Mark in the first century CE.

As European missionaries worked in Africa, they imported their own European style of Christianity. They brought with them European styles of buildings, dress, music, beliefs and values. Seldom did they make any real or sustained effort to understand or even consider traditional African religions which were thousands of years old and contained a great wealth of ideas and practices. This ignorance by many missionaries often led to the Africans being treated very badly, and helped to fuel such evils as the slave trade, which resulted in eight million people being torn away from their land and shipped to places like America.

However, in the twentieth century, as more African countries gained political independence, Christianity in Africa began to change. Many African Churches began to break away from the patterns and ideas that they had received from the missionaries. They remained as Christians, but began to use African ideas and patterns to express their beliefs and faith. These Churches have become known as the Independent African Churches and their beliefs and practices vary tremendously throughout Africa.

SOME CHARACTERISTICS

Many African Independent Churches have grown by using traditional African dances, music, story-telling, symbols and rituals. Christian themes are expressed in truly African ways through ancient African customs, and some Churches include African ideas about worshipping ancestors. For some Churches Jesus Christ is 'the light' who disperses the evil powers of darkness, while for others he is the 'giver of life' and 'the healer'. Some of the most popular types of Church are the 'prophet healing' Churches. The founders and leaders of these Churches are called 'prophets', who claim to have received a vision from God, who empowered them to heal in his name.

Many of these Churches grew out of a response of the failure of missionaries to relate Christianity to the traditional African view of the world. Often the missionaries condemned the traditional African way of life. They wanted to transform Africans into 'black Europeans'. For example, until relatively recently, African Christians had to be baptized with Christian names. An African name which might mean 'God is with me' was unacceptable because it was African.

Over the years a new movement has emerged called African Theology (see unit 33). It tries to express the Christian gospel against an African cultural background, and to take as positive an attitude as possible to African traditions while remaining true to the Gospels.

THE COPTIC CHURCH

One of the oldest churches in the world is the Coptic Orthodox Church, traditionally founded in the first century CE by St Mark, in Egypt. In the fourth century CE St Anthony (c. 251–356 CE) founded the world's first monastery. At the age of 20, after reading Matthew 19:21 (*'If you would be perfect, go and sell all that you have and give to the poor, and come and follow me'*), he went to live alone in a mountain cave in the desert. He spent his time in prayer and study. He experienced violent temptations but he overcame them and, in time, a number of disciples gathered around him. Many people came to him for guidance healing and teaching. He gathered the hermits who were living in the desert into loosely knit communities, and monasticism began (see unit 35). St Anthony became known as 'God's doctor to Egypt'. He died aged 105. The monastery of St Anthony is still in use today, and is in the desert sands about 500 kilometres south of Cairo in Egypt.

The world's first monastery was founded in the desert

entral to Coptic worship is the Eucharist

IFE IN THE DESERT

Iermits and the monastic communities are an mportant part of the Coptic Church, whose bishops l come from monasteries. In St Anthony's, the onks get up at 3 a.m. and spend the next five ours praying together. They then work through the ay, usually on the land. They are skilled farmers nd can grow crops even in the desert. One of the onks, Father Dioscorus, explains why he and the ther monks live in the desert:

'Many people think we come to the desert to punish ourselves, because it is hot and dry and difficult to live in. But it's not true. We come because we love it here. We love the peace, the silence. When you are in love you want to be alone with your lover – you want to sit together in a quiet place and talk, not to be in the midst of a crowd of other people. How can you talk in a crowd? So it is with us. We come here because, well, we want to be alone with our God. As St Anthony once said, "Let your heart be silent, then God will speak".'

OPTIC WORSHIP

entral to Coptic worship is the Eucharist, which is elebrated more often than in the Byzantine adition (see units 22 and 24). Music plays a very nportant part in worship. It is claimed that many of ie chants and hymns come directly from the temple usic of ancient Egypt. There have been many artyrs in the Coptic Church. The relics of these artyrs are considered holy and are given a

prominent place in worship. The Coptic Church, existing as it does in the middle of the Muslim world, has often been persecuted, and sometimes still is today. The desert monasteries, therefore, have been a place of refuge for Coptic Christians.

The biblical tradition of the Holy Family escaping into Egypt (Matthew 2) plays an important part in Coptic practices. There are many pilgrimage sites in the Delta and Nile valleys, associated with the Virgin Mary and the Holy Family. Coptics call Mary *Theotokos* (God bearer) and she is greatly honoured. Coptic Christians believe that Mary appeared at Zeitoun in Egypt, between 1968 and 1970. Visions, mysticism, miracles and healing all play an important part in the Coptic tradition.

Although the Coptic Church is steeped in history it is very alive in the modern world today. A high proportion of its members, both in Egypt and in Britain, are involved in medicine. Many others are involved in education and agriculture. The head of the Church is Pope Shenouda III who is based in Cairo. In 1994 the British Orthodox Church became part of the Coptic Orthodox Patriarchate.

FOR YOUR FOLDERS

▶ What problems did Christian missionaries sometimes cause in Africa?

▶ Explain some of the characteristics of the African Independent Churches.

▶ What is African Theology?

▶ How old is the Coptic Church?

▶ Who was St Anthony and what did he do?

▶ According to Father Dioscorus why do monks live in the desert?

▶ Explain some aspects of Coptic worship and practice.

▶ Why do you think the Coptic tradition is regarded as being so important by many Christians?

INTRODUCTION

Christianity is just *one* of the world's major religions. In the world today there are millions of people who follow Buddhism, Hinduism, Islam, Judaism, Sikhism and other religions. Some of these religions are older than Christianity, whereas others like Islam and Sikhism have developed since Christianity.

In the past there has often been conflict and strife between these religions and they have sometimes been the cause of wars and violence. Missionaries from some religions have tried to convert people of other religions to their beliefs. Some people who follow their own religion have shown little regard or sympathy for other religions, believing that it is their religion which is the 'true' one and all the others are false. This attitude has often been the result of ignorance and is a refusal to look at the beliefs and ideas of other religions.

Christians have often been guilty of this, regarding followers of other religions as being 'heathens' or 'infidels' or 'pagans'. This has been a dangerous attitude because it has often bred intolerance and misunderstanding. Indeed there are still today some Christians who strongly believe that the *only* way to God and salvation is through belief in Jesus Christ and that all other ways are of little worth. This attitude, which disregards other people's faith, is deeply destructive and divisive.

THE RELIGIOUS ANIMAL

Human beings have often been called 'religious animals'. This means that through every period of history, and in every culture in every part of the world, people have believed in forces and powers that lie beyond and within this world. We have as a species been powerfully aware of a 'spiritual world'. The way that this belief in a spiritual world has been expressed in ideas and practices has varied with different cultures. In Tibet, India, the Middle East, China, Africa and Australia, in fact in places all over the world, these beliefs in a spiritual dimension to life have been expressed through the local cultural patterns. The external practices might seem very different but many scholars believe that beneath the externals there is an underlying similarity of belief.

In the past, although these religious beliefs have met through trade, 'voyages of discovery' and sometimes missionary work, people often still clung onto the idea that their religion was the 'true' one and little was done to explore and exchange ideas.

There will be no peace in the world until there is peace between the world religions

GLOBAL VILLAGE

However, today we live in a 'global village'. The world has got smaller, not geographically but in the sense that communication and travel have developed. We are far more knowledgeable about other parts of the world and their peoples. We can travel across the world in a matter of hours. We can switch on the television and see pictures from China. With this increased knowledge has come an awareness that people in different parts of the world have their own beliefs, ideas, cultures and customs. These are as important to them as ours are to us. The second part of the twentieth century has witnessed, among religions, a growing awareness of each other and a growing desire to have 'dialogue': to talk, listen and learn about and from other religions. Also, because many people from places like India and Pakistan have settled in Britain, there has been a growing awareness of their beliefs and customs.

SIMILARITY

Although each religion is unique and has its own patterns of belief and practices, there is a growing awareness that there are similarities between them too.

Look at these sayings from the sacred scriptures of Hinduism, Judaism, Islam and Christianity:

'The life, or self, of this whole universe, is the same as that tiny seed from which it came. You are that self.'

(Upanishad 6:12:3)

'The Lord is near to all who call upon him, to all who call upon him in truth.'

(Psalm 145:18)

'We are nearer to him than his jugular vein.'

(Surah 50:15)

'... for, behold, the Kingdom of God is within you.'

(Luke 17:21)

DIALOGUE

Dialogue between the world religions is slowly beginning to increase. In the past, Christianity tended to adopt either a standpoint of 'exclusivity', which was a blanket condemnation of other faiths and their truths, or a standpoint of 'superiority' which rated Christianity as 'better'. Christian scholars believe that in this dialogue all the religions must realize that they have a lot to learn from others, and can teach others as well. This is not to say that they want to make all religions the same, or aim to make one world religion, but simply to learn what others have to say. By doing this they can deepen their understanding of their own faith.

THINKING POINT

- *'Wherever the teachings of all the religions of the world strike the eternal core of humanity, the teachings of Jesus, Muhammad, Lao-Tzu, The Buddha, are all the same. There is only one religion. There is only one happiness. There are a thousand forms, a thousand heralds, but only one call, one voice. The voice of God does not come just from the Bible. The essence of love, beauty and holiness does not reside in Christianity or in antiquity – it resides in you and me, in each one of us. This is the one eternal truth. It is the doctrine of the "Kingdom of Heaven" that we bear within ourselves. Demand more of yourselves. Love and joy and the mysterious things we call happiness are not over here or over there, they are only "within ourselves".'*

(Herman Hesse – twentieth-century writer)

FOR YOUR FOLDERS

▶ After reading this unit write an article called 'Inter-faith dialogue in our global village'.

▶ Why do you think dialogue is so important?

▶ The theologian Hans Küng has said *'There will be no peace in the world until there is peace between the world religions.'* What do you think he means?

33 LIBERATION THEOLOGY

INTRODUCTION

Over recent decades, a new movement has emerged in the worldwide Church, called Liberation Theology. It is particularly strong in Latin America although its influence is increasingly being felt around the world.

The movement consists of Christians, mainly Roman Catholics, who believe that the Gospels demand that people stand up and fight against poverty, exploitation, injustice and the lack of human rights. They are inspired by such passages in the Bible as:

> 'He has sent me to bring good news to the poor, to proclaim liberty to the captives and to set free the oppressed.'

> (Luke 4:18)

In the past, the Roman Catholic Church in Latin America did little to fight injustice. However, today many priests identify themselves with the poor, as Jesus did. They have begun asking questions such as:

● What is our Christian responsibility as we face the death and oppression in which our people live?

● Why is there such poverty in our continent, when there are enough resources for everyone?

● What actions should we take as Christians in response to the sufferings of our people?

BASE CHRISTIAN COMMUNITIES

In recent years there has been a growth of 'base Christian communities'. These are groups of ordinary people who come together to share everyday experiences and to work for change in their communities. They are centres for community Bible study in which members seek to relate human actions to the work of God in the world, as well as being centres of worship. Because these communities challenge those in power, they are often criticized by governments and even by powerful Church leaders. Christians who live in societies where torture, poverty, assassinations, corruption and death squads are normal, believe that their faith demands that they act against a system that creates such oppression and injustice. However, the system which protects the rich and powerful obviously does not want to encourage change.

Liberation Theologians want to see a Church that is a more loving community, with no difference between rich and poor members. They want to see a Church that is less authoritarian, with ordinary people more involved in making decisions. They want to see a Church that is more committed to ridding the world of injustice, corruption and inequality, and not *only* interested in people being converted to the Christian faith.

STATE VIOLENCE

In countries such as El Salvador, anybody who stands up against the government becomes a target. In 1980 Archbishop Oscar Romero (see unit 16), who had continually spoken out against the state, was gunned down by assassins while he celebrated mass. On Christmas Eve 1979, he had made clear what his view of Christianity was:

> 'We must not seek the child Jesus in the pretty figures of our Christmas crib. We must seek him among the undernourished children who have gone to bed tonight without eating, among the poor newsboys who will sleep covered with newspapers in doorways.'

In 1989 armed soldiers entered the Central American University in San Salvador, the capital city of El Salvador, and shot dead six Jesuit priests, along with their housekeeper and her 16-year-old daughter. Many other church workers, priests and nuns have been imprisoned, tortured and killed. A widely circulated death squad leaflet read: 'Be a patriot – kill a priest.' This reflected the deep hostility which greeted and *still greets* church workers who side with the poor. This same sort of intimidation has occurred

Bodies of Church members murdered in Nicaragua

n Nicaragua, where the Church has also sided with he poor. Some Christians, after seeing that non-iolence did not work, resorted to taking up arms. hey felt that these governments would not listen to on-violent protest. In these countries, many hristians feel that they cannot turn their backs on olitical struggle. In Columbia, Father Camilo Torres 929–66), who became a freedom fighter and who as later killed by the Colombian government, rote:

> '*The basic thing in Catholicism is loving one's neighbour. For this love to be true it has to be effective... We must take power from the privileged minorities in order to give it to the poor majority. The revolution can be peaceful, only if the minorities do not offer violent resistance.'*

lost Liberation Theologians still believe that iolence is wrong and only under extreme rcumstances would they agree to its use. However, s Camilo Torres wrote, it is the government which, y its policies, uses violence *every day* against the oor.

Liberation Theology has also had an impact on hurches in Britain and the developed world. Some shops in Britain, over recent years, have spoken out gainst government policies, which they see as being xtremely damaging to the poor. For instance, the nglican Bishop of Liverpool, David Sheppard, rote an important book called *Bias to the Poor*, which rges Christians to be involved in social change. In it e expressed concern about high unemployment, nner-city deprivation, bad housing and inadequate elp for the poor by the government.

In South Africa, many Church leaders, inspired by e ideas of Liberation Theology and Black Theology, ruggled against the evils of apartheid for many ears. Christians like Desmond Tutu, Trevor uddleston and Alan Boesak worked tirelessly, and ith great courage, to help liberate black South fricans from a system that trampled on their human gnity. In 1994 their efforts were rewarded when the rst multi-racial elections were held. It is widely knowledged that the apartheid system would not ave been destroyed without the courageous edication to truth, freedom and justice shown by any Christians in South Africa.

THINKING POINTS

● '*The Church has devoted her attention to formulating truths, and meanwhile did almost nothing to better the world. This must now cease.'*

(Gustavo Gutierrez – Liberation theologian)

● '*When I give food to the poor, they call me a saint. When I ask why the poor have no food, they call me a communist.'*

(Helder Camara – Brazilian bishop)

● '*The cry of the poor is for justice not charity. Dignity is as important as bread.'*

(Asian Ecumenical Conference)

FOR YOUR FOLDERS

▶ Explain briefly what Liberation Theology means. In your explanation, give examples of some Biblical teachings that have inspired Liberation Theologians.

▶ What are 'base Christian communities'?

▶ What sort of society do Liberation Theologians wish to see?

▶ Write an article about state violence in El Salvador.

▶ Explain who Archbishop Romero and Father Torres were.

▶ '*Every person must submit to the supreme authorities*' (Romans 13:1). How might some of the people quoted in this unit respond to these words of St Paul?

▶ Do you think Christians are sometimes justified in taking up arms? Give reasons for your answer.

In this unit Dr Melissa Raphael explains the main ideas of feminist theology.

'Christian feminism has been active since the nineteenth century, but since the early 1970s it has taken the vision of the women's liberation movement one radical step further, saying that true liberation – freedom from abusive relationships – cannot be achieved by new laws alone. **Sexual equality** of opportunity is only the beginning. What is needed is a new vision of the connectedness of women, men and nature in God.

The women's movement demonstrates how **patriarchy** (literally "the rule of the fathers") divides up the world into inferior and superior people: where there are people and things which can be used and a few people who can do the using. Today Jewish and Islamic as well as Christian women are among the many feminists who have shown how patriarchy has distorted religious thinking and practice.

Feminist theology is now widely researched and published. It is studied in universities and, above all, it is put into action in ordinary women's and men's lives. But it is surprising how many people think that feminist theologians believe that God is a woman instead of an old man. Feminist theologians are not saying that God is a woman. Nor is feminist theology just demanding that women be given the choice of ordination as priests instead of raising money for charity, making tea and arranging the flowers in Church, simply because they are female.

There is far more to it than that. What key writers like Rosemary Radford Ruether (US) and Mary Grey (UK) want to say is that we need to re-think the language we use about God. We are so used to hearing about God as if God were male, that we do not even notice the absence of female imagery. This is because theology has almost always been written by privileged men, for men, and about men. When women are discussed in theological texts, they are spoken about, and then usually stereotypically as either saintly mothers – Mary, who was a virgin – or as temptresses like Eve.

Tertullian, one of the Church fathers, referred to women as "the devil's gateway". Nowadays theologians take a much less harsh view of women. Yet the belief that God the Father became incarnate in Jesus the Son has had the effect of glorifying men and damaging women's self-esteem. The mother-daughter relationship is not represented at all in our idea of God's relationship with the world. The Bible and theology nearly always use masculine words for God, such as Father, King, Shepherd, and Lord, which means that women – over half of humanity – are left out of our ideas of God. These terms allow human kings and fathers to rule on behalf of God, and to speak on behalf of everyone and everything else. This effectively silences any record of women's experience of God and makes many women feel both less than human and less than divine: as if whatever else God is like, God is not like women.

Feminist theology claims that it is the male experience of ruling from above which has also shaped the way we think about sin, as if it were just personal disobedience to divine commands. Feminist theology disagrees with this idea of sin. It redefines **sin** as 'wrong relationships'. 'Sin' is when men base their economies and religions on using humans (especially women and non-whites) and the earth's resources as if they owned them. By contrast, feminists and many other religious thinkers today believe that God is present in all creation. This means that all life is sacred. Creation cannot be exploited and must be respected as telling us something about God.

It is urgent that we learn reverence for all God's world. The contemporary world needs the wisdom and energy of all human beings if it is not to collapse under the burden of racist nationalism, inter-religious hatred and destruction of the natural environment. If religion is going to be relevant or even understandable, the ancient Greek and medieval patriarchal worldviews which still colour so much Christian thinking must be replaced by a more caring, unifying vision. Feminist theologians suggest that we could do this by broadening our theological imagination and using the "inclusive" language of motherhood as well as fatherhood, and friendship to express the fullness of divine love. Other feminists prefer to use more abstract terms for the divine such as the **Holy One** or God/ess.

However, most Christians today think that it is wrong to talk of God in female terms because

Jesus did not. And many Christians follow St Paul's (and other writers') view that creation is a hierarchy in which the chain of command passes from God at the top, down through Christ to husbands and finally to wives and children at the bottom. Men have held on to their power by saying that the husband must be head of the family (and therefore society) because Eve – a woman – was responsible for sin. As a result, all women are punished by having menstrual periods ('the curse'), painful childbirth, and submission to their husbands. (For examples of this teaching, look at Genesis 3:16 ; 1 Timothy 2:12–16 ; Ephesians 5:22–3 ; 1 Corinthians 11:3; for a more 'feminist' vision see Galatians 3:28.)

Christian feminists still use the Bible as their central source of inspiration because some of the prophets, Jesus' teaching and the role of women in the early Church, point towards the just, peaceful, world that feminism is working for. But where the

Bible explicitly supports the patriarchal worldview, feminist theologians say that it does not reveal God and has no authority over them. This means that they use the Bible very carefully and offer distinctively 'woman-centred' interpretations of the stories and teaching.

Feminist theologians look towards **Shalom** *(the Hebrew word for peace) – that state of reconciliation and equality which in patriarchal language has been called* Kingdom *of God. But feminists often feel isolated in churches which reject their vision, and many are deciding to worship with other women (and men too) in more informal 'woman church' groups such as the St Hilda community in the East End of London where inclusive language and new rituals mean that all participants experience a foretaste of* Shalom.'

(Dr Melissa Raphael teaches and writes about feminist theology and spirituality)

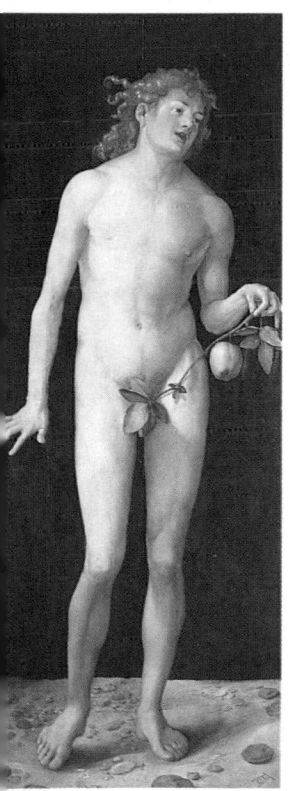

lam

Eve

FOR YOUR FOLDERS

▸ Find out the meaning of the following words and phrases: sexual equality; patriarchy; sin; Holy One; Shalom.

▸ *'We need to re-think the language we use about God.'* What do feminist theologians mean by this? Why do they think patriarchal language makes women feel both less than human and less than divine?

▸ How do feminist theologians redefine the word 'sin'?

▸ What have been the results of sin, according to them?

▸ Why do they believe that the medieval patriarchal worldviews need replacing?

▸ *'Feminist theologians look towards Shalom.'* After reading Dr Melissa Raphael's article, what do you think this means?

'The monk is there to show that one can be perfectly happy without depending on any worldly success or achievement'

Long before the rise of Christianity, 'monasticism' existed in many parts of the world. Monasticism means that people live in seclusion, obeying religious vows they have taken. The first Christian hermits lived alone in the deserts and in the fourth century CE St Anthony had founded the world's first monastery in Egypt (see unit 31). By about 530 CE an Italian called Benedict had also founded a monastery in Europe. He wrote a set of rules for the monastic life and these rules became known as the Rule of St Benedict. They covered every aspect of monastic life and St Benedict described the monastery as 'a school of the service of the Lord'.

Over the centuries other monastic orders were formed. In 1209 St Francis formed the Franscican Order. He set out to form an order of brothers who would be carefree disciples of Jesus living in poverty. During the same period, Dominic, a Spanish priest, founded the Dominican Order. His brothers too were travelling preachers, seeking learning and knowledge, but they did not endure the same level of poverty as Francis' brothers.

Members of religious communities take vows of poverty, chastity, obedience and prayer. The monastic day is filled with prayer, reading, meditation, worship and many different types of work involving much manual labour. Over the centuries Christian women have become involved in their own religious communities called convents – places where nuns live according to their religious vows.

People who join religious communities have made a personal commitment to dedicate their whole lives, minds, bodies and souls to worshipping God and developing themselves as spiritual men and women. A monastic life is not an escape from the world. People living so close to each other have to face all the problems that human relationships cause. They have to work hard both physically and on themselves to try to develop and grow.

One of the most influential Christian monks of this century was the Trappist monk called Thomas Merton. The Trappist order have taken a vow of silence, along with their other vows. Merton's writings have had a great influence on the lives of many Christians. Ironically Merton, a member of a silent order, played an important part in the political and social protests of his times, including the struggle for racial equality in the USA, and in the struggle against nuclear weapons and the Vietnam War. He explained this involvement in one of his books:

> *'This is an age that, by its very nature at a time of crisis, of revolution, of struggle, which calls for the special searching and questioning which are the work of the monk in his meditation and prayer... the monk abandons the world only in order to listen more intently to the deepest and most neglected voices that proceed from its inner depths.'*

> (Thomas Merton, *Contemplative Prayer*)

The Rule of St Francis

'This is the Rule and way of life of the brothers of mine: to observe the holy Gospel of our Lord Jesus Christ, living in obedience, without personal possessions and in chastity.'

LAUDS: PRAISE — MORNING PRAYER

PRIME: FIRST HOUR — 6 AM

TERCE: THIRD HOUR — 9 AM

SEXT: SIXTH HOUR — NOON

NONE: NINTH HOUR — 3 PM

VESPERS: EVENING — EVENING PRAYER

COMPLINE: COMPLETE — FINAL NIGHT PRAYER

typical day in a Benedictine monastery

Samples of Benedict's Rules

'Above all, let not the evil of grumbling appear, on any account, by the least sign or word whatever.

Let the monks sleep clothed girdled with belts or cords – but without knives at their sides lest they injure themselves in sleep. And thus let the monks be always ready; when the signal is given, let them rise without delay.

Let all guests who arrive be received like Christ, for he is going to say "I came as a guest and you received me".'

REFLECTIONS

'When I was sixteen I realized that I had to be a nun. There was no sudden flash; it was rather as if the truth had been there in my mind for a long time. I believe we are chosen, but that also experience of God can come through events that are part of the weave of our ordinary lives.'

(Dame Maria Boulding)

'When people ask me why I became a monk, I feel very like the engaged couple who are asked why they have fallen in love. We don't really know. Certain things happen in our lives which make us come to a decision.'

(Dom Leonard Vickers)

'The monk is there to show that one can be perfectly happy without depending on any worldly success or achievement. The monk bears witness to the fact that the happiness of the Christian does not depend on the promises of this world.'

(Thomas Merton, *Contemplation in a World of Action*)

FOR YOUR FOLDERS

▶ Briefly explain who Benedict, Francis and Dominic were.

▶ *'People who join religious communities are not escaping from the world but rather confronting it.'* Comment on this statement.

▶ Explain why Dame Maria Boulding and Dom Leonard Vickers joined holy orders.

▶ Try to explain in your own words what Thomas Merton is saying in his two books.

▶ What vows do members of religious communities take? What do their vows mean and how do you think taking them helps members of the community in their religious lives?

KEY WORDS

Contemplation – 'to think deeply; to consider with attention; to look quietly; deep thought.'
Contemplative – 'someone who spends much time in contemplation.'

(Longman, *Dictionary of Contemporary English*)

St Francis of Assisi in meditation

As unit 35 showed, people who join religious communities are engaged in many different types of activity. One very important feature of life for monks and nuns is **contemplation**. This can take many forms, but generally it entails thinking deeply and quietly about the meaning of life, or stopping all thoughts and associations, to be open to silence and inner peace. The word 'contemplative' applies to the individual's spiritual life.

Throughout Christian history men and women have adopted the contemplative life. Their lives and writings have inspired Christian seekers for centuries. Here are just two profiles of famous contemplatives:

Basil the Great (330–79 CE)

Basil is one of the honoured names in the Greek Orthodox Church. He gave up all the attractions of the world and became a hermit. Later, joined by his friend Gregory, he formed a monastery which was soon surrounded by hospitals and hostels for the poor and sick. He wrote the *Long Rules*, a series of questions and answers on the Christian life. Although these were intended for monks, much of what he has to say have an immediate relevance to all Christians – for example, loving God and loving one's neighbour in the love of God, the imitation of Christ as the goal of Christianity and guidance on work and prayer. In one answer he wrote:

'If a man says he finds the teaching of the divine scriptures sufficient to correct his character, he makes himself like a man who learns the theory of building but never practises the art... For, behold, the Lord Jesus, because of the greatness of his love for men, was not content with teaching the word only, but in order to give us accurately and clearly a pattern of humility in the perfection of love, he girded himself and washed the feet of his disciples in person. Whose feet will you wash? For whom will you care?'

Teresa of Avila (1515–82 CE)

Among all the saints of the Roman Catholic Church none is more greatly respected and loved, as a teacher of genuine spirituality, than Teresa. At the age of 20 she entered the Carmelite Convent, where she wrote many spiritual classics that still inspire Christians today. In her book *Life* she describes some of the spiritual experiences that enriched her life. Here is one:

'I used unexpectedly to experience a consciousness of the presence of God, of such a kind that I could not possibly doubt that he was within me or that I was wholly engulfed in him. This was in some sense a vision: I believe it is called mystical theology. The soul is suspended in such a way that it seems to be completely outside itself. The will leaves: the memory I think, is almost lost: while the understanding, I believe, though not lost does not reason – I mean that it does not work, but is amazed at the extent of all it can understand.'

After her death these words, sometimes called 'St Teresa's Bookmark' were found on her:

Let nothing disturb you;
Let nothing dismay you;
All things pass:
God never changes.
Patience attains
All that it strives for.
He who has God
Finds he lacks nothing:
God alone suffices.

◇

FOR YOUR FOLDERS

▶ Read the reflection. What does the contemplative life mean for Brother David?

▶ What does Brother David mean by:

a uprootedness

b spiritual

c flesh?

▶ Do you agree with everything he says?

▶ Do you think that most of 'our time' we are not 'rooted in time at all'? What do you think it means not to be rooted in time?

▶ Explain in your own words what you think Basil and Teresa are saying.

REFLECTION

'If we speak about the spiritual work of our time, there are three questions I would like to ask. What characterizes our time? What is the spiritual work for our time? And, how are we to go about it?

If we ask what characterizes our time, I offer one word: uprootedness.

Think, for instance, of the uprootedness that comes as a by-product of mobility. Now, it is very good that we can move quickly and easily from place to place. But there are families in the United States who move more than 20 times while their children are growing up. Think of our uprootedness from our families. There are many people who have had little or no contact with their grandparents, who hardly know their names.

Or think of our uprootedness from the Earth. Do you know the garden from which your fruits and vegetables come? How many people in the world know the well from which their water comes? They never give a thought to it, yet this used to be rather important.

Think of our uprootedness from our bodies and what it takes to experience our bodies as the embodiment of spirit and of our lives and to experience ourselves as body-spirits.

How many of us can say with conviction that we are really rooted in a tradition, rooted in the sense of getting nourishment from it?

We are speaking of our time. How rooted are we in time at all? Most of the time, 48 per cent of us is clinging to the past, 51 per cent is stretching out frantically towards the future and 1 per cent is left to be present where we are in this moment. So, it isn't even our time; it's just passing us by while we are busy with nostalgic memories or impatient fantasies.

How can we root ourselves in time? By facing first of all, the problem of our uprootedness; facing the challenge that emerges from it; and therefore facing the task. The task is re-rooting ourselves – in a place, in social structures, in this Earth, in our body, in tradition, in time.

When people say 'spiritual' they mean a great variety of things, so we ought to ask ourselves what we mean by spiritual. It means aliveness. Spiritual means alive – super-alive, if you want.

The spiritual work of our time is the task of making things alive, of rerooting – because if something is cut off from its roots, it will sooner or later die. That's the image of flesh – something that's cut off from its life, its roots.'

(Brother David – a modern Benedictine monk)

KEY WORD

Worship – 'the act of paying divine honour to God, especially in religious services; an act or feeling of adoration; to show reverence with supreme respect and admiration.'

For Christians, worship, like all other aspects of belief and practice, is centred around beliefs about Jesus Christ. An important feature of Christian worship is the way that Christians regularly gather together with other believers for public acts of worship. Another feature is the way that Christians will sometimes worship privately, on their own or with their families. Most public acts of worship take place on a Sunday and in a church building. In most Christian denominations, individual members of the congregation take part in the practices of regular worship. Many Christian denominations have a full-time professional staff of clergy (see unit 39) who are in charge of the churches and lead the worship.

DIFFERENCES OF STYLE

Liturgical or formal worship

'Liturgy' is a Greek word meaning 'public worship'. In this style of worship, the activities are all set out in a **liturgy** (certain pattern). Liturgical worship is often very formal, elaborate and colourful, with many rituals. This type of worship is usually common in Christian churches that have a high regard for the sacraments (see unit 41), for instance the Roman Catholic and Orthodox Churches. In these churches beliefs are expressed through the use of many symbolic objects and actions.

Non-liturgical worship

In this style of worship, set rituals and symbolic actions are avoided. This worship is common among many Protestant churches. The emphasis is more on practices like Bible readings, prayers, hymns and sermons. Although the sacraments of Baptism and Holy Communion may still be used, the main emphasis is on the spoken and written message of Christianity. An example of a less formal style of worship can be found among the Society of Friends (see unit 42).

These two styles of worship reflect different emphases. Christians who follow liturgical styles of worship see worship as being 'sacramental'. The word **sacrament** (see unit 41) means 'a religious rite followed as an outward and visible sign of an inward and invisible spiritual grace'. In other words, emphasis is put on many outward signs and symbols which express deep religious and spiritual feeling and meaning.

For Christians who follow less formal styles of worship, the emphasis is on the 'Word of God' (see units 4 and 22). Because of this, worship tends to focus on spoken presentations and responses.

Generally, for Christians, acts of worship:

- enable them to express and declare their faith
- inspire and strengthen them in their daily lives
- provoke responses like praise, thanksgiving, joy, love, wonder, commitment and repentance
- can be expressed through art, music, burning incense, clapping, communion, ringing bells, prayers, kissing icons, lighting candles, reciting creeds, silence, Bible readings, sprinkling holy water, greeting others, making the sign of the cross, story telling, wearing special clothes, offering money.

For some Christians, worship does not take place just in church. They feel that in their everyday lives they should try to carry out all their tasks with thanks and praise to God, the Holy One. Whether they are gardening, studying, cooking, playing the guitar or painting, everything should be done bearing in mind the wonderful gift of life that the Creator has bestowed upon the earth. Worship then becomes a certain way of living, when attitudes change from being self-centred, to an awareness of the beauty and wonder of the universe.

Sometimes this awareness can be like a meditation when the restless mind is stilled and a person's whole attention can be put into the task at hand.

FOR YOUR FOLDERS

▶ What are the differences between liturgical and non-liturgical styles of worship?

▶ What differences in styles of worship would you expect to find between a Society of Friends and an Orthodox Church service?

▶ How might some Christians bring worship into their daily lives?

▶ Read the reflection. Explain in your own words what worship means to Simon Barrington-Ward.

REFLECTION

Bishop Simon Barrington-Ward tries to explain how, at emotional times in our lives, we may spontaneously give thanks together.

' "*Everyone suddenly burst out singing
And I was filled with such delight
As prisoned birds must find in freedom
Winging wildly across the white
Orchard and dark green fields; on; on; and
out of sight.
Everyone's voice was suddenly lifted
And beauty came like the setting sun.
My heart was shaken with tears, and horror
Drifted away... O but everyone
Was a bird and the song was wordless
The singing will never be done.*"

Siegfried Sassoon's famous poem (above) for Armistice Day 1918 celebrated the end of four years of war. Previously he had described terrible glimpses of life in the trenches. Now, in one moment, the cloud parted. A long-dreamed-of breakthrough had come.

Can you imagine the scene? The voices rising, blending, the overwhelming music surging up and singing its way through the singers.

In a less dramatic way, most of us have known moments like that: a sudden unexpected climax; a reunion of friends or a final gathering.

The faces of some people whom perhaps you love surround you in the crowd. A song begins. It is taken up. People begin to sway to the music. They put their arms round each other's shoulders perhaps. Then it happens. Your inner feeling and the world round you and the people with you all flow together into some greater unity. You are caught up into some kind of movement, some tide of the Spirit carrying you upward, forward, out of yourself into the possibility of some new world.

A movement like that seems to be a kind of harvest festival. We suddenly feel ready to put all we have got into it. We offer ourselves. The past is gathered in with the present. All that we have, all that we are, is taken up and laid open, ready to be changed, ready to be poured out: expended; wholly given. Our only thought is an inexpressible thankfulness and gladness.

*"Then was our mouth filled with laughter,
And our tongue with singing..."*

At such times a door seems to open in the surface of life and lead us deeper in; into the real heart of the world, into that greater wholeness which lies hidden beyond our so-called "everyday" life. All of us sometimes have hints, little flashes of this underlying unity. All too often we dismiss it.'

'We bow before his infinite majesty and holiness, trembling with awe at his unapproachable light and radiance'

REFLECTION

'We all have the need to worship – to worship something or someone greater than ourselves, to whom we wish to dedicate our whole lives. Sometimes they say we all have a God-shaped space inside us and only God can fill it. This means that we are created by God, we are created like God, and we are created for God. And since God is infinite, you and I are made for the infinite and nothing less than God can really ever satisfy our hunger for God.

Others try to worship things that are less than God – it may be money, or ambition, or drugs or sex. In the end they find out that they are worthless idols. To worship means to give due worth to someone or something. We give worth to God. Worship is absolutely central to our faith where God comes first, always. We bow before His infinite majesty and holiness, trembling with awe at His unapproachable light and radiance.

Many times we feel that words are utterly inadequate, so we keep a deep silence in the holy presence. But true Christian worship can never let us be indifferent to the needs of others, to the cries of the hungry, of the naked and the homeless, of the sick and the prisoner, of the oppressed and the disadvantaged.

True Christian worship includes the love of God and the love of neighbour. The two must go together or your Christianity is false. We are Christian not only in church on Sunday. Our Christianity is not something we put on like our Sunday best. It is for every day. We must worship our God for ever and ever, and serve Him by serving our neighbour today and always.'

(Archbishop Desmond Tutu, *Hope and Suffering*)

In general, the Christian religion has three important features – doctrine (statements about beliefs), deeds and worship. Although all three are distinct they cannot be separated. To understand what Christians are doing when they worship you need to consider these other features, because Christian worship is linked to what Christians believe and what they do. If we look at Desmond Tutu's reflection on worship (opposite) we can see that for him true Christian worship includes 'serving our neighbour today and always'.

CHRISTIAN BELIEF

As we have seen in previous units, Christians believe that this visible and physical world is not the only reality. They believe that above, within and beyond the sights and sounds of this world lies another reality. The word **transcendent** is often used to describe this other reality. 'Transcendent' means 'going beyond ordinary limits'.

The idea of a 'transcendent reality' has been expressed by poets and writers through the ages. In this poem by the Christian writer Francis Thompson (1859–1907), the link between the physical world and the transcendent world is made:

'O World Invisible, we view thee,
O World Intangible, we touch thee,
O World Unknowable, we know thee,
Inapprehensible, we clutch thee.'

(Francis Thompson, 'The Kingdom of God')

Christians feel that there are many ways of 'viewing, touching, knowing and clutching' this 'invisible, intangible, unknowable, inapprehensible' reality. Expressions of such things within the Christian religion can take many forms. Just a few examples might include:

● listening to great works of music

● reading the holy scriptures

● expressing transcendent ideas in great architecture

● by prayer, contemplation, silence and deep thought.

CHRISTIAN DEEDS

For Christians, what they do in their lives is clearly connected with what they believe about life. Christian belief cannot be separated from worship, so in their lives Christians try to act out of love, as

they believe Jesus Christ did. However, they believe that because they are far from perfect they cannot act without God's help – this help is called **grace** (see unit 9). Worship helps Christians to get close to God, who gives them the grace to face life with all its problems and challenges.

TALKING POINT

● *'The worship of God is not a rule of safety – it is an adventure of the spirit, a flight after the unattainable.'*

(A. N. Whitehead – scholar)

KEY IDEAS

There are generally two important activities in Christian worship:

● offering – this means all that goes out from the worshipper, e.g. praise, adoration, confession

● receiving – this means all that comes back, e.g. fellowship, forgiveness, inspiration, strength.

FOR YOUR FOLDERS

▶ *'We all have the need to worship.'* Explain Desmond Tutu's words.

▶ Explain in detail what Desmond Tutu means by *'True Christian worship'*.

▶ Explain what the word 'transcendent' means. Explain some of the ways that Christians might try to 'touch' the transcendent.

▶ Explain the word 'grace'. How do you think worship helps Christians in their everyday lives?

Ely Cathedral

Chiu Chiu Calama, Chile

For most local Christian groups the centre of their religious lives revolves around a church building. This unit looks at some of the many differences to be found in Christian places of worship, and the way that these differences reflect different Christian attitudes to belief and practice.

Some Christian groups believe that the building or place of worship is not important at all. For them, too much emphasis on material things like church buildings can be an obstacle to their faith. Others, like Quakers, might have a building which they keep as simple as possible, with few furnishings or decorations. However, many Christian groups see places of worship as being sacred or holy. They believe that these holy places must have their own special character and atmosphere which enable worshippers to sense the presence of God and respond with reverence and devotion.

Here are some characteristics of Christian places of worship. Note how they often reflect the different emphases that Christian groups have:

- Many places of worship, like cathedrals (from Latin *cathedra* meaning 'bishop's throne'), are beautifully decorated and furnished to create an atmosphere that helps the worshipper to experience God's splendour and glory.

- The central and most holy part of many churches, like Anglican and Roman Catholic churches, is the 'holy table' or **altar**. Many Christians feel that the altar is the place where Jesus' presence is most deeply felt during the Eucharist.

- In most church services somebody preaches, and the place they preach from is usually high enough for the congregation to see and hear them. This is known as the 'pulpit'. It is usually made of wood or stone and is reached by a few steps. In some churches like Methodist churches the pulpit is more prominent than the altar, because Methodists generally place more stress on the presence of God through his Word (see diagram 1).

- Many churches and cathedrals have tall spires pointing to the sky. A spire makes the church easier to see. Others may have a square tower.

These remind Christian worshippers to look up to God. Some churches have a bell tower and the bells are rung at special times.

- Many churches and cathedrals have stained glass window decorations, often telling a story or expressing a belief. These windows help to add to the atmosphere of the building.

- Most churches have a carefully thought out structure. Traditional Christian churches have developed the cruciform (in the form of a cross) shape (see diagram 2). When the worshippers face the altar they are facing east (where the sun rises), which many Christians feel is symbolic of the resurrection of Jesus.

- In Baptist churches a central feature is the **baptistry**, or pool. In some Baptist churches the baptistry can be very big. Baptists believe that people should be baptized only when they are fully aware of what they are committing themselves to, so the baptistry occupies a prominent position (see unit 25).

- In other churches a **font** (a large bowl made of stone that contains the water used for baptism) is often found near the church entrance, because being baptized means entering the church.

- In churches that teach the sacraments there are 'confessionals'. These are wooden constructions that separate the person who is **confessing** his or her sins (the 'penitent') from the priest who is hearing him or her. The person confessing kneels in one part and talks to the priest through a small grille. However, in the Roman Catholic Church it is becoming more usual to remove this barrier, and people confess face-to-face with a priest.

- In the Roman Catholic Church there are small chapels dedicated to the Virgin Mary, containing a statue of her. Also, a light is always kept burning by the altar of Roman Catholic churches, reminding worshippers that God is always present.

FOR YOUR FOLDERS

▶ Explain the following words: pulpit; spire; altar; cruciform; baptistry; font; confessionals; penitent.

▶ Write a sentence about each of the photographs.

▶ How do church buildings reflect some of the beliefs of:

a Methodists

b Baptists

c Roman Catholics?

▶ Why are places of worship very important to many Christians?

▶ *'Places of worship are full of symbolism.'* Explain what you think this means.

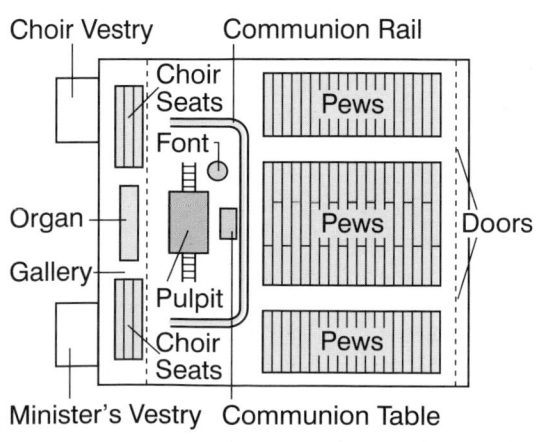

Diagram 1: Plan of a Methodist church

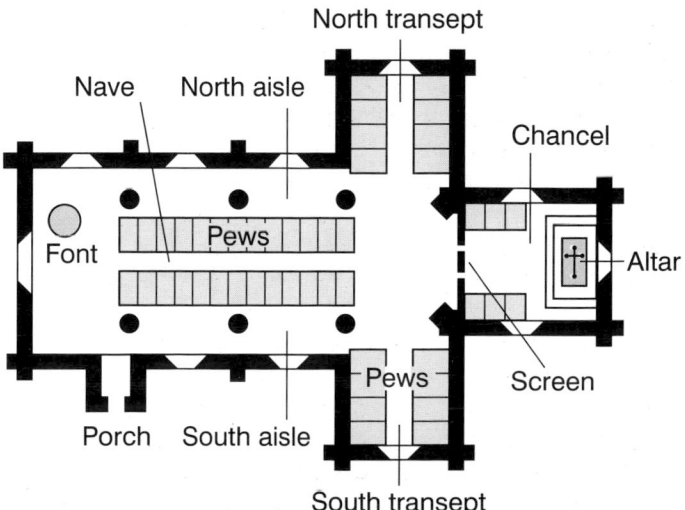

Diagram 2: Plan of a cruciform church

INTRODUCTION

This unit looks at two places of Christian worship that are among the most magnificent buildings on earth. Both were built around the same period of history (the twelfth century onwards) and they are in France, only 90 kilometres away from each other. They are the Gothic Cathedrals of Chartres and Notre-Dame.

What is remarkable about these beautiful buildings is that they were built during a time of terrible cruelty. The Roman Catholic Church had begun hunting and murdering **heretics**, who were people who didn't agree with its teachings. The violent and bloody crusades, carried out in the name of God, brought death and destruction to Europe and to the Holy Land. Yet, in the midst of this chaos, Chartres and Notre-Dame – their spires reaching to the heavens – were constructed, reminding men and women of their Higher Purpose on earth.

MYSTERIOUS ORIGINS

Although much has been written about these two architectural masterpieces, they are both shrouded in mystery. It is known that there existed Schools of Builders. They have left us their work, *but very little is known about these schools and the men and women in them*. Certainly, the Catholic Church of the eleventh and twelfth centuries, which used torture and the stake for heretics, and stifled all free thought, did not build them. Some scholars have suggested that an Order of Knights was responsible for planning the cathedrals. This group was known as the Knight's Templar, and under the instructions of Bernard of Clairvaux, the founder of the Cistercian Order of Monks, they abandoned their earthly possessions and spent ten years in the Holy Land. It is thought that during this time they searched for certain secrets believed to be buried in the most ancient ruins of Solomon's Temple in Jerusalem. They returned with great knowledge about astronomy, architecture, mathematics, stonemasonry, glass-making, psychology and physiology. They put their knowledge into practice by building the cathedrals. This is one theory, but, like other masterpieces of world architecture, nobody really knows their secrets.

Both cathedrals have been called places of *spiritual action*, with the power to change people and put them into a higher spiritual state. Pilgrims came not just to worship Our Lady the Virgin, but rather to find deeper understanding and refresh their soul. Over the ages, numerous pilgrims have written that

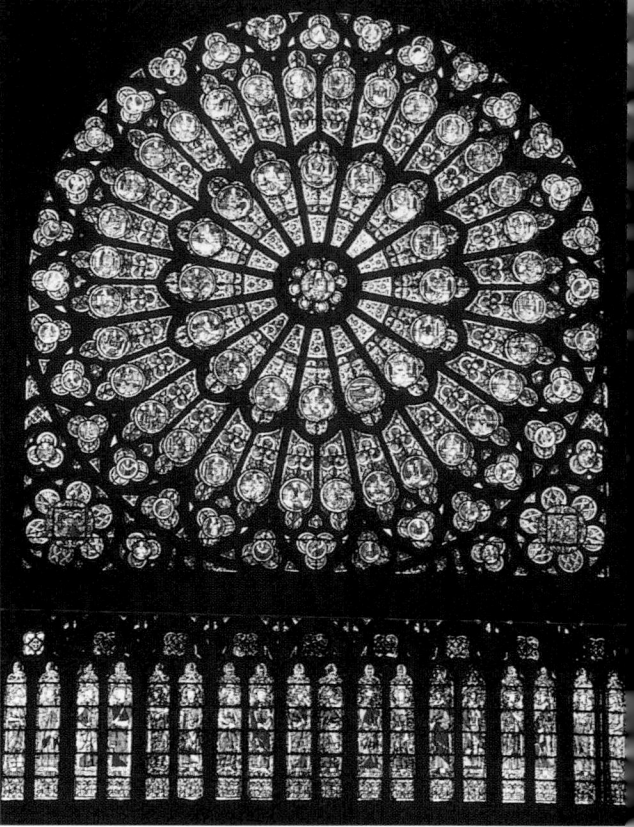

The rose window, Notre-Dame, Paris

the *buildings themselves* have the power to move a person into a higher state of awareness.

When the first Christians arrived in France in the third century CE they made an amazing discovery – a carving of a Virgin with child, blackened with age, at an ancient shrine in Chartres. It is believed that on this site, many years before the birth of Christ, the Druids (Celtic priests) had received a vision that a virgin would give birth to a child. The astonished Christians built a church on the site. There were six churches in all, five of them were destroyed by fire.

REFLECTION

'Many strange thoughts have always been evoked in me by the view from the top of the tower of Notre-Dame. How many centuries have passed beneath these towers, how many changes and how few changes.

A small medieval town surrounded by fields, vineyards and woods. A growing Paris which several times outgrows its walls... And the people, forever going somewhere past these towers, forever hurrying somewhere, and always remaining where they were, seeing nothing, noticing nothing, always the same people. And the towers always the same, with the same gargoyles looking on at this town, which is for ever changing, for ever disappearing and yet always remaining the same.

Here two lines in the life of humanity are clearly seen. One is the line of life of those people below; and the other, the line of the life of those who built Notre-Dame. And looking down from those towers you feel that the real history, the history worth speaking of, is the history of the people who built Notre-Dame and not that of those below. And you understand that these are two quite different histories.

One history passes by in full view and, strictly speaking, is the history of crime, for if there were no crimes there would be no history. All the most important turning points and stages of this history are marked by crimes: murders, acts of violence, robberies, wars, rebellions, massacres, tortures, executions ... This is one history, the history which everybody knows, the history which is taught in schools.

The other history is the history which is known to very few. For the majority it is not seen at all behind the history of crime. But what is created by this hidden history exists long afterwards, sometimes for many centuries, as does Notre-Dame...

I was wandering about the town for the last time. It was already growing light and the air was becoming cold. The moon moved swiftly among the clouds. I walked round the whole cathedral. The huge massive towers stood as though on alert. But I already understood their secret. And I knew that I was taking with me a firm conviction, which nothing could shake, that this exists, that is that there is another history apart from the history of crimes, and that there is another thought, which created Notre-Dame and its figures.'

(Peter Ouspensky,
A New Model of the Universe)

Notre-Dame Cathedral, Paris

FOR YOUR FOLDERS

▶ After reading this unit, write an essay called 'The Mystery and Meaning of Chartres and Notre-Dame'.

INTRODUCTION

The Christian scholar St Augustine (354–430 CE) defined a **sacrament** as: *'the visible form of an invisible grace'*.

There are a total of seven sacraments:

- The Eucharist
- Baptism
- Confirmation
- Marriage
- Penance
- Ordination
- Anointing of the sick (Holy Unction).

All the sacraments involve some physical elements (e.g. bread and wine in the Eucharist). These physical and visible elements represent spiritual and invisible things (e.g. the bread and wine in the Eucharist represent the body and blood of Jesus Christ).

The Roman Catholic and Orthodox Churches accept all the seven sacraments. Christians sometimes call the sacraments 'mysteries'. Most Protestant churches recognize only the first two, the Eucharist and baptism, as being sacraments. Some Christian groups, like the Society of Friends, may not use any sacraments at all.

THE SEVEN SACRAMENTS

- **The Eucharist/Holy Communion** (see unit 43) This central act of worship re-enacts the death and resurrection of Jesus in ritual form. It remembers the words and actions of Jesus at the Last Supper (see Mark 14:17–25).

- **Baptism** (see unit 55) This is a ceremony in which a child or adult is cleansed of sins, to begin a new life with God.

- **Confirmation** (see unit 55) This is when a baptized person becomes fully accepted into a church. The vows made at his or her baptism are 'confirmed'.

- **Marriage** (see units 56 and 57) This is the sacrament in which a man and a woman promise themselves to each other for life.

- **Penance** This is sometimes called 'confession'. People confess their sins to a priest, express their sincere sorrow for having sinned, and promise to

Holy Communion is the central act of worship for many Anglicans

try not to sin in the future. The priest forgives the sinner in God's name. The effect of penance is to bring the person back to God and the Church. Roman Catholic Christians must confess their sins at least once a year, but the Church encourages people to receive penance more frequently than this.

- **Ordination** This is the sacrament in which people are made deacons, priests or bishops. Bishops themselves usually take the ordination service and part of this ceremony includes the ancient practice of the 'laying on of hands'.

- **Anointing of the sick** This is a sacrament given to people who are very sick or very old. The priest anoints the person with oil – a sign of healing. In the Greek Orthodox Church, the anointing of the sick is performed annually in church for the benefit of the whole congregation, on the evening of Holy Wednesday.

SACRAMENTS AND THE CHURCH

For Christians, a sacrament is only powerfully effective when it is performed in and by the Church acting through recognized ministers who intend to act for the Church. This point is important. A sacrament is seen as being meaningless by most Orthodox, Roman Catholic and Protestant Christians if it is not part of the community of the Church. To be a Christian they would argue, demands involvement in the community where the effects of Christ's redemption may be carried out. Therefore a sacrament is not just a visible token of God's grace. It is an instrument whereby the individual is made a member of a wider Christian community with all its duties, disciplines and responsibilities. This doesn't mean that God's grace is only given through the sacraments; but it does mean that an individual becomes involved (partakes) in Christ's redemption, by being related to others who share the same benefits. In the sacraments therefore, both the personal and social relationships of Christian salvation are publicly confirmed, accepted and communicated.

Throughout Christian history Roman Catholic and Protestant Christians have not always agreed upon the meaning of the sacraments. The most bitter controversy centred around the Lord's Supper (also called Holy Communion, Eucharist, Mass) (see unit 43). The Roman Catholic Church taught the doctrine of **transubstantiation**; believing that the substances of bread and wine were miraculously changed into Christ's body and blood during Mass. Protestant reformers could not accept this – although they did accept that Christ in some way, was present in the Supper for those who had faith.

Another major difference between Roman Catholic and Protestant Christians concerned the number of sacraments. Roman Catholics claimed there were seven sacraments. Most Protestants accepted only the two undertaken by Christ himself in the Gospels (i.e. the Baptism and the Lord's Supper). Lutherans, however, were inclined to receive also the Sacrament of Penance. In recent times, many Anglicans have accepted not only Penance to be a sacrament, but also Confirmation, Matrimony, Unction and Holy Orders. They agree that these five rites are sacred signs, but they do not place them in the same rank as the Gospel Sacraments of Baptism and the Lord's Supper.

THE IMPORTANCE OF THE SACRAMENTS

In the sacraments the wholeness of the Gospel of Jesus Christ is proclaimed and offered. The great and powerful acts of God in Christ, enacted in the life, death, resurrection and exaltation of Christ for humankind's redemption, become living and powerful experiences for members of the Churches. The sacraments are therefore mysteries in which the limitations of time are transcended. These mysteries are seen to be accomplished by the power of the Holy Spirit.

With the increasing influence of modern psychology (the study of the mind and the emotions) more Christians are coming to see the important part the sacraments can play in helping them find more fulfilment in their lives. Many of the basic actions of the sacraments (such as eating, drinking and washing) can be seen as fulfilling deep human needs; as instruments in helping people communicate with one another at deeper levels of meaning.

FOR YOUR FOLDERS

▶ Try to explain in your own words St Augustine's definition of a sacrament.

▶ Why do you think the sacraments are often referred to as mysteries?

▶ Write a sentence on each of the seven sacraments.

▶ When, according to Christians, is a sacrament most powerfully effective?

▶ Why would they argue that the sacraments can be seen as more than just a visible token of God's grace?

▶ Briefly outline some of the disagreements about the sacraments that have arisen over the centuries.

▶ What do the sacraments proclaim and offer to Christians?

▶ Why, in modern times, are more Christians beginning to see the importance of the sacraments?

THE EASTERN ORTHODOX CHURCH

Two of the main features of worship in the Orthodox Church are the use of **icons** and the importance that is attached to symbolic actions.

Icons (see unit 24) are religious pictures of Jesus, scenes from the Crucifixion, or saints such as Peter or Mary, the mother of Jesus. Their purpose is to remind worshippers that in worshipping God, they are joining with the saints in heaven. All Orthodox churches have a screen dividing the main part of the church from the inner sanctuary. This screen is called an **iconostasis**, which means 'place of the icons, or pictures'. The iconostasis is usually covered with icons. In the centre of the screen there are doors which are opened at several points during Holy Communion to reveal the **altar**. The iconostasis screen stands for the separation between heaven and earth, God and people. When the doors are opened it reminds the worshippers that God has ended that separation in the person of Jesus Christ.

The other main feature of worship in the Eastern Orthodox Church is the importance of symbolic actions. During the actual service members of the congregation often move around. A worshipper might feel the need to light a candle and will walk around the church in order to do so. When worshippers arrive at the church they buy a small candle, light it and place it on a stand before an icon.

In Eastern Orthodox churches there are no pews or rows of chairs. The worshippers stand together in groups and they kneel, or bow the knee (called **genuflecting**), or touch the ground with their foreheads during certain parts of the service. All these movements have symbolic meaning. For example, by touching the forehead on the ground, worshippers express their submission to God.

THE RELIGIOUS SOCIETY OF FRIENDS (QUAKERS)

A Quaker meeting for worship begins when the first Friend (the official name for a Quaker) enters the meeting room, sits down and waits in silence to become aware of God's presence. At first, thoughts may come crowding into the mind but gradually as the meeting continues the silence deepens. Each individual Quaker will have a different way of settling into the silence, but the aim is to reach a sense of fellowship (or communion) with God and the others present. When this stage is reached Quakers call it a 'gathered meeting'. The stillness deepens and it can feel very powerful, yet peaceful at the same time.

A Society of Friends' meeting for worship

Sometimes, a meeting for worship can continue without any words being spoken for the whole hour, but usually, after a fairly long period of silence, someone will stand up and speak. They may speak of the life and teaching of Jesus, or they may use words from other sources, or they may talk about events in the news or they may offer a prayer in their own words. This is known as 'vocal ministry' and is spontaneous. Anyone may feel the call to speak, man, woman or child, but they must feel that God's Spirit is moving them to speak. They may feel very reluctant to get up but nevertheless find themselves on their feet and speaking. There may be two or three spoken contributions during the meeting.

After about an hour the meeting comes to an end when the **elders** shake hands. (Usually everyone joins in, shaking the hands of the people near to them.)

This simple form of worship needs very few aids or props. The meeting room will be very plain, with chairs arranged in a square or circle, perhaps around a table with some books such as the Bible and *Quaker Faith and Practice* which people may want to refer to.

A meeting for worship can be held almost anywhere and although there are Friends Meeting Houses, these are for convenience. Quakers do not think it is necessary to consecrate special places, times or people to serve God. They have no ordained priests – instead they say that everyone is a priest. They stress the importance of serving God in everyday life, and believe that God's **grace** can be found there. For this reason they do not have outward sacraments like the Eucharist, but say instead that every meal and every meeting for worship can be a time for thanksgiving, remembrance, celebration and communion.

THE ROMAN CATHOLIC CHURCH

Stained glass windows depicting the life of Jesus or the saints, statues or pictures of the Stations of the Cross (which illustrate the story of Jesus carrying the cross) and statues of angels, saints or the Virgin Mary are all features of a Roman Catholic Church. They are there to remind worshippers of God's glory. The main features include the **altar** and a **font** for baptisms

The focal point is the altar where the priest conducts the Word of God, and from where **Mass** is served (see unit 43). There are daily Masses, and also High Masses. These are solemn occasions when choirs and congregations sing praises to God and incense is sprinkled around. Incense, a sweet smelling substance, is a symbol of the sacred. Often, it is sprinkled on the altar, the priest and congregation and on the coffin during funerals. To believers, Mass is not a one-off event. It should affect the whole of a person's life. In Mass, worshippers get a sense of Christ's presence which they try to carry with them throughout their daily lives. The **tabernacle**, a small metal box fixed on the wall, contains a few pieces of consecrated bread, called the **host**, representing the actual living presence of Christ. These will be used when communion is taken and given to the sick.

Since the Second Vatican Council (see unit 23), more emphasis has been placed on the participation of **lay** (ordinary) members of the Church. Services are no longer in Latin and, as well as the priestly ministry, there is the ministry of readers, servers of Mass, and those who take communion to the sick.

THE UNITED REFORMED CHURCH

The United Reformed Church (URC) was formed in 1972 when the Congregational and Presbyterian Churches joined together. Each congregation is independent and elects its own minister. The Church is overseen by twelve moderators. The decor and layout of the United Reformed churches is simple. The communion table is the focal point of the church, as the Lord's Supper (see unit 43) is seen as the climax of worship, representing Christ Risen and Victorious. An empty cross, representing Christ's resurrection stands on the communion table. Services are simple with little ritual. A sermon, prayers, readings from Holy Scriptures and hymn singing are the main activities. Hymn singing has a long tradition in the Church and is experienced as being prayer and an expression of faith, as well as praise. Churches will have a font for the sacrament of Baptism.

FOR YOUR FOLDERS

▶ Explain the following words: icons; iconostasis; tabernacle; host.

▶ Briefly explain the chief features of these four styles of worship.

43 THE EUCHARIST

INTRODUCTION

For many Christians the **Eucharist** is the most important act of worship. The word 'Eucharist' comes from a Greek word that means 'thanksgiving'. The Eucharist remembers Jesus' Last Supper as recorded in the Gospels:

'And as they were eating Jesus took the bread, and blessed it, and broke it, and gave it to the disciples, and said, Take eat; this is my body. And he took the cup, and gave thanks, and gave it to them, saying, Drink ye all of it. For this is my blood of the new testament, which is shed for many, for the remission of sins.'

(Matthew 26:26–8)

This great act of Christian thanksgiving appears under many different names:

- Breaking of bread
- Eucharist
- Lord's Supper
- Mass (a title often used by Roman Catholic Christians)
- Holy (or Sacred) Liturgy (a title popular among Eastern Orthodox Christians)
- Holy Communion (**communion** means 'common sharing').

Christians have sometimes disagreed about what Jesus meant when he said that the bread was his body and the wine his blood. At the centre of the Eucharist, for Christians, is the idea that Jesus died on the cross for all human beings. By taking part in the meal, Christians feel that they are obeying Jesus' own command to do this in remembrance of him.

CELEBRATING THE EUCHARIST

There are differences in the way the Eucharist is celebrated among the Churches but almost all celebrations have a similar pattern:

- **The ministry of the Word** – This is the first part of the service, containing prayers, Bible readings, hymns, acts of confession and perhaps a sermon.

The second major part of the service is the Eucharist proper, and contains the following acts:

- **The taking of the bread and wine** – here worshippers are reminded of the origins of the Eucharist and the bread and wine are put on the altar or table

- **The great thanksgiving (i.e. the Eucharist Prayer).** Here is an example of the prayer:

'It is indeed right,
it is our duty and our joy,
at all times and in all places
to give you thanks and praise,
holy Father, heavenly King,
almighty and eternal God,
through Jesus Christ your only Son our Lord.'

The breaking of the bread

The bread and wine are blessed or consecrated by the minister or priest. In some churches the words of the Lord's Supper, from the Gospels, might be read out. Some of the following practices can be associated with this reading:

- bowing or genuflecting (bending the knee) among the congregation
- **censing** (putting incense) around the altar
- lifting up the bread and the wine
- ringing the bells.

In some churches members of the congregation might greet each other with the 'sign of peace'. This might involve shaking hands with the people around or embracing them. The sign of peace can represent unity.

The sharing of the bread and wine

In the Orthodox Church, Holy Communion is distributed to the congregation by dipping a piece of bread in the wine and then giving it to them on a long spoon.

In Baptist and United Reformed Churches, the wine is often distributed in separate glasses by church leaders. People do not drink from the same cup, or **chalice**, but do so from their own little cups together.

In the Church of England the congregation receives the bread kneeling at the altar. However, in some Protestant churches the congregation stands round the altar or table in small groups.

The dismissal

After the sharing of the bread and wine there is a short act of dismissal which might include prayers, a hymn or a blessing.

In many Protestant churches the Eucharist may take place once a month. In Roman Catholic churches, Mass takes place daily. In some churches only those people who have been confirmed (see unit 55) are able to take part in the Eucharist, whilst others have no such restrictions.

When Roman Catholic Christians attend Mass they follow a sequence which represents a path they believe they must follow in their lives and in their relationship to God. The main steps are as follows:

- they come together as a community in the presence of God (*Fellowship*)
- they turn away from their sin (*Penitential Rite*)
- they listen to the words of God in the Scriptures (*Liturgy of the Word*)
- they give thanks to God (*Eucharistic Prayer*)
- they receive the bread and wine, which they believe has been changed into the body and blood of Jesus Christ (*Communion*), (see unit 41)
- they are sent out to serve other people (*Dismissal*).

ONE IMPORTANT PRAYER IN THE EUCHARIST

The 'Agnus Dei' (Lamb of God), said or sung at the time of the breaking of the bread, has been used in the Christian churches since the end of the seventh century CE:

> *'Lamb of God, you take away the sins of the world; have mercy on us.*
> *Lamb of God, you take away the sins of the world; have mercy on us.*
> *Lamb of God, you take away the sins of the world; grant us peace.'*

This is just one important prayer; there are many others.

REFLECTIONS

'When we receive Communion, I believe that God reaches out to us on the most primitive and simple level. A babe can receive a small particle of bread and a drop of wine, and with it be reached by God.'

(The Most Reverend Metropolitan Anthony of Sourozh – head of the Russian Orthodox Church in Britain)

'I cannot do without Mass. If I can see Jesus in the appearance of bread then I will be able to see Him in the broken bodies of the poor. He has said, "I am the Living Bread".'

(Mother Teresa)

'I believe that I receive Christ, not because he is in the bread and wine but because He is in the heart of those who receive the bread and wine believingly.'

(Reverend John Stott)

'The bread and wine are distributed to the worshippers on conditions of absolute and complete equality. There is no table of **precedence**, *no priority of duke over dustman, it is an act of total sharing and it is in this act that the Church claims that the life of Christ Himself is shared.'*

(Reverend S. Evans)

FOR YOUR FOLDERS

▶ Explain the following words: Eucharist; communion; genuflecting; censing; chalice; precedence.

▶ What does the Eucharistic Prayer tell us of Christian beliefs about:

   a Jesus Christ
   b the Eucharist?

▶ Write an article of about 150 words on the different practices that take place in the Eucharist.

▶ Explain in your own words the feelings and meanings of the four reflections.

▶ Why is the Eucharist so important for many Christians?

Priests prostrating themselves during their ordination into the priesthood. Their lying down signifies humility and a mysterious beginning when they can administer the sacrament of the Catholic faith

'*Then he poured water into a basin and began to wash the disciples' feet.*'

(John 13:5)

In this act of service, Jesus set an example to all Christian leaders. He reminded them that they were there to serve others, and to **minister** to and help them. This is why some Churches use the word 'minister', when they talk about their religious leaders. In the Roman Catholic Church, the Eastern Orthodox Church and the Church of England, the Eucharist (see unit 43) is always carried out by a priest. In some Churches, for example the Methodist Church, it has to be carried out by a fully ordained minister.

Ordination is the ceremony by which a Church appoints its ministers. The most usual ceremony includes the very ancient practice of 'laying on hands'. This is seen, by some Christians, as a direct way of passing on spiritual power and authority; although some Christian denominations feel that ordination is not necessary. However, in some Churches ordination is seen as being extremely important because people feel that the priest or minister is doing work that is so sacred, and so important, that they need the authority of the Church to do it.

Before ordination, Roman Catholic, Orthodox and Anglican priests undergo a long period of training. The length of time for this varies, but it can be more than four years before full-time service can begin.

STRUCTURES

Churches which have the ministry of bishops are called **episcopal** (from the Greek word for bishop). They are the Roman Catholic, Orthodox and the Anglican Churches. These churches have three orders of ministry – bishops, priests and **deacons**. Bishops are in charge of large areas called dioceses. Most priests work in a parish, or local community. In Britain, deacons are people about to become priests.

Archbishops (who are senior bishops) have more responsibility than bishops. They can sometimes be in charge of the whole Church in one country. In the Orthodox Church the senior archbishops are called **patriarchs** (which means 'great fathers'). In the Roman Catholic Church an important group called the **cardinals** is responsible for electing the Pope. In England, Anglican bishops and archbishops are appointed by the monarch who is the Supreme Governor of the Church of England. Many Protestant churches elect their national leaders (sometimes called **moderators**) every year, and these people rule their groups through councils which are elected by individual churches.

WOMEN PRIESTS

The Roman Catholic and Eastern Orthodox Churches have no women priests. Some Churches that do have women priests include the Lutheran Churches, the French Reformed Church, the Congregationalists, the Methodists and the Baptists.

KEY WORD

Ordination – 'the act or ceremony of ordaining a religious leader.'

In 1994 after enormous debate the Church of England began ordaining women. Not everyone was happy with this and some people have since joined the Roman Catholic Church.

WORK

Generally speaking, in Christian worship, ministers have two jobs: they act as the representative of the community; and they are used as the means by which God addresses the people, by preaching and reading from the scriptures. A minister's work within the community can cover a whole range of activities. These can include things like running youth groups; visiting prisoners, elderly people and people in hospital; counselling the bereaved, the sick, the lonely and the depressed; helping with fund-raising activities; organizing the running of the parish; and much more. Some ministers are chaplains. They do not have a parish but work in the armed forces, or in prisons, universities or factories instead.

FOR YOUR FOLDERS

▶ Explain the following words: minister; ordination; episcopal; deacon; cardinal; patriarch; moderator.

▶ Why do you think Christian leaders are sometimes called 'servants in authority'?

▶ Construct a diary for a priest or minister. You will have to use your imagination to describe how his or her week is spent.

THINGS TO DO

▶ Look at this extract from the ordination service of the Anglican Church and the prayer which follows it. Make a list of some of the duties of a priest.

'Priests are called by God to work with the bishop and with their fellow-priests, as servants and shepherds among the people to whom they are sent. They are to proclaim the word of the Lord, to call their hearers to repentance, and in Christ's name to absolve, and to declare the forgiveness of sins. They are to baptize, and prepare the baptized for Confirmation. They are to preside at the celebration of the Holy Communion. They are to lead the people in prayer and worship, to intercede for them, to bless them in the name of the Lord, and to teach and encourage by word and example. They are to minister to the sick, and prepare the dying for their death. They must set the Good Shepherd always before them as the pattern of their calling, caring for the people committed to their charge, and joining with them in a common witness to the world.'

(Alternative Service Book)

Almighty God, give us priests:
to establish the honour of your holy name;
to offer the holy sacrifice of the altar;
to give us Jesus in the holy sacrament;
to proclaim the faith of Jesus;
to baptize and to teach the young;
to tend your sheep;
to seek the lost;
to give pardon to the penitent sinner;
to bless our homes;
to pray for the afflicted;
to comfort mourners;
to strengthen us in our last hour;
to commend our souls.
Almighty God, give us priests!

Holy father, you gave us Christ as the Shepherd of our souls; may your people always have priests who care for them with his great love.

We make our prayer through Jesus Christ our Lord, who lives and reigns with you and the Holy Spirit, one God, for ever and ever. Amen.'

INTRODUCTION

Different Churches put different emphases on the Christian calendar. For instance, the Roman Catholic Church keeps a very full calendar, observing a great many feasts and saints' days. Some Protestant Churches, on the other hand, keep a much simpler calendar, with only major festivals being observed. Some Evangelical Churches ignore the traditional Christian calendar completely, except for Christmas and Easter.

The Christian calendar falls into two main sections, revolving around the festivals of Christmas, when Christians celebrate the birth of Jesus, and Easter, when they remember His death. The festivals are observed by Christians all over the world.

The major Christian festivals all revolve around the life of Jesus as depicted in the four Gospels. Units 46–51 study some of these festivals in more detail. This unit looks briefly at some of them.

In the Christian calendar many festivals, sometimes called fasts and feasts, do not fall on the same date each year. The only two feasts that have the same date every year are Christmas (25 December) and Epiphany, which is related to Christmas. Saints' Days, which celebrate the death of Christian saints, also fall on the same date each year. However, if that date happens to fall on a Sunday (which is always a feast day), then the Saint's Day will be moved to another date.

The reason why festival dates vary is because they depend on the date of **Easter**. The rule for determining the date of Easter is quite complicated: Easter Day is always the first Sunday after the full moon which happens around 21 March. If the full moon is on a Sunday, then Easter Day (which is always a Sunday) is the Sunday afterwards.

In the Western Church, a tradition has evolved of using different coloured robes for the leaders of worship at each season of the Church year. For instance, purple robes are worn during periods of fasting, for example during **Advent** and **Lent**; white robes are worn for the major festivals of Easter, Christmas, Ascension Day and some Saints' Days.

MAJOR CHRISTIAN FESTIVALS

Western

Epiphany – 6 January

Epiphany comes from a Greek word meaning 'revealing'. This feast day is older than Christmas; it has been kept since the fourth century CE in the West, and the third century CE in the East where it originated. To Christians it celebrates the revealing of Christ's divinity, born in the flesh; and remembers the Wise Men who came from the East to see the newborn Christ. It is the last day of the Christmas period; Christmas decorations and the symbolic crib are put away for the year.

Ash Wednesday – February/March

This marks the beginning of Lent, a period of forty days which recalls the time Jesus spent in the wilderness in preparation for public ministry. During the service, held on Ash Wednesday as a reminder of our mortality, some Christians draw a cross of ashes on their foreheads. In the past, Lent was a time of fasting; today some Christians give up a favourite food, such as chocolate, for forty days.

Maundy Thursday – March/April

A special communion service on this day remembers the last evening Jesus spent with his disciples, and the sacrifice he made by his death. In Britain the Queen (as Supreme Governor of the Church of England) distributes 'Maundy money' – traditionally to poor people – in memory of Jesus washing the feet of his disciples (see John 13:1–20).

Good Friday – March/April

This day marks the death of Jesus on the cross. It is called 'good' as Christians believe that because Jesus died, they can gain forgiveness for their sins. Hot cross buns are eaten on this day. The spiced buns decorated with a cross on the top are thought to have originated in pagan times, when they represented the moon and its four quarters.

Easter Day – March/April

This is a movable feast day that marks Jesus' Resurrection and his appearance to his mother Mary and his disciples. Some Christian parents hide Easter eggs, symbols of new life, for their children to find.

Ascension Day – May/June

This is the day on which Christians remember Jesus' ascension into Heaven. In the Western Church, the paschal candle, lit during Easter, is snuffed on Ascension Day to mark Jesus' departure from the apostles.

Whit Sunday – May/June

Christians celebrate Pentecost, the day when God sent his Holy Spirit to the apostles and the Christian Church was founded. In some places there are public processions, such as the North of England's Whit Walk. It is a popular day for baptism, when a person is immersed in – or sprinkled with – water as a sign that they are cleansed from sin and have become a full member of the Church.

Celebrating Easter in Guatemala, Central America

Advent Sunday – November/December
This is the beginning of the Church's calendar year.

Christmas Day – 25 December
The holy day that celebrates the birth of Jesus actually began as a pagan festival. No one knows when Christ was born, but by the middle of the fourth century CE Christians were celebrating his birth on the winter solstice which, according to the astronomy of that time, was 25 December.

Eastern
Orthodox Churches are linked with ancient Greek civilization. The word 'orthodox' – meaning 'right in opinion' – emphasizes their strong and living links with the worship and teaching of the first Christian centuries (see unit 24). Festivals in Eastern Churches include:

Lenten Monday – February/March
This is the first day of a period of fasting and preparation for Easter. Orthodox and Western religious calendars disagree on the timing of Lent, largely because there has been no agreement on how to make adjustments to the lunar calendar on which Easter is plotted.

Easter Day/Pascha – March/April
Christians celebrate the Resurrection of Christ.

Pentecost – May/June
The word comes from the Greek for 'fifty' (see unit 20) and is the same feast as the Western Christians' Whitsun.

FOR YOUR FOLDERS

▶ Write a few lines about each of the major Christian festivals.

▶ Choose one festival. Make a card illustrating this festival and give it to another member of your class, unsigned. He or she will sign it (after reading it) and give it to another person in the class.

▶ Explain to a member of your class how the date for Easter is worked out.

▶ Write a paragraph explaining why you think the Christian calendar is important for a Christian. Explain how some Christian festivals also affect people who have no religious faith in the UK.

Before looking at this unit, read the stories about the birth of Jesus in Matthew's Gospel, chapters 1 and 2.

Christmas is the second most important festival of the Christian year, after Easter. It begins four Sundays before Christmas Day, with the season of Advent.

ADVENT

The period known as Advent provides an opportunity for Christians to retell and reflect upon many of the Biblical stories and passages which they believe point to Jesus as God's promised Saviour for the human race. For Christians, most of this preparation and reflection takes place during church services when the congregation hears readings from the Scriptures. Some Christian families have an Advent calendar and Advent candles at home which they use in the days leading up to Christmas Day.

CHRISTMAS

The word 'Christmas' comes from the old English 'Chrestes Maesoes', which means 'Christ's Mass'. Nobody really knows the exact date of Jesus' birth; it was not considered important by the early Christians who were more concerned with who Jesus was and what he did.

On Christmas Day itself, the great majority of Christians take part in an act of congregational worship. The style of worship varies in different Christian churches. However, the focus of all the different rituals is the birth of Jesus and the proclamation of beliefs in him, as the Son of God and Saviour of the world.

For some Christians, the most important event of Christmas is the Eucharist, or **Communion** service. It bears the marks of a celebration – with music, the Eucharistic meal and a procession dominating the service. The first Eucharist of Christmas often starts at about 11.30 p.m. on the night before Christmas Day (called Christmas Eve). This service is often called the Midnight Mass, and it is one of the most popular services in the Christian calendar. The next Eucharist will be on Christmas morning, and Christians try to attend this. In the Eucharist, Christians believe that they 'receive' Christ in the bread and wine, and so the idea of God giving himself to human beings at Christmas is echoed in the service.

Christians believe that at Christmas, they are thanking God for giving the world his only Son who was born as a human being. This idea is known as the **Incarnation** (see unit 7). At many Christmas services the first words of John's Gospel are read out, highlighting the idea that the **Word**, i.e. Jesus Christ (although he came from God) *is* God.

'In the beginning was the Word, and the Word was with God, and the Word was God.'

(John 1:1)

During the service on Christmas Day many Christians read the prophecy of Christ's birth, revealed 500 years previously by the Old Testament Prophet Isaiah:

'The people who walked in darkness have seen a great light: those who dwelt in a land of deep darkness, on them has light shined. For to us a child is born, to us a son is given: and the government will be upon his shoulder, and his name shall be called "Wonderful Counsellor, Mighty God, Everlasting Father, Prince of Peace". Of the increase of his government and of peace there will be no end, upon the throne of David, and over his kingdom, to establish it, and to uphold it with justice and with righteousness from this time forth and for evermore. The zeal of the Lord of hosts will do this.'

(Isaiah 9:2, 6–7)

FOR YOUR FOLDERS

▶ Explain the following words and phrases: Advent; Christmas; Incarnation; the Word.

▶ Read the reflection opposite on the meaning of Christmas. Why do people have to 'forget the tinsel and the gaudy lights' to discover the true meaning of Christmas, according to Reverend Roberts?

▶ Why does he believe that Christmas is about involvement?

▶ Why is Christmas so significant (see bold type)?

REFLECTION

'Forget the tinsel and the gaudy lights; forget the carol singing and the carousing parties; forget the shops and trees laden with presents – all very enjoyable in the middle of winter, but mostly irrelevant and in no way useful to discover the meaning of the great Christian festival.

We forget, or at least tend to forget, that when "Jesus was born in Bethlehem of Judea in the days of Herod the king", as the Gospel story tells us, it was not like that at all. The hotel where the holy Family had hoped to shelter was full and so the Christ child, the "Light of the World", first saw the light of day in an outhouse among the litter and the hay.

In a world of dire poverty and cruel injustice, a world of greed and selfishness, a child is born, not in some expensive cot in a private nursery but in a mean manger, "where oxen feed on hay". A thing to scandalize the conventional comfortable well-off people of every nation in every age – and yet for Christians the world over, the birth of Jesus signifies the coming of God into our world; of God taking our human nature to reveal to us his Divine Nature – and at His coming, He found His first home to be a very make-shift affair.

The Christmas message is really about involvement. People with ideas who want to change things and influence others, people who feel passionately about something important, have to be involved and Christians believe that when Jesus was born God himself became involved in the life of humanity, in order to change the existing order of things for the better.

For centuries the Jewish people looked forward to a time when poverty, injustice, war, cruelty would give way to a reign of peace and righteousness, when the "lion would lie down with the lamb".

For Christians, this change was inaugurated by the birth of Jesus and that is the event we joyfully commemorate at Christmas. God himself was involved, to give the whole of His creation a better deal and a purpose to living. Of course many Jewish people found it difficult to accept this and today many people find it difficult to accept the stark reality of this event, and prefer to hide behind the tawdry sentimentality of the occasion.

God became involved. He took the form of a slave, a servant, meeting people as they were and where they were. How unbecoming. How undignified. What sordid behaviour in the sight of those so concerned about their status, their wealth, their power, and who always hide behind the conventional.

But every year, Christmas throws down the challenge to all that is false and evil in the world and calls people to decide what is really important in the process of living.

Our indifference to the needs of those who are suffering hunger or poverty, injustice or sickness is a symbol of our rejection of God. Times don't seem to have changed for it was written down 2000 years ago that, "he entered his own realm, and his own would not receive him" (John 1:11).

Christ's birth tends to upset people's comfortable little lives, and they don't want this to happen. So, they try to keep him out in that outhouse where he was born. So they hide the true message in heaps of pretty tinsel and flashing neon lights.

But those who truly believe in him will try to follow his example. They know that he speaks to them of God in action and in their involvement they will try to change the order of things and make the world a better place to live in. Especially for those who are sick in body and mind, those who are downtrodden, beaten, exploited and hungry in body or in mind. But above all Christ was a Messenger of God. The message for all of us is to wake up from our slumber, see the world as a passing through, and realize our Divine origins.'

(Reverend Richard Roberts, Church of Wales)

The festival of **Easter** is the most important festival in the Christian calendar, celebrating the death and Resurrection of Jesus. It is so important that, for instance, Orthodox Christians often call it 'the Feast of Feasts'.

Many non-Christians think that Easter is a festival that lasts only a few days, from Good Friday to Easter Monday. In fact, the festival lasts for ninety days in all. This period includes the forty days of **Lent** (not including the Sundays) before Easter, and fifty days after Easter (including the Ascension and Whitsuntide).

The period called Lent is associated with the time Jesus spent alone in the wilderness, as recorded in Matthew's Gospel (4:1–17) and Luke's Gospel (4:1–13).

THE TEMPTATION OF JESUS

'Full of the Holy Spirit, Jesus returned from the Jordan, and for forty days was led by the Spirit up and down the wilderness and tempted by the devil.

All that time he had nothing to eat, and at the end of it he was famished. The devil said to him, "If you are the Son of God, tell this stone to become bread." Jesus answered, "Scripture says, 'Man cannot live on bread alone.'"

Next the devil led him up and showed him in a flash all the kingdoms of the world. "All this dominion will I give to you," he said, "and the glory that goes with it; for it has been put in my hands and I can give it to anyone I choose. You have only to do homage to me and it shall be yours." Jesus answered him, "Scripture says, 'You shall do homage to the Lord your God and worship him alone.'"

The devil took him to Jerusalem and set him on the parapet of the temple. "If you are the Son of God," he said, "throw yourself down; for Scripture says, 'He will give his angels orders to take care of you', and again, 'They will support you in their arms for fear you should strike your foot against a stone.'" Jesus answered him, "It has been said, 'You are not to put the Lord your God to the test.'"

So, having come to the end of all his temptations, the devil departed, biding his time.'

(Luke 4:1–13)

In the early Church, Lent was observed by eating only one small meal in the evening; all animal and fish products were forbidden. Today the observance of Lent is more relaxed and people can choose what to eat. However, some Christians still go on a strict fast (they give up eating) for part of the time. Other Christians might observe Lent by giving something up, e.g. sweets, cakes, alcohol, etc.

The meaning and purpose of Lent, however, has remained the same. It is a time when Christians are

Christ in the wilderness

eminded that Jesus sacrificed his life for the
alvation of all people. Lent is a time when
hristians remember too the suffering Jesus
ndured, in stark contrast to the joy of Easter when
hristians remember Jesus' Resurrection from the
ead.

HROVE TUESDAY

he last day before Lent is called Shrove Tuesday.
hrove' means 'being forgiven'. It is a time when
hristians **confess** their sins and ask God for
orgiveness. They often go to a priest who gives
em 'absolution' (forgiveness of sins). By doing this
ey feel that they can have a completely new start
or the period of Lent, and can prepare for Easter
ithout feeling burdened by their sins. In Britain,
hrove Tuesday is often called 'Pancake Day', when
eople eat pancakes, which are made out of flour
nd eggs. Traditionally, people feasted to eat up all
e good things that they might have in their
tchens, before beginning the serious fasting
ssociated with Lent.

SH WEDNESDAY

he first day of Lent is called Ash Wednesday. In the
ast, notorious sinners would perform public
enance and punish themselves in public to show
at they had done wrong and were sorry.
raditionally, small crosses, made from palm leaves
hich had been used at the previous year's Palm
unday service, were burnt and the ashes put on
eople's foreheads in the shape of a cross.

UNDAYS

ent is broken up by the weekly festivals of
undays. The fourth Sunday in Lent is called
tefreshment Sunday'. It is also known as
Mothering Sunday', when people show their
ratitude to their mothers for their love and care.
he fifth Sunday is called 'Passion Sunday' and is a
me when Christians think about the final week in
sus' life (often called '**Holy Week**'). Around this
me Lent becomes a very solemn and sad time.
ome churches cover up all icons, ornaments,
osses, etc. with purple cloths, to introduce feelings
f sorrow, sadness and mourning. This is because
uring Holy Week, Christians believe that God's
nly Son was brutally and violently killed on the
oss by an ignorant humanity. For Christians it is
e darkest time in human history.

THINKING POINT

- Origen (185–253 CE) was an educator and
priest in Alexander and Caesarea. His
father was martyred for his Christian
faith and it is believed that Origen was
martyred as well. In this piece of writing
on temptation he says that people must
not feel guilty about temptation but
rather see that temptations can help them
to understand themselves.

*'The gifts which our soul has received are
unknown to everyone except God. They
are unknown even to ourselves. Through
temptations they become known.
Afterwards we can't be ignorant of what
we are. We know ourselves and can be
aware of our wrongdoings. Temptations
that come upon us serve the purpose of
showing us who we really are and make
clear the things that are in our heart.'*

FOR YOUR FOLDERS

▶ Explain the following words: Lent;
homage; fast; Shrove; confess.

▶ Explain what happens on Shrove
Tuesday and Ash Wednesday.

▶ Why do Christians see Lent as being a
preparation for Easter?

▶ How might Lent be observed by some
Christians?

▶ What is the meaning of Lent for
Christians?

▶ How is the account of the temptation of
Jesus related to Lent?

▶ Explain why Origen believed that
temptations can help us to get to know
ourselves.

Palm Sunday procession

Holy Week, the last week of Jesus' life, is the most solemn time in the Christian year. Holy Week is often called 'The Passion'.

SUNDAY – PALM SUNDAY

On this day Christians remember the entry of Jesus into the city of Jerusalem, as recorded in the Gospels.

> '… and those who went ahead and the others who came behind shouted, "Hosanna! Blessings on him who comes in the name of the Lord!" '
>
> (Mark 11:9)

In the Gospel accounts it is recorded that people welcomed Jesus by carpeting his path with palm leaves as he rode into the city. On Palm Sunday worshippers are given a small cross made out of a palm leaf. Then the worshippers, led by somebody carrying a cross, make a small procession around the church. This is the last celebration for Christians before they enter the sadness of the rest of Holy Week.

THURSDAY – MAUNDY THURSDAY

The word 'Maundy' comes from the Latin word 'mandatum', which means commandment. On Maundy Thursday Christians remember Jesus' last supper with his disciples before his arrest and trial. In the Gospels it is recorded that Jesus shared the meal with his disciples and used the bread and wine as mysterious symbols of his own body and blood:

> 'During supper he took bread, and having said th[e] blessing he broke it and gave it to them, with the words: "Take this; this is my body." Then he took a cup, and having offered thanks to God he gave i[t] to them; and they all drank from it. And he said, "This is my blood, the blood of the covenant, shed for many." '
>
> (Mark 14:22–[5])

This meal has become known by different names, e.g. the **Eucharist**, **Mass**, Holy Communion. It is regarded by Christians as being the most holy act of worship in the Church (see unit 43). In John's Gospel, it is recorded that Jesus gave his disciples a new commandment at the Last Supper:

> 'I give you a new commandment: love one another; as I have loved you, so you are to love one another. If there is this love among you, then all will know that you are my disciples.'
>
> (John 13:34–[5])

FRIDAY – GOOD FRIDAY

In the Gospels it is recorded that after the Last Supper Jesus was arrested and put on trial. On the Friday he was crucified by the Romans. The Friday of Holy Week is called 'good' because Christians believe that on that day Jesus displayed the greatest possible sort of goodness, by sacrificing himself on the cross for the sake of humanity.

'They brought him to the place called Golgotha, which means "Place of a skull". He was offered drugged wine, but he would not take it. Then they fastened him to the cross. They divided his clothes among them, casting lots to decide what each should have.

The hour of the crucifixion was nine in the morning, and the inscription giving the charge against him read, "The king of the Jews". Two bandits were crucified with him, one on his right and the other on his left.'

(Mark 15:22–8)

This is the most solemn day of the whole Christian year, a day of great sadness and deep emotion. Church services might take place from noon until three in the afternoon. On Good Friday the churches are dark and sombre, reflecting the mood of Christians who believe that the death of Jesus marked the ultimate turning away from God.

'The Crucifixion' by Salvador Dali

THINKING POINTS

● *'Wouldst thou learn thy Lord's meaning in this thing? Learn it well: love was this meaning.'*
(Julian of Norwich, c. 1342–1420)

● *'Nails would not have held the God-man fast to the cross had not love held him there.'*
(Catherine of Siena, 1347–80)

● *'A man's self is his greatest cross.'*
(François Fenélon, 1651–1715 – French thinker)

FOR YOUR FOLDERS

▶ Explain in detail:

a the events of Holy Week as recorded in Mark's Gospel

b the ways that Christians remember Holy Week in their beliefs and practices.

▶ Explain in your own words what you consider to be the significance of the Crucifixion for Christians.

▶ Explain what you think Julian of Norwich, Catherine of Siena and François Fenélon mean.

▶ Why do they believe the death of Jesus marked the ultimate turning away from God?

FOR DISCUSSION

▶ *'Then said Jesus, "Father, forgive them: for they know not what they do." '*

(Jesus' words on the cross, Luke 23:34)

SUNDAY – EASTER SUNDAY

It is recorded in the Gospels that three days after His death on the cross, Jesus 'rose from the dead'; this is known as the **Resurrection**.

> *'When the Sabbath was over, Mary of Magdala, Mary the mother of James, and Salome bought aromatic oils intending to go and anoint him; and very early on the Sunday morning, just after sunrise, they came to the tomb. They were wondering among themselves who would roll away the stone from the entrance to the tomb for them, when they looked up and saw that the stone, huge as it was, had been rolled back already. They went into the tomb, where they saw a youth sitting on the right-hand side, wearing a white robe; and they were dumbfounded. But he said to them, "Fear nothing; you are looking for Jesus of Nazareth, who was crucified. He has been raised again; he is not here; look, there is the place where they laid him." '*

(Mark 16:1–6)

The Resurrection of Jesus is regarded by nearly all Christians as being the single most important event in the New Testament. Although scholars and theologians have often debated the facts and meanings of the Resurrection, especially over the last century, for Christians it is a wonderful and miraculous act of God.

The significance of the Resurrection is, for many Christians, explained by the words of St Paul:

> *'But the truth is, Christ was raised to life – the first fruits of the harvest of the dead. For since it was a man who brought death into the world, a man also brought resurrection of the dead. As in Adam all men die, so in Christ all will be brought to life; but each in his own proper place: Christ the firstfruits, and afterwards, at his coming, those who belong to Christ.'*

(1 Corinthians 15:22–4)

THE RESURRECTION IN THE NEW TESTAMENT

Belief in the Resurrection is mentioned in all the New Testament books. The Resurrection lies at the heart of Christianity. The whole of Christian

For Christians, the resurrection is the central event of cosmic history

theology – all its thinking about Christ and God – is based on belief in the Resurrection. According to the Gospels, when Jesus was crucified the disciples had run for their lives, terrified and in despair. *Yet something happened* that made them meet up again and later gave them the courage to go out into a brutal and hostile world to preach his message.

The New Testament letters do not describe the Resurrection in any detail. Generally, they refer to it as the victory of Jesus over death, and as the feelings of new life that Christians felt inwardly:

> *'If the spirit of God, who raised Jesus from death, lives in you, then he who raised Christ will also give life to your mortal bodies... '*

(Romans 8:11)

The four Gospel writers see the Resurrection as a triumph, a transformation and a promise of hope. It is seen as God's blessing on Jesus, when in the view of many his life had been a failure, ending with his eath on the cross. The Resurrection is seen as a omise that all is not lost, and that darkness, espair and death will be turned to light.

WORSHIP

churches all over the world, the atmosphere anges from one of deep sadness for the rucifixion, to one of deep joy and thanksgiving at e Resurrection. Ornaments are brought back into e churches, silver and gold colours appear and ring flowers decorate every corner. On Easter Eve, any Christians stay awake (keep a 'vigil'). In oman Catholic churches, large Easter candles alled 'Paschal candles') are lit and carried in. veryone in the congregation lights his or her own ndle from the Paschal candle and the church is oded with light. The Easter Proclamation is sung, *ejoice. Christ has conquered.'* The church bells are ng for the first time in three days and Mass is lebrated. Easter Sunday is the most important day the Christian year. It celebrates the victory of sus' Resurrection – the victory of life over death, of ht over darkness. For Christians, it is the central int of history – the time when death was nquered and God gave the world his only Son, ho **atoned** for the sins of the world.

FOR DISCUSSION

▶ Read the accounts of the Resurrection in Matthew 28, Mark 16, Luke 24 and John 20. Afterwards discuss the following:

Do you think the empty tomb alone could have made the disciples believe in the Resurrection? Why do some Christians think Jesus rose spiritually, but not physically? Is it possible that Jesus did not die on the cross and recovered later in the tomb? Would he have been able to move the stone if he had? Was the risen Christ a ghost? What do you think must have happened to change the disciples' fear, and make them bravely go out and preach in a dangerous world? Could somebody be a Christian and not believe in the Resurrection? Do you think there is a life after death?

THINKING POINTS

● *'If Christ was to raise a new life like his own in every man, then every man must have had in the inmost spirit of his life, a seed of Christ, or Christ as a seed of heaven . . .'*

(William Law)

● *'Jesus dares to confuse the space known as earth. The resurrection is nothing if not a conquest of time and place (death on Golgotha) by space – that is by an empty (space-filled) tomb where sadness and death are no longer granted place. Where grief comes to an end. Where life, new but mysterious, is resurrected against all odds and all pessimism and all cynicism and all sadness.'*

(Matthew Fox)

FOR YOUR FOLDERS

▶ *'If Christ has not been raised, then our preaching is in vain'* (1 Corinthians 15:14). What do you think St Paul meant by these words? Why is the Resurrection so important for Christians?

▶ Explain and describe some of the practices that are associated with the Resurrection in Christian worship.

▶ Read the thinking points and discuss them in groups. Write down your ideas.

As we have seen, **Easter** is the most important festival in the Christian year. To begin to understand the impact it has on Christians throughout the world, read these three accounts of the Easter experience. The first account is from Tim Richards, a Protestant from Wales; the second from Mario Constantinou, a young Greek who is a member of the Greek Orthodox Church; and the third from Caitlin McKenny, a Catholic living in Belfast.

REFLECTION 1

'I try and go into a church every morning during Easter week, if not to a service then just to sit quietly, think, and sometimes pray. Easter is a mystery. Almost 2000 years ago, in a remote corner of the Roman Empire a new doctrine was taught. Jesus' preaching lasted only three years and ended in defeat. The preacher was executed. But on the eve of His death, He prophesied that the Good News he had brought would be preached "unto all nations". Today, the Gospel has been translated into more than 600 languages. This is a miracle, part of the ongoing miracle, that first took place when Mary Magdalene found that the stone of the tomb had been rolled away. Jesus Christ rose from the grave. Death has been conquered. The Gospel writers tell us that Jesus rose physically from the dead. Tertullian, the historian (c.160–230 CE), wrote that what is raised is, "this flesh, suffused with blood, built up with bones, interwoven with nerves... it must be believed, because it is absurd". I believe that a Supreme Power who can create the milky way, the sun, the planets and the tiniest bird, can do anything – most of all raise up a Messenger from the blood-stained hill of Calvary. Easter is a time of joy, new life, but most of all it's a time of thanksgiving.'

(Tim Richards, author's interview)

REFLECTION 2

'Lent, when people share in the fast, is a time for reflection and learning about oneself and Christ. Every day with thousands of others we descend upon the small churches in Athens and offer our prayers to God. Then on the Holy Friday, the day when Christ gave us his ultimate sacrifice, the bells toll throughout our land and the body of our Saviour lies shrouded in flowers in all the village churches. In the churches the great Liturgy takes place. Twelve passages are read from the Bible, while we hold lighted candles. The winding sheet, a cloth symbolizing the broken body of our Saviour, is placed in the middle of the church, like a coffin at a funeral. Although this Friday is the darkest day in the history of the world, our hymns and chants echo our hopes of the coming glorious Resurrection. On the Saturday we symbolize Christ's burial by carrying the winding sheet around the church three times. We begin to feel the transformation – the casting aside of death and darkness, the coming of life. The priests change their vestments from the colours of despair to the whiteness of joy and life. At midnight the bells throughout the world chime. The priests wait outside before the closed church door – a symbol of the tomb. The doors are opened and the priests come in with candles and lights. The church is a sea of light as we embrace each other, "Christ is risen" echoes through the church and we reply "He is risen indeed". Easter is not just a celebration of the past; it is a powerful experience of the present.'

(Mario Constantinou, author's interview)

REFLECTION 3

'On Holy Thursday we celebrate Mass. The priest will wash the feet of some of the congregation – a re-enactment of Christ's humility. Afterwards the altar is stripped of all ornaments. On the Friday, we have a three-hour service of readings and hymns.

The Saturday is a day of vigil. St Augustine calls it "the mother of all vigils", for all Christian worship springs from this night. Through drama and poetry we act out the central events of our faith. Here we hope and trust that a world of justice and unity will be born from our suffering world. A large candle is marked with alpha and omega, the first and last letters of the Greek alphabet, and is carried into the darkened church. Its light dispels the darkness. Then the Easter proclamation is sung: "Rejoice: Christ has conquered." A service of readings follows, when the whole of history is recalled – from the alpha of the Creation to the omega of the Resurrection. This is a time of great joy and hope; the bells ring; we sing "Glory to God in the highest". People are sometimes baptized, born anew to a life of promise and love. Mass is celebrated, tonight and again tomorrow the great mystery of Mass floods my soul with a peace that goes beyond any normal understanding. The sacredness of this shared holy meal is the highest form of human activity. We believe that the risen Lord, the risen Christ is with us in the bread we break and the wine we drink.'

(Caitlin McKenny, author's interview)

FOR YOUR FOLDERS

▶ Read Tim's reflection.

  a Why does he see Easter as being a 'miracle'?

  b What does he believe about the Resurrection?

  c Express in your own words what the Easter experience means to Tim.

▶ Read Mario's reflection.

  a Explain the 'Liturgy' and 'winding sheet'.

  b What symbolic actions are taking place?

  c Express in your own words what the Easter experience means to Mario.

▶ Read Caitlin's reflection.

  a Explain 'vigil' and 'alpha and omega'.

  b What symbolic actions are taking place?

  c Express in your own words what the Easter experience means to Caitlin.

An Easter procession in Brazil

Procession in South India, celebrating the Ascension

ASCENSION DAY

Jesus is taken up to heaven

'So, when they were all together, they asked him, "Lord, is this the time when you are to establish once again the sovereignty of Israel?" He answered, "It is not for you to know about dates or times, which the Father has set within his own control. But you will receive power when the Holy Spirit comes upon you; and you will bear witness for me in Jerusalem, and all over Judaea and Samaria, and away to the ends of the earth."

When he had said this, as they watched, he was lifted up, and a cloud removed him from their sight. As he was going, and as they were gazing intently into the sky, all at once there stood beside them two men in white who said, "Men of Galilee, why stand there looking up into the sky? This Jesus, who has been taken away from you up to heaven, will come in the same way as you have seen him go." '

(Acts 1:6–11)

On the Thursday which falls forty days after Easter Sunday, Christians remember Jesus' ascension –

when he was taken up into heaven. This was the day when his disciples saw him for the last time. In church services Christians remember the ascension with special prayers and readings from the scriptures.

WHITSUN

According to the Acts of the Apostles, seven weeks after Jesus' Resurrection another miraculous event took place on the day of the Jewish festival of Pentecost, or Shavuot. This was when the power of the Holy Spirit was given to the disciples (see Acts 2:1–4 and unit 20). In the Hebrew Bible there are many references to the way that the Spirit of God inspired the prophets. There is also the promise in Joel 2:28, that this spirit would one day be *'poured out on all flesh'*. Christians believe that the Holy Spirit was given to the disciples and to the whole of humanity on this day.

Pentecost (or **Whitsun**) is seen by Christians as being the birthday of the Christian Church. Traditionally, it is a time of admitting new members to the Church through the rite of **baptism**. People dress in white, symbolizing pureness and newness, and because of this the day became known as White Sunday, or Whit Sunday or Whitsun.

TRINITY SUNDAY

Trinity Sunday is a time when Christians think about and reflect upon the mystery of the **Trinity**. They are reminded that they do not believe in three Gods but rather only in one (see unit 8). Although they believe in only one God, they remember to think of him in three ways: God the Father, God the Son and God the Holy Spirit.

On Trinity Sunday some Christian denominations ordain people who have completed their training to the ministry. The Church year from Trinity Sunday until Advent is counted in terms of Sundays after Trinity.

All the festivals of Christianity make the claim that there are not three Gods but only one, and so it is appropriate that the last festival of the Church calendar should be devoted to remembering this idea in particular.

THE TRINITY

The doctrine of the Trinity (or Trinity of God) has been the central mystery of the Christian faith, since the early centuries of the Church. It holds the deepest beliefs of Christianity and is also acknowledged as the most difficult belief to explain. Although you may have studied the Trinity in unit 8, it will be useful to look at some of the main ideas again.

The idea of the Trinity was described in the early Church, as Christians tried to explain the meaning of Christ's life, teaching and mission. It is not mentioned explicitly in the Gospels, but only hinted at (Matthew 28:19, 2 Corinthians 13:14). At the first two general councils of the Church (at Nicaea in 325 CE and Constantinople in 381 CE), it was agreed that both Jesus Christ, as Son of God, and the Holy Spirit are the same Being as God the Father, i.e. fully God, yet without dividing God. The idea of the Trinity is seen as an attempt to describe the fullness of God as revealed in and through Christ's life on earth. This revelation can be understood as follows:

'God confronts humankind in Jesus Christ (i.e. God is truly present in the Son) but,
He is also known as the Father, who "sends" his Son and,
He is known as the Holy Spirit, opening the hearts and minds of men and women.
Yet it is the same God who is present throughout. The words Father, Son and Holy Spirit refer to one and the same God.'

FOR YOUR FOLDERS

Look at units 45–51 and answer the following.

▶ Briefly explain the meaning and significance of Ascension Day, Whitsun and Trinity Sunday.

▶ Try to explain the doctrine of the Trinity in your own words. Think of some examples in everyday life where three equals one and one equals three.

▶ Explain why you think it is important for religions to have a calendar.

▶ Write an article of about 150 words called 'The important landmarks in the year of the Christian Church'.

▶ Try to represent the Christian year in a large drawing or diagram.

▶ Explain in detail how the events of Jesus' life are reflected in the festivals of Christianity.

▶ Festivals are times of celebration. Show in detail how the idea of celebration is present in any one Christian festival that you have studied.

Christians believe that through prayer they can come closer to God

Most Christians practise private prayer, believing that they find their closest experience of God in prayer. They believe that God is a *personal* God and through prayer they can communicate with God.

TYPES OF PRAYER

Here are some of the types of prayer used by Christians:

● **Adoration** – the person praying thinks about God's greatness, power, wisdom and love.

● **Confession** – when confronting the power of God's love the person praying becomes aware of their own weaknesses and may ask God for forgiveness.

● Intercession – 'intercede' means 'speak in favour of somebody'. As well as asking for God's forgiveness, the person praying may become aware of the needs of others. They may pray for the sick, the poor, the lonely, for people who are close to them or for the whole world.

● Petition – this is when the person praying makes a request to God for help.

● Thanksgiving – this form of prayer expresses thanks to God and praises God for his love.

MEDIATORS

Most Christian prayers are addressed to God, and they end with the words 'through Jesus Christ our Lord'. This is because many Christians believe that

God is too great to approach directly and it is only through Jesus that they can approach him. This is why Jesus is sometimes referred to as an 'advocate' or 'intercessor', a mediator between God and humanity. Protestant Christians believe that Jesus Christ is the only one who can mediate between them and God. Some Christians, like Roman Catholics, believe that others, like Mary the Mother of God or the saints, can act as mediators.

Christians do not all pray in the same way. Some pray at regular times, others don't; some use their own words whilst others use set forms of prayer; some attach more importance to praying alone, others to praying communally (with others). Some Christians use another form of prayer called **contemplation** (see unit 36).

THINKING POINT

● *'The great psychologist, Jung, has written that there are two ways to lose your soul. One of these is to worship a God outside you. If he is correct, then a lot of church-goers in the West have been losing their souls for generations to the extent that they have attended religious events where prayer is addressed to a god outside.'*

(Matthew Fox)

THINGS TO DO

▶ Look at these three prayers. What types of prayer do you think they are?

*'Lord make me an instrument of thy peace,
where there is hatred, let me sow love;
where there is injury, pardon;
where there is discord, union;
where there is doubt, faith;
where there is despair, hope;
where there is darkness, light;
where there is sadness, joy;
for your mercy and for your truth's sake.
Amen.'*

(Prayer of St Francis)

*'And in the name of every creature under
heaven we too praise your glory as we say,
Holy, holy, holy Lord, God of power and
might,
heaven and earth are full of your glory.
Hosanna in the highest.'*

(Roman Catholic Sunday Missal)

*'Christ has no body now on earth but
yours;
yours are the only hands with which he can
do his work,
yours are the only feet with which he can
go about the world,
yours are the only eyes through which his
compassion
can shine forth upon a troubled world.
Christ has no body now on earth but
yours.'*

(Teresa of Avila)

TALKING POINTS

● *'Why, O Lord, is it so hard for me to keep my heart directed toward you? Why do the many little things I want to do, and the many people I know, keep crowding into my mind, even during the hours that I am totally free to be with you and you alone? Why does my mind wander off in so many directions, and why does my heart desire the things that lead me astray? Are you not enough for me? Do I keep doubting your love and care, your mercy and grace? Do I keep wondering, in the centre of my being, whether you will give me all I need if I just keep my eyes on you?*

Please accept my distractions, my fatigue, my irritations, and my faithless wanderings. You know me more deeply and fully than I know myself. You love me with a greater love than I can love myself. You offer me more than I can desire. Look at me, see me in all my misery and inner confusion, and let me sense your presence in the midst of my turmoil.

(Henri Nouwen – Trappist monk)

● *'Instead of supposing that one great God is thinking about the answer to millions of different problems of all the individuals in the world, is it not more reasonable to suppose that some action is set in motion by prayer which gives us the answer from our subconscious minds? In saying this I'm not saying that God doesn't exist. I'm saying that it might well be that this uplifting power somehow activates the subconscious solution-providing mechanism which would otherwise not be possible.'*

(Sir Alistair Hardy)

● *'When I pray for something, I do not pray;
When I pray for nothing I really pray.'*

(Meister Eckhart)

Many Christians use the Bible, the **rosary**, the crucifix and icons to help them in their prayers.

THE BIBLE

REFLECTION

'In order to hear God in the silence it is useful to fix your mind on some image which will help inspire meditation. There is no better source for such inspiration than the Bible. There are many different "methods" in which the Bible can be used. We learn from the Bible how to offer our prayers and the guide lines we should follow.'

(The Reverend P. B. Martin)

THE ROSARY

Many Roman Catholic Christians use a rosary when they are praying. A rosary is made up of five sets of ten beads. Each set of beads is called a 'decade' (A); each decade is separated by a bead which is more spaced out than the others (B). By counting the beads as they pray, Roman Catholics are able to contemplate some of the central events in the lives of Jesus and Mary. At each bead the person praying repeats the 'Ave Maria':

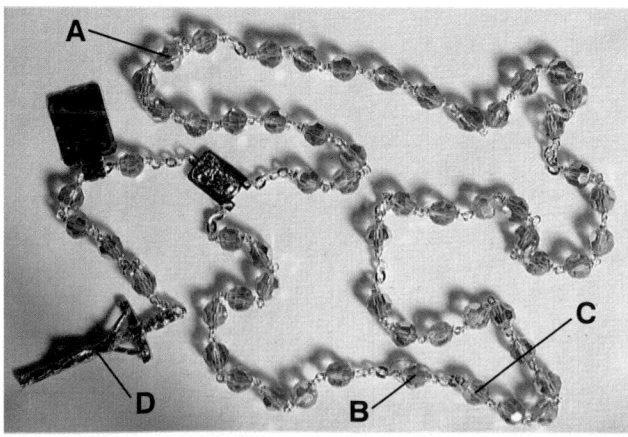

A rosary

*'Hail Mary, full of grace,
The Lord is with you.
Blessed are you among women
and blessed is the fruit of your womb, Jesus.
Holy Mary, Mother of God,
Pray for us sinners now
and at the hour of our death. Amen.'*

At the first bead of the decade (C) the **Pater Noster** ('Our Father...', see opposite) is said. At the last bead of the decade the person will say the 'Gloria Patri':

'Glory be to the Father and to the Son and to the Holy Spirit, as it was in the beginning is now and ever shall be, world without end. Amen.'

THE CRUCIFIX

Hanging from the string of beads is a crucifix (D), a cross with an image of Jesus on it, and five more beads. These beads represent a Pater Noster, three Ave Marias and a Gloria. When the person comes to the crucifix they say the Apostles' Creed (see unit 5). As well as being parts of rosaries, crucifixes can also be worn. A crucifix can also be a statue.

ICONS

Icons are very important for Orthodox Christian prayer. Icons are religious paintings of Jesus, Mary (see opposite), the saints and angels. They are usually richly decorated. They are not simply portraits of people; they are intended to express their inner characters. It is the meaning behind the picture that is important. Orthodox Christians treat icons with great reverence and offer devotion to them. They are not praying to the icons, but rather using the icons as a means of offering prayers to God.

THE LORD'S PRAYER

In the New Testament (Matthew 6:9–13) Jesus tells his disciples *'This is how you should pray'*, and gives them a prayer which is known as the Lord's Prayer. The Lord's Prayer is used by all Christian denominations and is the most important prayer in Christianity. Within this prayer are examples of adoration, petitionary and penitential prayers.

'Our Father in heaven,
thy name be hallowed;
thy kingdom come,
thy will be done,
on earth as in heaven.
Give us today our
daily bread.

Forgive us the wrong we have done,
as we have forgiven
those who have wronged us.
And do not bring us to the test,
but save us from the evil one.'

(Matthew 6:9–13, New English Bible)

THE JESUS PRAYER

The Jesus Prayer, 'O Lord Jesus Christ, Son of God, have mercy on me', is of special significance to Orthodox Christians. Believed to be based on the words of the blind beggar healed by Jesus, this prayer was repeated continuously by mystics in the Orthodox tradition. Indeed, it was believed by some that, because the name of Jesus was itself divine, continuous repetition of it brought direct communion with God, who is present in Jesus' name. The prayer was associated with a particular posture (head bowed, chin on chest, eyes fixed on the place of the heart) and controlled breathing as a means to concentration.

THE PRACTICE OF THE PRESENCE OF GOD

Brother Lawrence (1605–91), was a French soldier who became a hermit and then a Carmelite monk. He lived his life in a state of constant prayer which he called 'the practice of the presence of God'. At the beginning of the day he prayed to continue in the presence of God as he worked. During the day he tried to be present to God as he went about his duties in the kitchen. He would say 'the time of business does not with me differ from the time of prayer'.

An icon of the Black Madonna of Czestochowa

KEY WORDS

Doxology – this is a formula, usually used at the end of a prayer, praising God, e.g.

'For thine is the kingdom, the power and the glory, for ever and ever. Amen.'

Amen – a word which means 'Let it be'.

FOR YOUR FOLDERS

▶ Write an essay of about 100 words on the way that Christians use the Bible, the rosary, the crucifix and icons to help them in their prayers.

▶ What types of prayers are to be found in the Lord's Prayer?

▶ Explain Brother Lawrence's attitude to prayer.

INTRODUCTION

A pilgrimage is a religious journey and the people who go on pilgrimages are called **pilgrims**. They are not like tourists on holiday. Pilgrims travel to places that they believe are holy or sacred because they want to get close to God. Pilgrimage is a very popular form of worship in all religions and every year millions of pilgrims from many different religions make special religious journeys. Anyone can be a pilgrim, whether they be rich or poor; male or female, old or young.

A pilgrim will try to reach a holy site where they can feel close to their God and to their religion. Some of these places can be very busy, in the middle of huge, bustling cities. But some holy sites are high up in the mountains and pilgrims may have to walk for many miles.

PILGRIMAGE – A JOURNEY IN SELF-UNDERSTANDING

As well as being a physical journey to a place, pilgrimage can also refer to our journey through life, from birth to death. It can also refer to an inner journey, whereby as we grow we begin to understand more about ourselves. A very ancient saying says *'Know thyself and thou wilt know the universe'*, which means that getting to know yourself is like a *journey in understanding*.

PILGRIM'S PROGRESS

For Christians a pilgrimage can mean all these things. One of the most famous books written by a Christian is *Pilgrim's Progress* by John Bunyan (1628–88). It became a best-seller. Bunyan wrote it while he was in prison because he had preached the Gospel without proper authorization. It is a story about the Christian life, describing the journey of a man named Christian and his friend, Hopeful, from the City of Destruction to the Celestial City. On the journey he meets many obstacles and difficulties.

PLACES OF PILGRIMAGE

In the Middle Ages pilgrimage was a very important part of many Christians' lives. Some places in Europe became great centres of pilgrimage, and still are today. There are many Christian holy sites all over the world. Here we can only touch on some of them briefly. It is important to remember that, for devout pilgrims, they all represent *places where divine*

Pilgrims flock to pay homage

power has been expressed and by visiting them the believer can be rooted in God's grace.

At *Santiago de Campostela*, in Spain, pilgrims flock to pay homage to St James, a disciple who is believed to have preached the gospel in Spain. It has been claimed that after he was killed by Herod Agrippa, his body was brought from Jerusalem to Spain. His shrine in Santiago (which means St James) de Compostela, is visited by millions of pilgrims from all over the world. Some Christians walk across the rugged mountains of northern Spain to the tomb of St James – this is called the way of St James. They may wear or carry a cockle shell, because the site is near the sea and St James is often depicted as wearing one in works of art. In the Middle Ages pilgrims used the shell as a spoon or food scoop.

Rome in Italy is an important place of pilgrimage because of its many associations with the early Church. Deep underground are the Catacombs where early Christians, the victims of cruel persecution, secretly met and worshipped. The Vatican, the seat of power of the Roman Catholic Church and where the Pope resides, is also in Rome.

Lourdes in the Pyrenees in Southern France attracts multitudes of pilgrims every year. It was here, in a small grotto in 1858 that a 14-year-old girl called Bernadette Soubirous is believed to have seen eighteen visions of the Virgin Mary. A spring appeared, healings were reported, and an official pilgrimage was declared in 1862. Christians from all over the world came to pray and worship and many hoped to be healed of diseases and sicknesses. In the centenary of 1958, Lourdes attracted six million pilgrims. Bernadette Soubirous was canonized in 1933 (see unit 10).

Like Lourdes, other shrines have come into existence, usually because of a vision after which miracles were reported. *Grenoble* in France (1846); *Ilare* in Croatia (1865); *Knock* in Ireland (1879) and *Fatima* in Portugal (1917) are just some examples.

In Britain during the Middle Ages *Canterbury* became a major centre of pilgrimage. As with other pilgrimages, pilgrims believed that to go on a pilgrimage created much merit for the faithful and wiped away their sins. As well as being the centre of power of the Anglican Church, Canterbury also contains the shrine of St Thomas Becket (1118–70) who was murdered in the cathedral by four knights of Henry II, after Becket had disagreed with the King.

Walsingham in Norfolk is another important place of pilgrimage. In the Middle Ages pilgrims flocked to this small town believing that the Holy House of Nazareth, where Jesus and his earthly parents had lived, had been miraculously transported to Norfolk. The shrine had been destroyed during the Reformation but was revived as a place of pilgrimage in 1897. Over this century both Roman Catholics and Protestant Christians have come on pilgrimage to the priory, dedicated to Our Lady of Walsingham.

Further afield, pilgrims from all over the world travel to the Holy Land. They visit the places where Jesus lived out his earthly existence. These include *Jerusalem*, where they will see the Via Dolorosa (the Stations of the Cross) where Jesus carried his cross to the Church of the Holy Sepulchre, the place of his execution; the Garden of Gethsemane where he spent his last night; *Bethlehem*, the birthplace of Christ now marked by the ancient and beautiful Church of the Nativity; *Nazareth* where Jesus lived as a boy and *Galilee* and *Capernaum* where he carried out his ministry.

Pilgrims in Mexico go to a shrine at *Guadalupe*, where in 1531 a man had a vision of the Virgin Mary. Some pilgrims in Poland will walk 240 kilometres from the capital Warsaw to the shrine of the Black Madonna in *Czestochowa* (see icon on page 109), where it is believed the Madonna miraculously helped the Polish army defeat the Swedish invaders. In Greece many pilgrims visit the Holy Mountain of *Athos*, the chief centre of Orthodox monasticism since the tenth century. Today there are twenty monasteries on the mountain where, according to one present day hermit, 'every stone breathes prayer'. In Russia pilgrims will visit the spectacular church of the Transfiguration in *Kizhi*, which has a total of twenty- two domes.

TALKING POINTS

- *'Since we live in space and time it is not surprising that our religions select special places and times to symbolize and make real the eruption of the divine into the earthly sphere.'*
- *'The earthly voyage is an echo of life, which is in itself a pilgrimage.'*

(Ninian Smart – modern theologian)

FOR YOUR FOLDERS

▶ Have you a special place you like to go to? Why do you go?

▶ Explain in your own words what a pilgrimage is and why they are important to Christians.

▶ What reasons do you think Christians would give for going on a pilgrimage?

▶ Pretend you've had a round-the-world tour of some Christian sacred sites. Write a letter home explaining what you've seen.

▶ Explain in your own words the two talking points by Ninian Smart.

The second sacrament accepted by all Christians, except the Salvation Army and the Society of Friends, is baptism. It is the rite of initiation by which people enter the Church. Because of this, in many churches (but not the Baptist Church) the font, which contains the water for baptism, is found near the door of the church.

Baptism is an extremely important part of Christian worship, and it has much meaning and significance. Baptism is seen by Christians as an act of:

- renunciation ('giving up'). The parents of the baptized child, or the baptized adult, are asked if they repent of their sins and renounce evil
- renewal – baptism marks the beginning of a new life with God
- spiritual cleaning – the water used in baptism is a symbol for spiritual and inner cleanliness.

REFLECTION

'Water is one of life's most important commodities. Small wonder that most religions therefore regard water as a powerful symbol. The early church adopted the practice of baptizing converts in obedience to the instructions Jesus had given to his disciples (Matthew 28:19–20). It was through studying the importance of baptism to the early church that Baptists laid so much stress on the practice which has given them their name.

From time to time Baptists still make use of rivers or seas for baptism. But most Baptist churches nowadays have a baptistry built into the floor of the church. It's a great day when the pool comes into use. The candidate approaches the Minister some weeks before and requests baptism. The Minister questions the candidate to make sure he/she has made a personal commitment to Jesus Christ and understands a little of what it means to follow him. Then comes the long-awaited day when the candidate is to confess his or her faith in Jesus Christ. If the candidate is a girl, she will be dressed in a special white baptismal gown. If a boy, he will come dressed in shirt and flannels.

There will be the usual hymns, prayers, readings and sermon. Then, during the hymn before the ceremony, the Minister will leave the church and don his special waders, before returning to the service, and descending the steps leading down to the baptistry. In many churches, the candidate is expected to stand by the pool and to give some sort of statement about how he or she came to faith in Christ. Then once the candidate has entered the water, the Minister pronounces his or her name and plunges the candidate beneath the waters, baptizing him or her "in the name of the Father, the Son and the Holy Spirit". The congregation sings a hymn of faith, while the candidate leaves the baptistry and makes for the dressing room. Quite often the baptismal service is followed by a short celebration of Holy Communion.

What does baptism mean? It is hard to put into words. Baptism, like art or drama, needs to be experienced rather than explained. But clearly the New Testament teaches that baptism is a kind of death and resurrection. It marks the end of an old way of life and the commencement of a totally new quality of life, lived out in the company of all other Christians. Looking at the New Testament baptism is a kind of "statement" – the ceremony speaks very clearly of the way Jesus died and rose again, and how a person needs to be made clean; it is also an act of "commitment" – just as the candidate has taken off his normal clothing and put on his special baptismal attire, so in life he has put the past behind him, and put on a totally new kind of life altogether. Baptism is also a "gift", it is the place where one may receive forgiveness of sins and a means of receiving God's Holy Spirit into life. It is also the gateway into membership of Christ's Church.'

(John Wood)

KEY IDEA

For most Christians, baptism is an outward, visible sign of rebirth. It marks the start of a new life and the water is a symbol of the removal of sin from human life by the death and resurrection of Jesus.

A believer's baptism

INFANT BAPTISM

Most Christian denominations practise infant baptism. However, some Christians, in particular Baptists, argue that infant baptism is meaningless because the infant is too young to realize and appreciate what is going on. Also, some parents have their children baptized but have no intention of bringing them up in the Christian Church.

CONFIRMATION

In the early days, when infant baptism became widespread, it became necessary to have a later service which could 'confirm' the undertakings made during baptism. This became known as **confirmation**. The promises made on behalf of the infant are made again, publicly. The person being confirmed is old enough to understand the promises

they are making. Confirmation services are usually conducted by a bishop. Methodists and United Reformed Christians do not have a service of confirmation. People become full Church members when they publicly confess their faith.

Candidates for confirmation will be asked to answer certain questions as a group. These will include the questions their parents had to answer for them when they were babies:

'Do you turn to Christ?'
'Do you repent of your sins?'
'Do you renounce evil?'

The Bishop will ask set questions such as, 'Do you believe and trust in God the Father, who made the world?' The candidates will then kneel at the altar rail and the Bishop will place his hands upon the head of each of them, in turn, and pray. In the Roman Catholic Church, and in some Anglican Churches, the Bishop will put some oil on their foreheads – the anointing of the holy oil symbolizes the gifts of the Holy Spirit. In the Orthodox Church, the prayer for the blessing of the Holy Spirit will be said straight after baptism, at a ceremony called **Chrismation**. The oil, or **chrism**, will have been blessed by a bishop who will pray that people marked with it may 'bear Christ in their heart, in order to become a dwelling of the Trinity'.

FOR YOUR FOLDERS

▶ Explain what Christians think about baptism.

▶ Look up Matthew 28:19–20 and copy the passage.

▶ Describe in your own words a Baptist baptismal service.

▶ Explain the New Testament teachings on baptism.

▶ Briefly explain what happens during confirmation services and the meaning of confirmation.

MARRIAGE

'I take thee to be my wedded husband (or wife)
to have and to hold
from this day forward
for better for worse
for richer for poorer
in sickness and in health
to love and to cherish
till death us do part
according to God's holy law
and thereto I give thee my troth (promise).

(The Book of Common Prayer)

Christians have always valued marriage. The joining of a wife and husband in 'holy matrimony' is thought to reflect the union of Christ with his followers. Christians believe that in their love for each other, married couples will experience and learn of God's love for creation. In the Gospels Jesus taught that God's purpose was that marriage should be a lifelong union:

'In the beginning of the Creation, God made them male and female. For this reason a man shall leave his father and mother, and be made one with his wife; and the two shall become one flesh.'

(Mark 10:6–8)

Christians believe that marriage is the right relationship for sexual intercourse, for having children and for mutual support.

In order to understand the importance Christians place on marriage we will briefly look at some of the Churches' teachings.

The Baptist Union of Great Britain

In the marriage ceremony the couple make promises to remain married, in the words of the service 'until death us do part'. A vow (promise) such as this, taken before God, is to be considered seriously. A marriage is for life and the couple must be committed only to each other. Baptists believe that though the words of the marriage ceremony are spoken by the couple, the marriage is made by God. They believe that in the marriage service God makes the two people one.

The Church of England

The Church of England marriage ceremony is conducted by members of the clergy. The occasion is regarded as being an opportunity to celebrate God's gift of marriage. The Church teaches that marriage should always be undertaken as a life-long commitment.

The Methodist Church

According to the Methodist marriage service, marriage is 'the life-long union of one man and one woman'. The union of man and woman, for companionship and mutual support, in equal partnership, and the procreation and bringing up of children is believed by the Church to be God's will for most men and women.

The Roman Catholic Church

Roman Catholics see marriage as a vocation and a sacrament. Here are some extracts from a Roman Catholic marriage service, which show some of their beliefs:

'Father, you have made the union of man and wife so holy a mystery that it symbolizes the marriage of Christ and his Church.

Look with love upon this woman, your daughter, now joined to her husband by marriage. She asks your blessing. Give her the grace of peace and love. May she always follow the example of the holy women whose praises are sung in the scriptures. May her husband put his trust in her and recognize that she is his equal and the heir with him to the life of grace. May he always honour her and love her as Christ loves his bride the Church. Father, keep them always true to your Commandments. Keep them faithful in marriage and let them be living examples of Christian life. Give them the strength which comes from the Gospel so that they may be witnesses of Christ to others. (Bless them with children and help them to be good parents. May they live to see their children's children.) And after a happy old age grant them fullness of life with the saints in the kingdom of heaven. We ask this through Jesus Christ our Lord. Amen.'

DIVORCE

Sometimes, for a variety of reasons, marriages do not work, and couples decide to separate. Since the 1969 Divorce Act it has become less difficult to obtain a divorce in Britain. However, divorces can leave many emotional scars, especially if children are involved. Generally, Christians believe that everything possible should be done to keep couples together, but if this is not possible then couples should be allowed to divorce.

> *'Christian teaching is that marriage is the life-long union of the partners, and is therefore in principle indissoluble. However, with other Christians such as the Eastern Orthodox Churches, the Methodist Church recognizes that for a variety of reasons marriages do die. They can become destructive rather than creative experiences for all concerned. After making every effort to save the relationship, and taking care of the interests and future of children of the marriage, separation or divorce may be unavoidable.'*

(Methodist Conference statement)

The Roman Catholic Church recognizes that in some situations Catholics have to go through a civil form of divorce; however this is *only* a civil procedure and the Church would not be able to bless a second marriage if the partner of the first marriage still survived. The only way that Roman Catholics can have a second marriage blessed is if their first marriage can be declared null and void. They would have to show that there was lacking some essential quality in their first relationship which would mean that the couple did not actually fulfil all that was required for it to be a valid marriage. The Church teaches that if the marriage involves one partner who is not baptized then the marriage can be dissolved under serious circumstances (e.g. if one partner converts to Catholicism but the other 'refuses to live peacefully with the new convert'). Also, a marriage between two partners who are baptized can be dissolved if there is a just reason e.g. impotence.

The Roman Catholic Church can also annul a marriage. An **annulment** is a declaration that the marriage bond did not exist, whereas a **dissolution** is the breaking of a bond that did exist. A marriage can be annulled if there is:

- a lack of *consent* (e.g. somebody has been forced into a marriage)
- a lack of *judgement* (e.g. if somebody marries without being fully aware of what marriage is really about)
- an *inability* to carry out the duties of marriage (e.g. somebody might be mentally very ill)
- a lack of *intention* (e.g. if one of the partners intends at the time of the marriage not to have children).

FOR YOUR FOLDERS

▶ Look up the following words in a dictionary and explain in your own words what they mean: vow; cherish; troth; matrimony; union; companionship; procreation; impotence; vocation; sacrament; repentance; indissoluble; annulled; dissolution.

▶ Explain briefly in your own words what you think the words about marriage in the *Book of Common Prayer* mean.

▶ In your own words, write a paragraph about what Christians generally believe about marriage.

▶ Why do Methodists believe that marriage is 'God's will'?

▶ Explain what happens in a Roman Catholic marriage service.

▶ How is the relationship between Christ and his Church compared to marriage in the Roman Catholic service? (See the marriage service.)

▶ Give some reasons why you think people divorce.

▶ After making promises before God, do you think Christians should be allowed to divorce?

▶ How do you think Christians might work to save a marriage?

▶ Why might a Roman Catholic marriage be dissolved? Explain what an annulment is. How might an annulled marriage have come about in the first place?

INTRODUCTION

This unit looks in more detail at the Roman Catholic and Anglican views on marriage, the family, divorce and contraception.

For about 1500 years the Church in the West struggled to keep a single, living tradition of communion in worship, faith and practice. In the sixteenth century (see unit 21) this network of shared experience was broken. Movements for reform could no longer be contained in one Church. The Roman Catholic Church and the Churches of the **Reformation** went their separate ways. Over the years, differences occurred in how, in isolation from each other, the Churches have developed their structures of authority and their judgements on moral issues. During recent years the Roman Catholic and Anglican Churches have talked together and tried to understand each other. They have found that they still have a *shared vision* about the Christian life and have many beliefs in common. Here are two areas where there is total agreement:

Human sexuality

- Human sexuality, as spoken about in scripture, is part of God's creation (Genesis 1:21; Genesis 24; The Song of Songs; Ephesians 5:21–32).
- Sexual energy can be both creative and destructive. It therefore needs to be part of an ordered life that will nurture a person's spiritual relationship with others and with God.
- Sexual self-centredness is a sin, leading to individual and social destruction.
- Sexual energy must be directed towards either marriage or celibacy. Only this directing of sexual energy can bring about human happiness and fulfilment.
- Sexual relationships have a social dimension as well as a personal one, i.e. they affect other issues such as poverty, justice, the exploitation of women, the protection of children, etc.

Marriage and the family

- Marriage and family life are institutions given by God for human well-being and happiness.
- Within the institutions of marriage and family life, the physical expression of sexuality finds its true expression and fulfilment.
- In the *procreation* (the act of having children) and rearing of children, the couple share in the life-giving generosity of God (Genesis 1:27–9).

- Marriage is not a human institution, it is God-given.
- Marriage requires commitment, *reciprocal love*, trust and mutual respect.
- Marriage is a **vocation**.
- The mutual pact (covenant) made between husband and wife bears the mark of God's abundant love (Hosea 2:19–21). Marriage is the order of creation, it is both a sign and a reality of God's faithful love, and therefore it has a **sacramental** dimension (see unit 41). Since it also points to the saving love of Christ, it is open to a still deeper and more mysterious sacramentality within the life and communion of Christ's own body.

However, the vision of marriage and family life as a fruitful life-long covenant full of the grace of God, does not always happen in the harsh realities of life. Its very goodness, when corrupted by human frailty and self-centredness, causes pain, despair and tragedy. This pain does not just involve the separated couple, it also deeply touches the children, the wider family, the community and the whole social order. The whole question of separation (divorce) and re-marriage is an area where Roman Catholic and Anglican viewpoints differ.

DIVORCE

Before the break in the sixteenth century, the Church in the West had developed a doctrine of *indissolubility*: the marriage bond *ought not* to be dissolved; indeed it *could not* be dissolved. At the Reformation some Protestants in Europe interpreted the teachings of Jesus in Matthew 5:32 and Matthew 19:9 differently, arguing that *divorce was permissible on grounds of adultery or desertion*. However, at the Council of Trent (1545 CE) the Roman Catholic Church (see unit 23) reaffirmed the teaching that *the marriage bond could not be dissolved, even by adultery*. Also the Church taught that neither partner, not even the innocent one, could re-marry during the lifetime of the other.

The Anglican Church

In 1857, when matrimonial matters in England were transferred from Church authority to *civil* (non-Church) authority, divorce on the grounds of adultery was legalized. However, the Anglican Church refused to give official approval to re-marriage. This has been the subject of worldwide debate in the Anglican Church. Some Anglicans have held the traditional view of indissolubility. Others have argued that once the marriage relationship has been destroyed beyond repair, the marriage itself is dead, the vows have been frustrated and the bond has been broken. Different provinces (areas) within the Anglican Communion have devised different practices. Among some of them, permission is granted for a marriage, after divorce, to be carried out in church. In other cases, after a civil ceremony, a service of prayer may be offered instead.

The Roman Catholic Church

The doctrine of indissolubility was confirmed at the Council of Trent. The Church makes a distinction between marriages that are sacraments (in which both partners are baptized members) and *marriages that are not sacraments* (*natural* marriages in which one or both partners are *not* baptized). In Roman Catholic teaching, both forms of marriage are in principle indissoluble. A sacramental marriage which has been fully *consummated* (the couple have shared full sexual intercourse) cannot be dissolved by any human power. But if the marriage has not been consummated it *can* be dissolved. It has also come to be accepted that a non-sacramental marriage, whether consummated or not, can in certain cases be dissolved. The Roman Catholic Church also allows for the annulment of marriage (see unit 56).

CONTRACEPTION

Contraception can be defined as 'various methods by which a couple can avoid unwanted pregnancy'. Although both the Roman Catholic and Anglican Churches may agree on many points about sexual intercourse within marriage, they disagree on methods of birth control. However, both traditions would agree that:

● Procreation is God's greatest gift to the married couple.
● God calls married couples to responsible parenthood, which means accepting parenthood and being totally committed to the nurture, education, support and guidance of children.
● Part of God's will is that children are born within marriage.
● There are some situations in which it would be acceptable to avoid bringing children into the world (these might be social, environmental, physical or psychological reasons).

However, the Churches do not agree on the *methods* of contraception.

The Roman Catholic Church stresses that when deciding on the number of children to have, and when to have them, couples are encouraged to use the natural rhythms of the body and practise *natural family planning*. This refers to the woman becoming aware of her own fertile and infertile cycles by recording the natural signals of her body. Artificial methods of birth control (condoms, the coil, diaphragm, pill, etc.) are considered not to be fully in keeping with the full human expression of sexual love. In the Catechism of the Roman Catholic Church (1994) it states that any methods, other than natural family planning, are 'intrinsically evil'. It teaches that the two *goods of marriage* (i.e. loving union and procreation), must be part of all sexual intercourse. They may not be separated by artificial means during marital intercourse.

The Anglican Church view is that although the two basic goods of marriage should characterize a marriage as a whole, they don't necessarily have to characterize *every* act of intercourse. A couple can, in loving union, have full sexual intercourse but not every act always has to be 'open to procreation'. As long as, at some stage in their marriage, they wish to procreate, this is fine. So, during some acts of intercourse, they can decide to use contraception. Most other Protestant Churches agree with this view.

FOR YOUR FOLDERS

▶ Explain in your own words the meaning of the following: contraception; the Reformation; celibacy; repression; procreation; reciprocal love; vocation; covenant; sacramental; indissolubility; adultery; civil authority; natural marriage; consummated; natural family planning; two 'goods' of marriage.

▶ Explain why the Reformation has led to different views on some aspects of sexual issues.

▶ Write an essay called 'Human sexuality, marriage and the family'. In it, explain the similarities and differences that exist between the Roman Catholic and Anglican Churches.

CHRISTIAN IDEALS

For all Christians the family is the ideal basic social unit. They believe that the family plays an important role in making sure that society is stable. They agree that:

- Family relations are mentioned in the Bible. The family unit is part of God's plan for humankind.
- Families just don't happen, they need to be worked at with commitment, effort and responsibility.
- Marriage is more than a piece of paper. It is a *sacred agreement*. Loving relationships aren't a human right without any responsibilities. To love requires *effort*, *discipline* and *sacrifice*. Relationships within the family between parents, between parents and children, between children and parents, between siblings (brothers and sisters) and within the extended family also require effort, discipline and sacrifice.
- The family plays an important part in controlling the sexual drive.
- The family is a responsible basis for having and rearing children.
- Through the family people can learn about the customs, religion and traditions of a society.
- The family provides a secure and loving environment where the aged, the young, the sick and the disabled can find support.

Christianity teaches that a person may only have one partner in marriage (monogamy). The basic Christian ideal of the family consists of husband, wife and children, with close support from and to other members of the extended family, especially elderly relatives.

However, Christians would argue that a family is not an end in itself. While parents are to be *honoured* (see Exodus 20:12) they are not always to be obeyed. Parents are not perfect and sometimes can make mistakes. The ideal, at all times, within the family relationship, is that members should be able to talk to each other about anything. *Communication* is essential. *Love*, *mutual trust*, *co-operation*, *respect* and *tolerance* are the ideals within Christian family relationships.

Although the ideal is that children, when they reach adulthood, will be married, most Christians feel that there is nothing wrong with situations in which people decide to remain single. Some Christians (see unit 68) believe that if people are homosexual they have the right to have gay partnerships. However, other Christians oppose this.

Many Christians who attend their churches would want to see their children brought up knowing about Christianity and some will send their children to *church schools*. They will have their children baptized, and later confirmed (see unit 55). However, some Christians do not want to force their own faith on their children. They hope that as their children get older they will, in the light of knowledge, be able to make up their own minds. *Parenting* is seen as an important part of family life. Christians believe that bringing up children in a loving environment will help them to develop their own loving relationships in later life.

Christian parents want their children to grow up with virtues such as: respect for all life, the ability to communicate with others, generosity, loyalty, the ability to form loving relationships, tolerance of others, the ability to think clearly for themselves, self-discipline, respect for others (especially members of the opposite sex and the disadvantaged), the ability to listen to others, always being true to themselves, and to take care of planet earth.

SINGLE PARENTHOOD

Many children are brought up by single parents. Although in a ideal world, it would be better if children had two loving parents at home, many Christians feel that, given enough support, single parenting by either the father or the mother need not be damaging. Many Churches feel that more needs to be done to support single parents in society. There should be better financial support and provision of cheaper housing. They also stress that single parents need moral and emotional support. They would like to see absent parents, the extended family and the local community more involved in giving this moral and emotional support. Many Christians also wish to see better sex education provided in schools, so that teenagers are taught to think about contraception, parenthood, pornography and sexual responsibility. They believe that good sex education is far more than just biology; it is about helping teenagers to understand that *responsibility* within all relationships is the key to happiness.

THE ELDERLY

In some societies around the world, the elderly are revered (honoured, respected). However, in the West, over the last one hundred years or so, changing attitudes have resulted in many elderly people being treated badly. They are treated with scorn and there are many prejudices about old age. The elderly seldom live with their families – they either live alone (if their partner has died), or in nursing homes and geriatric hospitals. Many Christians believe this to be wrong. Elderly people have a vast store of experience behind them, and old age often brings with it greater wisdom and understanding. Christians believe that the elderly deserve much greater respect than our present society gives them. Many Christians work voluntarily for organizations that help the elderly.

HOMELESS FAMILIES

An estimated 500,000 homeless families live in temporary accommodation. Much of this temporary accommodation is overcrowded, unhealthy, dangerous and run by greedy landlords. It is often situated in environments where drug abuse, alcoholism, violence, sexual harassment and bad language are common. Christian organizations such as the Children's Society (see unit 26) and the Catholic Housing Aid Society (CHAS) work to help these families. They try to challenge the injustice experienced by homeless families. Through working directly with homeless families the Children's Society and CHAS seek to counteract some of the damaging effects of homelessness, providing support, guidance and legal help to homeless families. Generally, these organizations believe that:

● Adequate housing is the fundamental right of all families.

● More houses at affordable rent should be available for families on low incomes.

● The government should work to end the evils of homelessness.

THE VICIOUS CYCLE

Over recent decades there have been massive changes in society and therefore in the family. Many Christians are concerned about the breakdown of the traditional family unit. Increasing divorce and separation, growing poverty, unemployment, breakdown in communications and the changing roles of men and women have all put growing pressure on the traditional family. Some Christians believe that if the family unit begins to break down, it will have disastrous effects on society as a whole. They argue that the vicious cycle of family breakdown → social breakdown → family breakdown will lead to social disintegration, unrest, disharmony and chaos.

Many Christians believe that all human relationships, whether they be friendships or marriages, need to be worked at. Relationships are not meant to be easy, they are one way we learn about ourselves. Those close to us know us – our faults and virtues – and because of this can help us to grow as decent human beings. *We should see our relationships as the most important aspects of our lives.* They deserve our effort and commitment. Many Christians would say that not enough time is given at school to help children understand and discuss personal and moral issues such as relationships, sexual ethics, friendship, marriage and parenthood. They would like to see more emphasis on these matters, which they believe to be just as important as learning about facts in different subjects.

FOR YOUR FOLDERS

▶ Why do Christians believe that the family is so important?

▶ What ideals would Christians like to see in family relationships? Explain what their ideals mean.

▶ How do Christians think children should ideally be brought up?

▶ What problems face many families today?

▶ What are the problems facing many single parents? Outline some of the things many Christians would like to see that would help single parents.

▶ What problems face the homeless? What are some Christians doing to try to ease these problems? Should the government do more?

▶ What difficulties face people as they grow older?

▶ Why do many Christians believe that the elderly deserve much greater respect in our society?

▶ What is the 'vicious cycle'?

▶ 'Relationships just don't happen and everyone lives happily ever after. They require *effort, discipline* and *commitment.'* What do you think this means?

INTRODUCTION

One of the most powerful drives for human beings is the sexual urge. It is a strong personal drive directed towards others. However, because it is so powerful, it has been heavily influenced by taboos, rules and teachings about right and wrong. In our society, sex has become something apart, an 'it', a *subject* of embarrassment, perversion, fascination and guilt. It is sniggered about in playgrounds, sold in newsagents, used by advertisers to sell anything from jeans to motor cars, and written about in cheap novels, films and pop songs.

PAST ATTITUDES

In the past, attitudes to sexuality in our society have been heavily influenced by the teachings of the Churches. Until very recently Christianity saw sex as a kind of 'naughty indulgence' to be practised only within marriage. The leaders of the Christian Church, from St Paul onwards, felt that the sexual urge was a threat to an individual's religious life. The body was a trap, sexual pleasure a sin, and women were second-class citizens. Many leaders of the early Church struggled to solve the conflict between their own bodies crying out for sexual fulfilment, and their duty, as they saw it, to reject the 'sins of the flesh'. They felt that the holy and the pure could not in any way be touched by the flesh. The physical and the spiritual were separate, distinct, different and in continual battle with each other.

SIN AND GUILT

It is amazing to find that these attitudes towards sexuality affected nearly 2000 years of thinking, and in a way still affect us today. Connected to these attitudes about the repression of sexuality are ideas about sin and guilt. Guilt has played a huge part in Christian thinking for 2000 years. In the past the priests and clergymen of all Churches have made ordinary men and women feel guilty about their sexual urges. Some have even preached and taught that *'the sins of the flesh lead to the gates of hell and eternal punishment'*. People have been made to live in fear, struggling with sex in a confused and ignorant way.

For young people this struggle has often seemed impossible. After reaching puberty and the onset of intense sexual desire, young people have had to release their sexual tension through masturbation. This used to be frowned upon by the Churches and the young were threatened with the 'fires of eternal damnation'. Such teachings about eternal damnation and the gates of hell, as punishment for having natural urges and needs, are a long way from the loving message of the Gospels.

Through attitudes like these, the magnificence and creative power of human sexuality were lost in a maze of fear, guilt and perversion – with the Churches on one hand causing the guilt and on the other hand offering ways to get rid of it.

Some Christian missionaries turned these negative emotions on to the people they went to convert. They took their ignorant ideas about sexuality with them, failing to see that these cultures had their own teachings on sexuality. In many of these cultures, human sexuality was accepted as an important and delightful fact of life, not as an embarrassment to be shuffled around with shame. Regulations already existed, not to repress the sexual urge, but rather to control and celebrate it for the good of all.

SEXUALITY TODAY

Over the last few decades attitudes to sexuality have changed drastically in our society. However, new attitudes have brought new problems. Sex has become commercialized. In some ways human love has been diminished. Pornography of a kind that would have been banned a few years ago is now for sale in newsagents. More and more people have sex before marriage. Thousands of young girls become pregnant every year. The crime of rape has increased drastically. Diseases, such as AIDS, are taking on plague proportions around the world. Hardcore pornography is being transmitted worldwide by satellite television.

Traditionally, the Churches have seen themselves as guardians of moral behaviour – teaching people what they consider to be right and wrong. However, in a society in which Church membership is decreasing the Church has not the authority it previously had. Put simply, the Churches have two choices:

- the **liberal view** – to *adapt* their teachings to fit the needs of a changing world
- the **traditional view** – to keep on repeating their *traditional* teachings, which they believe are eternal and thus relevant to every age.

CELIBACY

Celibacy in the Christian tradition is understood as the *choice to remain unmarried in order to devote oneself completely to God*. When people join a monastery or convent they make a public vow of chastity.

Sometimes Christians in ordinary life may make a private vow. Since the eleventh century the Roman Catholic Church in the West has required that its priests remain celibate. In the East married men may be ordained, but those who are already ordained priests are not allowed to marry. The Church's teaching on celibacy is taken from Christ's teaching in Matthew 19:10–12. Over the last twenty years the idea of celibacy among priests has become a controversial issue in the Roman Catholic Church, with many modern Catholics arguing that priests should be able to decide for themselves whether they wish to remain celibate or not. However, successive Popes have ruled that celibacy among priests must remain.

FOR YOUR FOLDERS

▶ 'In our society sex has become something apart, an "it".' What do you think this means?

▶ During the history of the Christian religion the physical and the spiritual were often seen as being distinct and different. What do you think this might mean? What consequences has this attitude had on our civilization?

▶ What new problems have arisen as a result of a more open approach to sexuality?

▶ Explain the difference between traditional and liberal views of sexuality. Give examples.

▶ What is celibacy? Who is celibate? What reasons can you think of why ordinary people decide to be celibate?

FOR DISCUSSION

'Sexual intercourse is, first of all, a body language, through which couples talk to and do things for one another. When couples make love they rejoice in each other's presence and the pleasure they exchange. For this they want to give thanks. Thus sex is a recurrent act of thanksgiving.

Second, because people want to make love repeatedly, they trust that their partners will respond to them again. So sex is also a recurrent act of hope; the hope of being desired again.

Third, in the course of the day couples hurt one another. Most of these hurts are forgiven and forgotten on the spot. But some are too painful to be forgiven so easily. Such hurts need a deeper level of love and communication to erase them. So sexual intercourse can also be an act of reconciliation.

Fourth, sexual intercourse confirms the sexual identity of the partners.

Finally, every time a couple makes love, they are saying to each other, 'I recognize you, I want you, I appreciate you.' In this way it is a recurrent act of

personal affirmation.

As a result, sexual intercourse has the capacity to give life in more than a biological sense. So sexual intercourse not only gives pleasure. It also has a powerful personal dimension in which the couple enrich one another's lives.

From this point of view marriage can be seen as providing the condition where the physical and personal can unite and transform the life of the couple. Marriage provides a continuous, reliable and predictable relationship within which the rich potential of sex can thrive. In this sense, sex actually requires marriage for the realization of its potential.

This is the case for Christian morality: not that sex is dangerous and needs marriage and procreation to protect it; but rather that sex is so powerful and meaningful that justice can only be done to it in a continuous and enduring relationship.'

(Jack Dominion – modern Roman Catholic theologian and psychiatrist)

Sometimes people don't like to think or talk about death. Most people are afraid of death. One reason is that we have no idea of what's going to happen when we die. Fear of the unknown can be worse than fear of what we know.

KEY QUESTIONS

Is death the end? Is there a hell? Is there a heaven? Do we return to earth in another form? What is the soul?

Is death the end? From the dawn of human history people have answered 'No'. Long before there were any written records, there is evidence that people believed in some kind of life after death. Today all the world religions believe in life after death, although their beliefs can vary.

Very generally speaking, Christianity teaches that God has qualities like mercy, goodness and love. He cares for the people in His creation, who were created with the purpose of having a relationship with God. While this relationship can be entered into within this life, it can be fully realized only after this life. Salvation is thought of in terms of a personal relationship and fulfilment. Christians generally believe that they retain their personal identity and individuality after death. Judgement is an important idea. They believe that everyone will eventually have to account for what they've done in their lives. Traditionally, Christianity has taught that a good life will be rewarded in heaven and a bad life will be punished in hell. Roman Catholics believe that only those Christians who have led a very good life will straightaway enter into heaven. Most will go to 'purgatory' – a type of purification process and preparation for heaven. Many modern Christians reject the idea of hell, and argue 'How could a God of love create a place of eternal suffering and torture?'. They believe that heaven is being with God. Hell is being apart from God. These are not places but rather states of mind.

For Christians, there is hope of eternal life confirmed by the life, death and Resurrection of Jesus Christ. This 'eternal life' refers neither to infinite life, nor to immortality, but describes a quality of being. Life is eternal, because we are in continuing fellowship with God, through life before death and life after death.

'The Angel of Death' by Evelyn de Morgan (1890) based on the poem of the same name, which she wrote as a teenager

The Angel of Death

'Oh Love in Glory
With crowned brow
I feel thine arms
Around me now.
Soft thy kisses
Warm thy breath
Vision of love
Angel of death.'

(Evelyn de Morgan)

CHRISTIAN FUNERALS

Some Christians are buried in coffins; others are cremated. It is traditional for people attending funerals to wear dark clothes. Although there is sadness about death, the service stresses the hope that the dead person will in time be resurrected. Often the following words are read out at a funeral service:

'Lo! I tell you a mystery. We shall not all sleep, but we shall all be changed, in a moment, in the twinkling of an eye, at the last trumpet. For the trumpet will sound, and the dead will be raised imperishable, and we shall be changed. For this perishable nature must put on the imperishable, and this mortal nature must put on immortality. When the perishable puts on the imperishable, and the mortal puts on immortality, then shall come to pass the saying that is written: "Death is swallowed up in victory. O death, where is thy victory? O death, where is thy sting?" '

(1 Corinthians 15:51–55)

REFLECTION 1

'The death of Christ, the second Adam, transforms death, sin's penalty, into a means of deliverance from its guilt and power. Because Christ has tasted death for every man. He has made death the gateway into eternal life. The crucified Son of God has drawn the sting to death – which is sin (which means "missing the mark"). The believer must still undergo "natural" death, but he or she has been delivered from the "second death" or final death. He lives in newness of life, because by the saving grace of God in Christ, he has learned how to die. His faith is itself a daily dying, in which the "old man" of sin is crucified and dies at every moment in order that the "new man" may be raised from the dead by the same power of God that raised Christ.

The believer has already begun his new life in the Spirit... The whole matter is summed up for us in the words of Jesus in the Fourth Gospel: "He that believeth hath" (even here and now) "eternal life".'

(H. Lovell – United Reform Church)

REFLECTION 2

'It's a sleep,
Christ, life and death is a watch.
While the earth sleeps in loneliness
there on watch is the white moon; there
on watch is the Man,
Watching from the cross, while men lie
asleep;
there on watch is the Man, drained of
blood, the Man white
as the moon in the blackness of the night.'

(Unamuno, 1864–1937
– Spanish poet and philospher)

FOR YOUR FOLDERS

▶ Briefly write down your views on the key questions.

▶ Try to explain the meaning of the words in 1 Corinthians 15:51–5.

▶ Read the reflections, then explain what you think they are saying.

▶ According to the reflection by Lovell, try to explain what Christ's death has done for humankind.

▶ What do you think it means to learn 'how' to die? What parts of us must die every moment, if we are to find the 'new man'?

▶ According to Lovell, how is it possible to find eternal life in the here and now?

REFLECTIONS

Thinking about death

'Your time here is short, very short; take another look at the way in which you spend it. Here man is today; tomorrow, he is lost to view; and once a man is out of sight, it's not long before he passes out of mind. How dull they are, these hearts of ours, always occupied with the present, instead of looking ahead to what lies before us! **Every action of yours, every thought, should be those of a man who expects to die before the day is out.** Death would have no great terrors for you if you had a quiet conscience, would it? Then why not keep clear of sin, instead of running away from death? If you aren't fit to face death today, it's very unlikely you will be by tomorrow; besides, tomorrow is an uncertain quantity; you have no guarantee that there will be any tomorrow – for you.

What's the use of having a long life, if there's so little improvement to show for it? Improvement? Unfortunately it happens, only too often, that the longer we live the more we add to our guilt. If only we could point to one day in our life here that was really well spent! Years have passed by since we turned to God; and how little can we show, many of us, in the way of solid results! Fear death if you will, but don't forget that long life may have greater dangers for you.

Well for you, if you keep an eye on your deathbed all the time, and put yourself in the right state of mind for death as each day passes. Perhaps, before now, you've seen a man die? Remember, then, that you have got the same road to travel.

Each morning, imagine to yourself that you won't last till evening; and when night comes, don't make bold to promise yourself a new day. Be ready for it all the time; so live, that death cannot take you unawares.

Plenty of people die quite suddenly, without any warning; the Son of Man will appear just when we are not expecting him. And when that last hour comes, you'll find yourself taking a completely different view of the life that lies behind you. How bitterly you will regret all that carelessness, all that slackening of effort!

If you hope to live well and wisely, try to be, here and now, the man you would want to be on your deathbed.

(Thomas à Kempis, c. 1379–1471 – monk. For the sake of clarity a few words and phrases have been altered.)

What is dying?

'A ship sails and I stand watching till she fades on the horizon and someone at my side says, "She is gone." Gone where? Gone from my sight, that is all; she is just as large as when I saw her. The diminished size, and total loss of sight is in me, not in her, and just at the moment when someone at my side says, "She is gone," there are others who are watching her coming, and other voices take up a glad shout, "There she comes!" and that is dying.'

(Bishop Brent)

The secret of death

'You would know the secret of death.
But how shall you find it unless you seek it in the heat of life?
The owl whose night-bound eyes are blind unto the day cannot unveil the mystery of light.
If you would indeed behold the spirit of death, open your heart wide unto the body of life.
For life and death are one, even as the river and the sea are one.
In the depths of your hopes and desires lies your silent knowledge of the beyond;
And like seeds dreaming beneath the snow your heart dreams of spring.
Trust the dreams, for in them is hidden the gate to eternity.
Your fear of death is but the trembling of the shepherd when he stands before the king whose hand is to be laid upon him in honour.

*Is the shepherd not joyful beneath his trembling,
that he shall wear the mark of the king?
Yet is he not more mindful of his trembling?
For what is it to die but to stand naked in the
wind and to melt into the sun?
And what is it to cease breathing but to free the
breath from its restless tides, that it may rise and
expand and seek God unencumbered?
Only when you drink from the river of silence
shall you indeed sing.
And when you have reached the mountain top,
then you shall begin to climb.
And when the earth shall claim your limbs, then
shall you truly dance.*

(Kahlil Gibran)

No trace of a shadow

*'Death is nothing at all. I have only slipped away
into the next room. I am I, and you are you.
Whatever we were to each other, that we still are.
Call me by my old familiar name, speak to me in
the easy way which you always used. Put no
difference in your tone, wear no forced air of
solemnity or sorrow. Laugh as we always
laughed at the little jokes we enjoyed together.
Play, smile, think of me, pray for me. Let my
name be ever the household word that it always
was, let it be spoken without effort, without the
trace of shadow on it. Life means all that it ever
meant. It is the same as it ever was; there is
unbroken continuity. Why should I be out of
mind because I am out of sight? I am waiting for
you, for an interval, somewhere very near, just
round the corner. All is well.'*

(Henry Scott Holland 1847–1918
– canon of St Paul's Cathedral)

FOR DISCUSSION

▶ Read the Thomas á Kempis reflection
slowly and carefully to yourselves. In
groups of four, discuss the sentences that
are in bold type.

▶ In groups of about four, discuss the other
three reflections. Report your findings
and insights back to the class.

FOR YOUR FOLDERS

▶ Write about your own thoughts on
death. If you wish, this can take the
form of a poem.

INTRODUCTION

Why do the Churches speak out on moral and social issues? In John's Gospel, Jesus says, *'This is my commandment, That ye love one another as I have loved you'* (John 15:12). Throughout the Gospels Jesus taught that as well as being about working to awaken us, religion is concerned with how we treat each other. Religion is not *just* a personal matter, it is also about relationships with others. The Churches believe that it is part of their work to speak out on relationships.

All Christians believe that the universe was created by God. Therefore, the universe and everything in it has *meaning*. Through the teachings in the Bible, Christians believe that God gives human beings *guidance* on how to live as harmoniously as possible. They believe that in the life and teachings of Jesus they can see God at work in the world. In the Gospel accounts Jesus, in his earthly life, was concerned about the world and the people in it. Following his example, Christians believe that they also have to try and express God's will in the modern world.

THE MODERN WORLD

These issues are, perhaps, more complicated than they were 2000 years ago. The pace of change today is incredible. Life in the second half of the 1990s is very different from how it was only a few years ago. Modern technology, although bringing many benefits, also raises many baffling questions about moral issues. For example what is right and what is wrong about genetic engineering, nuclear power, chemical drugs, testing on animals, the role of the media, surrogate motherhood, test-tube babies, organ transplants, etc?

Because life is always changing the Churches have found it necessary to try to explain what Christian moral standards are, in the light of modern issues. It is important for Christians that they do this. Therefore the Churches have tried to *interpret* the ideas in the Bible, so that they are *relevant* today.

On some moral and social issues the Churches disagree. For example on the question of birth control, the Roman Catholic Church teaches that artificial methods go against God's intention. On the other hand, the Methodist Church teaches that responsible contraception is a welcome means towards fulfilment in marriage. *Sometimes even within the same Church there is disagreement.* For example, some Roman Catholic Christians do not agree with their Church's teaching on artificial contraception; they argue that in a world that is already overpopulated it is global suicide to ban artificial contraception.

These differences illustrate how moral attitudes are formed. Some Churches will emphasize the importance of individuals developing and applying their own moral attitudes in the light of Christian principles and *coming to their own decisions*. Other Christians will put much greater emphasis on individuals remaining *loyal to the Church authority* and its teachings on moral attitudes.

HOW DO CHURCHES ARRIVE AT THEIR VIEWS?

All the Churches look to three sources of guidance when they are deciding on moral values. These are:

- scripture (the Word of God as revealed in the Bible)
- tradition (the experience of the Church through Christian history)
- reason (human understanding and knowledge).

Different Churches will put more emphasis on one of these sources than on others. They all take notice of biblical insights, but they will interpret these in the light of how Christians have traditionally understood them. They will also take into account new ideas and understanding gained from recent advances in human knowledge. All the Churches will discuss the issues, giving every member the chance to give their views, with the final decisions being made by a representative body of some kind. Here, briefly, is how four Churches come to decisions about moral and social issues.

Because life is always changing, the Churches have found it necessary to try to explain what Christian moral standards are, in the light of modern issues

The Baptist Union of Great Britain

The Baptist Church is built on two pillars: evangelism and liberty. So the Baptist Union does not usually make official statements on behalf of the member churches as this would restrict the liberty (freedom) of individual congregations. This is why the denomination is described as the Baptist Union (of member churches), rather than the Baptist Church. Nevertheless at the National Annual Assembly resolutions are passed relating to a variety of issues. These do not necessarily reflect the view of every church, but would still be regarded as the denomination's considered statement on matters of social and moral concern. Scripture has a dominant place in helping Baptists reach decisions.

The Church of England

The General Synod is the 'parliament' of the Church of England. It meets three times a year and has 560 members consisting of three 'houses' – Bishops, Clergy and **Laity** (ordinary Church members who are not ordained). The Church derives its authority equally from scripture, tradition and reasoning. During the debates in the Synod, members will express their own opinions and refer to scripture or tradition, depending upon their particular viewpoint.

The Roman Catholic Church

The Roman Catholic Church tries to understand contemporary issues by looking at scripture, the tradition of the Church, the wisdom of its scholars, the experience of modern Roman Catholics living in the world and the on-going theological thinking in different parts of the Church in different periods of history. Scripture and tradition are not seen as separate elements in the life of the Church but as inter-related. The Church will make statements through the Pope (speaking formally – *ex cathedra* – as the chief Bishop) in conjunction with all the Bishops of the Church and through its Councils, when the Church's teachings are made official.

The United Reformed Church

At the heart of decision-making in the United Reformed Church is scripture. A Church statement reads:

> *'The United Reformed Church acknowledges the Word of God in the Old and New Testaments, discerned under the guidance of the Holy Spirit, as the supreme authority for the faith and conduct of all God's people.'*

The Church meets once a year at the General Assembly when decisions are made on behalf of the whole Church. Decisions are reached by majority vote but resolutions usually include words like 'recommend', 'encourage' or 'urge', and consequently aren't seen as binding for all members.

FOR YOUR FOLDERS

▶ How do Christian beliefs affect the way the Churches speak out on moral and social issues?

▶ How do the Churches try to make decisions about modern issues?

▶ Is there always agreement among members of:
  a the same Church
  b different Churches?
  Explain why you think this might be so.

▶ Explain in your own words what are the three main sources of guidance that Christians appeal to.

▶ Explain briefly how any two Churches arrive at their decisions.

▶ Why do you think the Churches feel they have a duty to speak out?

INTRODUCTION

At the centre of Christian belief is the idea that the universe, the world and everything in it has been *created*. It did not happen by chance. Because of this Christians believe our world is **sacred**. This word means many things: holy, whole, precious, special, divine, hallowed, mysterious, worthy of respect and honour. Christians also believe that God made humankind in his own image (Genesis 1:27) and that we are *'crowned with glory and honour'* (Psalm 8:5). So we can see from these teachings that humankind holds a responsible place in God's creation.

THE GREATEST COMMANDMENT

In Mark 12, a teacher of the law of Moses asked Jesus which commandment was the most important of all. Jesus replied that the greatest commandment was to love God with all the your heart, soul, mind and strength, and the second commandment was to love your neighbour as yourself. Love lies at the heart of Jesus' teachings. Love of God and love of humanity cannot be separated. They are two sides of the same coin. Christians therefore try and live their lives according to this ideal – loving not only the Creator but also his creation. Dr Martin Luther King (1929–68) summed up his Christian views on the sacredness of human life in the following way:

> *'We need to affirm the sacredness of all human life. Every person is somebody because s/he is a Child of God.'*

REVERENCE FOR LIFE

Many Christians have taken this a step further and said that people must try to love *all of creation*. For example, Albert Schweizer (1875–1965), a Christian thinker and medical missionary in Africa, believed that the most important thing we can have is **reverence** for life. All our behaviour, he believed, should come from a deep understanding of the gift of life. He wrote:

> *'Reverence concerning all life is the greatest commandment ... we take this so slightly, thoughtlessly plucking a flower, thoughtlessly stepping on a poor insect, thoughtlessly disregarding the suffering and lives of our fellow men and women.'*

Some Christians have also stressed the uniqueness of each and every living thing. One such person was Thomas Merton (1915–68). Merton was a Trappist monk who wrote about contemporary monasticism. In one of his works, *Seeds of Contemplation*, he speaks about this uniqueness:

> *'No two created things are exactly alike. This particular tree will give glory to God by spreading out its roots in the earth and raising its branches into the air and the light, in a way that no other tree before or after it ever did, or will do... Each particular being in its individuality gives glory to God by being precisely what He wants it to be, here and now, in the circumstances ordained for it, by His love, and His infinite Art.'*

LOVE OF LIFE

'Lord, may we love all your creation, all the earth and every grain of sand in it. May we love every leaf, every ray of your light. May we love the animals; you have given them the rudiments of thought and joy untroubled. Let us not trouble them; let us not harass them; let us not deprive them of their happiness; let us not work against your intent. For we acknowledge unto you that all is like an ocean, all is flowing and blending, and that to withhold any measure of love from anything in your universe is to withhold that same measure from you.'

(Fyodor Dostoevsky, 1821–81 – Russian author)

'Reverence concerning all life is the greatest commandment'

ANIMALS

In the past, many Christians thought that animals were of little or no value and that they were merely put on earth for human use. However, this view did not come from the Bible. When God commanded that the earth should produce all kinds of animal life *'He was pleased with what he saw'* (Genesis 1).

Although the Bible teaches that humanity is at the pinnacle of creation God did not exclude the rest of creation. Through the ages many Christians, despite the attitudes of the Church, have shown a great concern for animals. St Francis of Assisi (1181–1226) – the patron saint of animals – is believed to have preached to the birds and tamed a wolf. William Wilberforce (1759–1833), who fought against slavery, also campaigned against blood sports like bull-baiting. As early as the 1840s, the Earl of Shaftesbury (1801–85) campaigned against vivisection (the practice of dissecting living animals for experiment). The RSPCA was founded by Christians. Many Quakers have been actively involved in animal rights for over 200 years. Quakers were among the first vegetarians of the nineteenth century and have opposed fox-hunting and other blood 'sports' for over 200 years. For many years they have refused to wear fur, visit zoos or circuses or wear products tested on animals. Other famous Christians such as John Wesley (1703–91) and C. S. Lewis (1898–1963) spoke out and acted for the rights of animals.

Although in the past the institutionalized Church has not had a great deal to say on animal rights, over recent years this has changed. Thanks to the work of such organizations as Greenpeace, the RSPCA, Animal Aid and the Worldwide Fund for Nature, the Churches have begun to speak out.

'Unnecessary and unjustifiable experiments and trials – as on the effects of cosmetics – should not take place. Intensive factory farming methods, which ignore the welfare of animals, are to be condemned. Every measure should be taken to preserve animal habitats.'

(Methodist Church statement 1990)

'The Christian tradition asserts that animals have been created by God and that they have an intrinsic value for that reason. Nevertheless, the value of animals has always been seen as secondary to that of human beings made in God's image and placed in a central position in creation. Human beings both have an affinity with, and an obligation to, animals.'

(Church of England report
Our Responsibility for the Living Environment)

REFLECTION

'Jesus is also a lover and pray-er of nature. Mountains, deserts, parks, lakes welcomed him for days at a time as he suffered his fame and his loneliness and his beauty and his decision-making in all these sacred temples. He chose the way and the lifestyle of the story teller, the parable maker who fashions a new creation out of the holy materials of the only creation we all share in common: the birds, the lilies of the field, the fish caught, the fig tree in bloom, the sheep versus the goats . . . . His reverence for nature was so great that the creatures of nature were indeed his teachers and his professors.'

(Matthew Fox)

FOR YOUR FOLDERS

▶ Using some of the ideas in this unit design a poster called 'The Love of Life'.

▶ Explain in detail what Christians mean by the sacred world. Use ideas from some of the quotations.

▶ Explain the Christian attitude to animal welfare.

▶ What are your views on vivisection; experimentation on animals; zoos; circuses; wearing fur coats? What do you think Christian views on these matters ought to be? Give reasons for your answer.

This unit looks briefly at a variety of social issues that concern Christians.

SUNDAY

Over recent years, government laws have changed regarding trading on Sunday in England, allowing shops to remain open. Many Christians believe that this is wrong. In 1993 the General Synod of the Church of England stated:

> 'This Synod affirms the importance of Sunday as a day for spiritual renewal, rest and re-creation and for the nurturing of family life. It deplores the deliberate flouting of the law governing Sunday trade, by powerful commercial interests.'

MONEY

In the reflection below the Salvation Army explains its views on money matters.

HOMELESSNESS

More and more people in Britain live on the streets. Homelessness is a social evil and deeply concerns many Christians. Some reasons for homelessness may include: poverty, not being brought up in a family, problems at home, physical and sexual abuse, divorce, unemployment, mental illness, having a criminal record, alcohol or drug abuse, being a battered wife, and racism. Christian organizations such as the Salvation Army, the Catholic Housing Aid Society and the Children's Society work tirelessly to help the homeless and put pressure on

REFLECTION

'In the early days of the Salvation Army much caring work was directed towards those who had little or no money. Poverty presented a challenge to the Salvationist.

William Booth, the Founder, was also concerned about man's "unhealthy longing after wealth, house, lands, trade or any worldly thing for its own sake". He felt that to desire money or position was good only if it was to be used to help others. The Bible teaches that stealing is wrong (Exodus 20:15) and that to covet is wrong (Exodus 20:17). The example of Jesus teaches us to put the needs of others before our own and to be content with a simple lifestyle.

The Old Testament teaches the principle of tithing (Genesis 28:22). Many Salvationists allocate a tenth of their means for the needs of others in their corps, community and overseas. Others give more than a tenth, since the New Testament stresses the idea of a 'freewill offering', made according to what a person can afford.

Salvationists do not gamble, because the main aim of a gambler is to gain at the expense of others, which contradicts the unselfish attitude a Christian should show. By avoiding games of chance altogether Salvationists guard against the problems and disappointments to which gambling so often leads. Salvationists are glad to support worthy charities which hold raffles by giving donations rather than buying tickets.

High pressure advertising has resulted in a rapid increase in the use of store and credit cards and other means of obtaining credit. With this has come a serious danger of incurring debt because of the very high rates of interest charged on credit. More and more people are falling into debt and research carried out by the Freedom from Debt campaign has shown that debt is a major factor in marital stress and family breakdown. The NSPCC claims that debt is one of the three major factors in child abuse within the family.

Salvationists urge great care to ensure that credit does not exceed ability to repay, especially in the purchase of luxury goods. Similar caution is needed when considering entering into hire-purchase agreements or securing bank loans.

The Salvation Army in its early days frequently had converts who were suffering materially because they had mismanaged their money. Their acceptance of the Christian principles of thrift, honesty and temperance often raised their standard of living by a remarkable degree. Salvationists find these principles are still the best guidance for managing the more bountiful resources of today. Much of the Army's social work is related to helping people who have financial problems.'

(Salvation Army)

the government to help solve a problem that many of its policies have created. It is estimated that 98,000 children and young people go missing in Britain every year.

In early 1993 the Children's Society highlighted in the media an alarming double standard in the law. While social services and police protection is given to children abused in the family home or in care, Society streetwork projects were finding that runaways as young as 14 years were being cautioned with *soliciting* and left with a record on their police files. The law states that girls under 16 are unable to consent to sex; yet they can be cautioned and charged with soliciting by the courts.

'We see child prostitution as sexual abuse,' says Peter Blackley, who runs the Society's Safe in the City Project in Manchester. 'These children are the ones the crime is being committed against.'

Under the Children Act, police have a duty to call in welfare agencies to help desperate young people picked up on the streets. The Children's Society believes that young people involved in the street-sex trade should be given the same support and protection by social services and police-child-protection teams as any other child who has been sexually abused.

UNEMPLOYMENT

There are around three million people without work in Britain, but some people fortunate enough to have jobs don't even seem to question the problem of unemployment. In this Church of England statement, some of the evils of unemployment are explained:

'There are social and personal costs. Local communities and amenities decline; social order is threatened; crime increases; the integrating effect of having a job and belonging in society is lost; individuals suffer psychological shock; they feel humiliated, angry and depressed; health problems increase; families suffer extra strain, (there are) increases in heart disease, suicide and other deaths, mental illness, loss of self-esteem, violence, the use of alcohol and tobacco.'

Many people – old and young – are living on very low incomes and have real difficulty making ends meet. Often their health and their family life suffer. The Churches are among those working to reduce poverty. *In the UK 5 per cent of the population own 40 per cent of the nation's wealth*, and to many Christians this distribution of wealth is unfair.

THINKING POINTS

- *'As long as there is poverty in the world I can never be rich, even if I have a million dollars. I can never be what I ought to be, until you are what you ought to be.'*

  (Dr Martin Luther King, 1929–68)

- *'The earth belongs to everyone not just to the rich.'*

  (St Ambrose, 334–97 CE)

- *'Christianity began with a dreamer and ended up with a well-fed clergy.'*

  (Karl Marx, 1818–83)

- *'You cannot serve God and money.'*

  (Matthew 6:24)

- *'The love of money is the root of all evil.'*

  (1 Timothy 6:10)

FOR YOUR FOLDERS

▶ Explain the meaning of the following words: tithing; gambling; debt; thrift; honesty; temperance.

▶ Briefly explain the Salvation Army views on money, debt, gambling and poverty.

▶ Why do many Christians think it is wrong that Sunday is no longer seen as a day of rest?

▶ What problems face the homeless? What are some Christians doing to try to improve this situation?

▶ What problems does unemployment cause do you think?

▶ Why do Christians believe that the unequal distribution of wealth is unfair?

▶ Explain what you think the words of Dr King, St Ambrose, Karl Marx and the two biblical quotes mean.

▶ Why do you think the Churches find it necessary to speak out on social issues?

INTRODUCTION

It is a fact of life that people often harm one another. Crime can take many forms, from shoplifting to murder. In the world of human behaviour, order is preserved by laws and customs. However, the law needs to be constantly checked and updated to make sure it is fair. Sometimes Christians and others who have believed that a law is unfair have protested against it in order that it be reformed. This may mean breaking the (old unfair) law, to put pressure on society to change it. Often when Christians have felt they must do this, they have taken part in non-violent direct action (e.g. Dr Martin Luther King, see unit 16).

In the past when the Church and the State were closely connected it was often believed that laws, created by the state or government, were the will of God. For example, in the past Kings of England, who were Supreme Governors of the Church, had enormous power because they could argue they were representatives of God. Today this has changed and ordinary people have more power to make decisions and elect their own representatives.

CRIME

People commit crimes for many different reasons. There are *intermediate* causes, such as boredom, frustration, anger, lust, thrill or jealousy, and deeper *underlying* causes, such as poverty, consumerism, materialism, poor housing, deprived upbringing and inequality. Over recent years many Churches have spoken about the undeniable connection between poverty, deprivation and crime. In 1985 the Church of England's report, called *Faith in the City*, made these connections. It stressed that present-day society is too materialistic and that people are encouraged by the constant influence of the media to want more and more.

PUNISHMENT

Traditionally in our society there are five theories of punishment:

- to *protect* (society/individuals/the offender from him/herself)
- to *deter* (put people off committing further crimes)
- to *reform* (try and make people responsible citizens)
- to *punish* (retribution – 'an eye for an eye')

- to *vindicate* (crime is punished, so the law is protected).

Generally, Christians recognize that governments have a duty, on behalf of society, to protect that society. However, they believe that any criminal justice system should be *merciful*. They also believe that although an offender must be punished, and this punishment will include an element of retribution, the sole aim of punishment is not retribution, still less revenge. *They believe that any punishment should also try to reform and rehabilitate the offender.*

Because of these ideas many Christians work with organizations that try to help prisoners, and many are involved in prison visiting.

Many Christians are concerned about the way offenders are punished by our current system. *Britain punishes more people by imprisonment than any other country in Europe.* They believe that the current system doesn't do much to help the prisoners themselves and many prisoners re-offend after they've been released. Christians also believe that too often the needs of the victim are ignored and that there should be schemes of *mediation between victim and offender*. The two would meet and try to understand each other in order that a healing process may take place between them.

THINKING POINT

- *'Punishment is useful only when it helps people to realize the hurt they are doing to the sense of worth in themselves and others.'*

(Quaker viewpoint)

CAPITAL PUNISHMENT

Capital punishment was abolished in Britain in 1970, although it is still carried out in an estimated 100 countries around the world today. Because so many countries worldwide still use the death penalty, and there are still occasional calls for its reintroduction in Britain, the Churches have made public statements about it. One of the key questions about capital punishment is *does it act as a deterrent?* Some people would say that it does, and that when planning a crime, the potential criminal would draw back at the thought of giving up their own life. Abolitionists (people who are against capital punishment) would say it is not a deterrent, because murder is a crime apart. The whole purpose in planning a killing is usually to avoid being found out and therefore it is not a deterrent. The Roman Catholic Church has never officially condemned the death penalty. However, over recent years many bishops in Canada, the USA, France and Ireland have called for its abolition. Most Churches in Britain are opposed to capital punishment.

FOR YOUR FOLDERS

▶ Think of some laws you consider to be unfair. Would you be willing to break the law in order to change it? Can you think of examples of people who have done this?

▶ What do you think are the main causes of crime? Are there some 'crimes against humanity' that governments have actually committed, that you know about?

▶ Explain in your own words the five theories of punishment. What do you think Christian views on punishment are?

▶ What concerns do Christians have about the prison system?

▶ What do you think 'schemes of mediation' might involve?

▶ Explain in your own words what the Christian teaching on redemption means. How does Amnesty International apply this teaching to the issue of the death penalty?

TALKING POINTS

● *'The real security for human life is to be found in a reverence for it... A deep reverence for human life is worth more than a thousand executions in the prevention of murder; and is, in fact, the great security for human life. The law of capital punishment while pretending to support this reverence does in fact tend to destroy it.'*

(John Bright – first Quaker Member of Parliament, 1868)

● *'All human life is sacred and each human being, however wretched, can become a new person.'*

(Salvation Army statement)

● *'For too long we have treated violence with violence and that's why it never seems to end.'*

(Coretta Scott King – widow of Dr Martin Luther King, who was murdered)

● *'Every saint has a past and every sinner a future.'*

(St Augustine, 354–430 CE)

● *'Perhaps the strongest argument in Christian theology against the death penalty lies in the notion of* redemption. *Christianity professes that human beings are free either to follow the path of Christ or to stray from it and that those who stray are sinners, but* great stress is laid on the ability and duty of sinners to repent, *to change their behaviour once they have been forgiven, and on the need for reconciliation between those sinned against and the sinner. After true repentance, a fresh start can be made in life. The death penalty, it has been argued, denies a "sinner", or truly repentant criminal the chance to make the fresh start promised by Christ.'*

(Amnesty International)

DEFINITIONS

Prejudice is defined as 'thinking badly of others without sufficient reason'. The word 'prejudice' itself means to *prejudge*, that is, we judge somebody without having knowledge or experience about them. So prejudice is a way of *thinking* about other groups of people.

Racism is defined by the formula 'prejudice + power'. Sometimes, our racial prejudices are made acceptable and supported by key institutions in our society. Racism is seen when racial prejudice is turned into action of some sort, and that action is to the disadvantage of some racial group or individual. So racism is about *acting* towards other groups of people.

INTRODUCTION

One of the problems in studying racism is that people tend to think of it only in terms of strong personal prejudice, violence, and racist organizations like the British Movement. However, these are often extremes. They can limit our understanding and make the vast majority of racist thought and action go unchecked.

All black people suffer from the effects of the subtle and far-reaching racist attitudes that exist in our society. Racist attitudes have been built into society over several centuries, and this makes them difficult to shake off. These attitudes for example mean that *in the UK, Asians are 50 times and West Indians 36 times more likely than whites to be the victims of racial violence*, and people from ethnic minorities

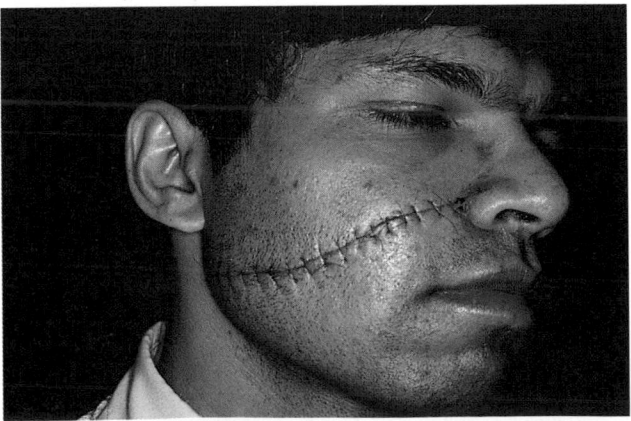

Asians are 50 times more likely than whites to be the victims of racial violence

are four times more likely to be homeless in London than white people.

Often, black people's reaction to racism has been to close in on themselves, to refuse to be absorbed into a racist society. Instead, as a means of survival they have learned to take pride in their blackness. An example is the religion of Rastafarianism. At the heart of this belief is the rejection of white dominance and the hope of an eventual return to Africa and from the evils of the capitalist and materialistic West, which Rastafarians call Babylon.

For some black Christians in the UK, the Caribbean and West African Churches play an important part in providing a sense of identity for black communities. Whether they are attached to mainstream British Churches or to separate black denominations, the Christian message is seen to offer security against racial discrimination, especially in its teachings about equality.

In the past the white male-dominated mainstream Christian Churches have, like all major institutions, been racist. The missionary movement (see units 30, 32 and 76) was painfully unaware of black cultures. Usually using violence, they forced people in Africa, the Americas, India and Australasia to accept a white Christian worldview. The results have been tragic with the wholesale destruction of ancient cultures. Over recent years, due to sophisticated communications systems and the arrival of working black people in Britain, there is a growing awareness of the richness of non-European cultures. With this has also grown a realization that *all men and women are equal*, and that we are all living in *one world*. Because of these changes, the mainstream Churches today speak out against racial prejudice, discrimination and inequality. However, there is no room for complacency. For instance, in North America, racist churches exist, like the Church of Jesus Christ Christian Aryan Nations, which teach white supremacy.

THE BIBLE AND RACISM

Many modern Churches' attitudes to prejudice and discrimination are based on the two biblical concepts of creation and redemption.

1 Creation

All human beings are made in the image of God (Genesis 1:26). Human beings are made for each other; to live in community and to have corporate responsibility for the whole of creation (Genesis 2:19–20). But unlike the rest of creation there are no separate species within humanity. *There is only one human race*. What we call 'races' are nothing more significant than slight variations of the basic human stock (Genesis 3:20 and Acts 17:26).

2 Redemption

In Jesus Christ the barriers between humankind and God are broken down and race, class, sex or status cease to be reasons for hostility and division (Galatians 3:28, Colossians 3:11, James 2:5–9).

TALKING POINTS

- *'Guided by the Light of God within us and recognizing that of God in others, we can all learn to value our differences in age, sex, physique, race and culture … These are God's gifts. We need one another, and differences shared become enrichments, not reasons to be afraid, to dominate or condemn.'*

  (Meg Maslin, quoted in *Quaker Faith and Practice*, the Religious Society of Friends, 1995)

- *'Every human being created in the image of God is a person for whom Christ died. Racism, which is the use of a person's racial origin to determine a person's value, is an assault on Christ's values, and a rejection of his sacrifice.'*

  (World Council of Churches statement)

- *'Definition*
  Racism results where prejudiced attitudes of superiority over others are combined with the power to shape society.
  History
  Western civilization is, and has long been, seriously flawed by racism.
  Acknowledgement
  British society nurtures racism through assumptions, stereotypes and organizational barriers which deny black people a just share of power and decision-making.
  Confession
  The church displays racism by failing to adapt so that black people can share fully in its life, its outreach and its decision-making.'

  (*A Declaration on Racism* by the United Reform Church)

FOR YOUR FOLDERS

▶ In your own words, explain the meaning of the following words: prejudice; racism; discrimination; violate.

▶ What do you think are the effects of racism on:

  a individuals' lives
  b society in general
  c the world?

  Give examples (from the past and present) of racism.

▶ List some of the benefits of a multi-racial society.

▶ How can Christians fight against racism?

▶ Look up the Biblical quotes mentioned. Copy down the quotes and use two of them to design an anti-racist poster.

▶ Generally what do Christians believe about racial equality?

▶ *'Western civilization is, and has long been, seriously flawed by racism.'* Explain what you think this means. Give examples.

67 SEXISM

INTRODUCTION

Sexism has been defined as *'the opinion that one sex is not as good as the other, especially that women are less able in most ways than men'* (Longman Dictionary). Throughout history, societies, especially in the West, have been dominated and ruled by men. This is known as **patriarchy**. It is often difficult to examine the status of women, because normally they have had none. History, culture, language and institutionalized religion have been patriarchal. Women have nearly always been dominated by men and regarded as men's personal property. Like all other patriarchal institutions, the Church has been guilty of sexism. Much of this sexual discrimination has come about through male church leaders interpreting the Old Testament in such a way that the power of the Church remained firmly in their hands (see unit 34).

THE OLD TESTAMENT

'So God created man in his own image, in the image of God created He him: male and female created He them.' Throughout Jewish and Christian history it was Eve's role as Adam's 'helper' and 'inferior' which was accepted universally, because her own likeness to God came only via the male spare rib. It was forgotten – or overlooked – that woman, like man, was created in the image of God. It was never forgotten, however, that in the story, it was because Eve yielded to the temptation of the serpent (by eating the forbidden fruit and giving some to Adam) that they were both expelled from the Garden of Eden (Genesis 3:1–24), ashamed of their nakedness. In the story Adam was condemned to work among thorns and thistles but Eve, as the cause of their 'fall' was given a 'worse punishment': *'I will greatly multiply your pain in childbearing; in pain you shall bring forth children yet your desire shall be for your husband and he shall rule over you.'* This literal interpretation of Genesis sums up woman's lot down the ages and reflects attitudes towards women at the time that the *Genesis* story was written. Because of her biology man must be woman's master.

Genesis reflects the social realities of that time. The whole of the Old Testament depicts a society which was rigidly patriarchal. A woman was a man's private possession. Rape or adultery were considered to be a violation of *his* property rights, whereas his own unfaithfulness was overlooked unless he interfered with the wife of another man. During much of their adult lives women underwent the additional burden of being considered 'unclean'. For instance, during menstruation they were untouchable for at least a week: 'If any man lies with her and her impurities on him, he shall be unclean seven days and every bed on which he lies shall be unclean' (Leviticus 15:24).

JESUS' ATTITUDES

Jesus' attitude to women was very different and it is widely believed that women played a very *active* role in his ministry and life. He always considered them as equal and as deserving of respect as any man. It was to the Samaritan women at the well that he first made himself known as the Messiah (John 4:7–30); the story of Martha and Mary demonstrates his belief that women were fit for other things besides domesticity (Luke 10:38–42); and he appeared to women first after he rose from the dead (Matthew 28:1–10).

ST PAUL'S ATTITUDES

St Paul stated *'... there is neither male nor female for you are all one in Christ Jesus'* (Galatians 3:28). He also taught that a husband should love his wife as himself (1 Corinthians 7:3). However, he also warned wives to *'... be subject to your husbands'* (Ephesians 5:22–23). When it came to teaching the Word to others, St Paul said *'Let the woman learn in silence with all subjection. But I suffer not a woman to teach, nor to usurp authority over the man, but to be in silence'* (1 Timothy 2:11–12).

CHRISTIAN HISTORY

During the 2000-year-old history of Christianity women have had no position in society, and the Church has reinforced the general sexist attitudes of the day. Here is just one example:

> *'Women should remain at home, sit still, keep house, bear and bring up children.'*
>
> (Martin Luther, 1483–1586)

PORNOGRAPHY

Many Christians are deeply concerned about the rapid commercialization of sex and the dehumanization of women in pornographic literature and films. In this extract, Anna Grear, a Christian, explains why pornography is an affront (outrage, insult) to human dignity.

'To be human means to be a responsible, responsive being, rejoicing in all of life before the face of God. We are created, unique, valuable individuals. Pornography portrays people as sexual commodities, consumer durables available for sale. It reduces them to objects, commercially and sexually available, performing their titillating antics at the turn of a page or the press of a video remote control. Pornography violates the integral, whole nature of human personality – ripping personhood from the woman splayed across their page and reducing their rich complexity to a glossy photo of their genitalia. Not only does pornography dehumanize the person portrayed, but it also dehumanizes the viewer, for to the extent to which we dehumanize others and fail to respect them as creations of God, we ourselves are dehumanized and dwarfed ... The biblical stress upon relationship helps to enlarge our understanding of human sexuality. A problem with pornographic literature is not that it emphasizes sexuality too much, but that it does not emphasize it enough. It totally eliminates relationship and restrains sexuality to the narrow confines of the genital. It has made sex trivial ...

The main affront of pornography to the sexual relationship is that it does overemphasize the genital. It makes sex incredibly shallow in meaning. It concentrates on the sexual act itself ... it tears genital sex out of the wider context of what human sexuality is. The deep but mysterious meaning of our creation as male and female is reduced to little more than a difference in sexual anatomy as a result.

Pornography rips the intimacy of the sexual act out of its loving, giving, mutually caring context of committed, faithful relationships. Pornography undervalues the sexual act drastically, and is a deep affront to the integrity of the marriage relationship and all that it stands for in the eyes of God ... it is utterly opposed to biblical truth on a number of counts. It violates the biblical view of what it is to be human, to be male and female in relationship, the view of the human body, and the biblical view of the sexual act. It is a perverse lie flowing out of heartless, idolatrous values ... At home we see the injustice of the pornographic portrayal of women resulting in rape and violence. We see increasing adultery and divorce as a result of dissatisfaction and the industry fed belief that the myth of sexual liberty will bring fulfilment. The social repercussions of this can be seen in the lives of countless devastated children growing into adults incapable of forming lasting relationships themselves. The subtle, degrading view of women which creeps into the market place in the form of pop videos and advertising leads to men and boys despising women ... the increasing use of younger and younger models cannot help but feed the problem of child abuse and incest. The circle is vicious and depressing.'

FOR YOUR FOLDERS

▶ What do the words 'sexism' and 'patriarchy' mean?

▶ How has the literal interpretation of Genesis affected the rights of women?

▶ What were Jesus' attitudes to women?

▶ What were St Paul's attitudes to women?

▶ After reading Anna Grear's views, answer the following:

a Find out what the following words mean: violate; dehumanize; trivial.

b How does pornography portray people? How does this portrayal violate the whole nature of human personality?

c How does pornography also dehumanize the viewer?

d What aspects of human sexuality are excluded by pornography?

e Why does it make sex trivial and shallow?

f Why does pornography undervalue the sexual act?

g How does it violate the biblical view of human relationships?

h What are some of the tragic consequences of pornography?

INTRODUCTION

The term 'homosexuality' was first coined by the medical profession in the last century. Nowadays, most homosexuals prefer to use the terms 'lesbian' and 'gay' because the word 'homosexual 'sounds rather like a psychiatrist's diagnosis. There is no general agreement about what causes homosexuality or whether it is just how people are born. The psychologist Alfred Kinsey wrote a report on sexuality in the early 1950s. He concluded that we are all somewhere on a scale of sexuality, with total heterosexuality at one extreme and total homosexuality at the other. He believed that most people are capable of feeling attracted to someone of the same sex, and that the absolute division between heterosexual and homosexual is a false one.

TALKING POINT

- *'There are not two discrete (separate) populations, heterosexual and homosexual ... Only the human mind invents categories and tries to force facts into separated pigeon-holes ...'*

(Alfred Kinsey – psychologist)

CHRISTIAN VIEW

Christians currently hold a wide range of views on homosexuality. Discussion is more widespread in the churches in Europe and North America. They have been confronted with this issue owing to the campaign for lesbian and gay rights in society that started in these continents in the 1970s. There are now several organizations for lesbian and gay Christians and some Churches openly welcome and accept them. However, some homosexuals find it very hard to match their sexuality with their faith. 'Coming out' may be very difficult when family or friends are the kind of Christians who believe that homosexuality is a sin. For someone brought up to take the Bible's rules literally, it can be very painful to break these rules. It can also be painful for lesbian and gay Christians to be unable to marry their partner before God. Sometimes couples are able to arrange a 'blessing' ceremony with a sympathetic priest or minister. Some would like to see the Church of the future offering the marriage service to lesbian and gay couples.

WHAT THE BIBLE SAYS

In the whole of the Bible, there are six passages that seem to talk about homosexuality. For centuries, Christians have understood these passages to be condemnatory. Recent scholarship has sometimes come up with a different view. It all depends on how you translate certain important words. Some scholars now say that translators of the Bible have read an anti-homosexual teaching into these passages because that is what they already thought.

FOR DISCUSSION

▶ Look at the following Bible passages.

Old Testament
Genesis 19:1–25, Leviticus 18:22, Leviticus 20:3
New Testament
Romans 1:24–7, 1 Corinthians 6:9, 1 Timothy 1:10

The Genesis passage says, *'Bring those men out, that we may know them.'* For this verse, the Hebrew verb 'to know' has always been translated as meaning 'to have sex with'. Some scholars have recently pointed out an interesting fact. This same word 'to know' is used 943 times in the Old Testament but it is only translated as meaning 'to have sex with' in ten places, and each time, it refers to heterosexual sex. However, this passage is often quoted as proof that homosexuality is condemned.

In Leviticus it says, *'You shall not lie with a man as you would with a woman: it is an abomination'* (a disgusting act). This sounds as though it can have only one meaning. So does the Old Testament condemn homosexuality? Notice that it is only addressed to men. Is being a lesbian allowed? Some Christians emphasize that Jesus taught acceptance of all people and say that this verse should not be taken as a strict role. After all, they point out, there is also a rule in Leviticus which says that you should kill all divorced people who remarry.

The three mentions of homosexuality in the New Testament are in letters thought to have been written by St Paul. A recent theory suggests that in Romans, Paul only condemns men who are heterosexual but who sometimes have sex with male prostitutes in the pagan temples. He may not be saying 'no' to all homosexual behaviour. This is a matter of controversy.

The passage in Romans is also the only part of the Bible that could be understood as a condemnation of lesbian sex. As with many passages, the meaning seems to change according to which translation is used. Some sound more definite than others.

Some experts say that we can never know the exact meaning of some of the original Greek words. The verses in 1 Corinthians and 1 Timothy use two Greek words that have always been translated as having a homosexual meaning. But scholars of ancient Greek say that neither word was used to mean 'homosexual' in any other Greek writings that were around when St Paul was writing. Biblical scholars are still trying to agree on just what these words meant to the people Paul wrote them to. There were words in Greek for 'homosexual', but Paul didn't choose those words.

OPINIONS EXPRESSED BY CHRISTIANS

1 'We should love the sinner but hate the sin.'
2 'We should accept people in a loving and faithful same-sex partnership because they are as valuable to and valued by God as heterosexual people.'
3 'Homosexual acts are disordered and can in no sense be approved of; but we must treat homosexuals with understanding because the Church must exclude no one.'
4 'No practising homosexual or lesbian should be rejected for training for ordination on the grounds of the expression of their sexuality alone.'
5 'Homosexuality is an abomination and homosexuals are possessed by the devil.'
6 'Sexuality is a divine gift and sexual activity is a morally neutral part of everyday life. It is motive and circumstances which degrade or ennoble any act.'

TEACHINGS BY SOME CHURCHES

A Roman Catholic view

'Tradition has always declared that "homosexual acts are intrinsically disordered". They are contrary to the natural law. They close the sexual act to the gift of life ... under no circumstances can they be approved. The number of men and women who have deep-seated homosexual tendencies is not negligible. They do not choose their homosexual condition; for most of them it is a trial. They must be accepted with respect, compassion and sensitivity. Every sign of unjust discrimination in this regard should be avoided.'

(Catechism of the Roman Catholic Church 1994)

A Methodist view

'For homosexual men and women, permanent relationships characterized by love can be an appropriate and Christian way of expressing their sexuality.'

REFLECTION

'I am a gay Christian. Because of the Church of England's teachings on homosexuality I find that my life is a constant struggle between my faith and my sexuality. At times this conflict is unbearable. The Church's teachings are, without a doubt, hypocritical. On the one hand, it publicly condemns homosexuality, bringing great suffering to Christians who are gay or lesbian – yet privately many of its leaders, including some of its bishops, are themselves homosexuals.

Ever since I came out and declared my sexuality, my fellow Christians argue that I can't possibly be a true Christian. They refuse to accept Christ's wonderful message of love, which embraces everyone. My partner and I have lived faithfully and happily together for twelve years. We love and care for each other very deeply. We have tried as best we can to live good, Christian lives. I am told that our love is wrong. How can something as deep and meaningful as the love between two human beings be wrong?'

(Author's interview)

FOR YOUR FOLDERS

▶ Define 'homophobia'.
▶ What might the problems be for a Christian who 'comes out'?
▶ Should lesbian and gay couples have the right to marry in church?
▶ Read the reflection. Why does the gay Christian think that the Church is hypocritical?

69 THE DISABLED

INTRODUCTION

Over recent years it has become more widely recognized that disabled people have the same rights, feelings, needs and emotions as able-bodied people. This does not apply just to rights regarding food, clothing, shelter and education, but also to the development of real friendship with other people.

People sometimes use the terms 'impairment', 'disability' and 'handicap', and it is useful to understand the differences between these words.

- The *consequence* of the diagnosis (disease or congenital malformation, injury) is known as *impairment*.

- The *impact on activities* of daily living results in *disability*.

- If a disabled person then suffers *social disadvantage* this is known as a *handicap*.

An example may be helpful. As the result of an accident a person may suffer a spinal injury – this is impairment. A consequence of this is that they are unable to walk and are confined to a wheelchair – this is the disability. There are certain things they cannot do because of access and other problems – this is the handicap.

THE MENTALLY HANDICAPPED

In the past, people with mental handicaps were locked away in hospitals. This did nothing to break down people's prejudices about them. Today, there is a steadily growing awareness that mentally handicapped people have plenty to give, and can develop within the community. As a result more of them are taking their place in community life. However, it is also the case that because of lack of government money people who are mentally ill are often forced to live on the streets.

The sacrament of marriage and disability

Within the Church there has been much debate about whether mentally disabled people should marry. This statement by the Roman Catholic Bishops of England and Wales states a view that is shared by nearly all Christians:

'The disabled person needs to love and be loved. The disabled person needs to feel loveable. This basic need – basic to all human people created by God who himself is love – is expressed in many ways: within family life, by a generous and trusting friendship and, in a unique way, between husband and wife in marriage. For some people a mental or physical handicap will exclude the possibility of such a relationship. But this must not be presumed. On the contrary, the natural right to marry must be respected unless the person concerned is clearly unable to understand what they are doing or unable to sustain the life-long commitment of marriage.

Within the group – the very large group – of people we call disabled there are many persons who are very suited for married life. The limited research done on the stability of marriage between disabled people suggests that there is a better prospect of a permanent commitment between people who marry while disabled than between people who have no apparent handicap. Because of this, support should be given to those who, although in some way disabled, show a serious desire to marry and are able to make a life-long commitment. Serious consideration would have to be given to the implication of having children and caring for them. However, we must recognize the right of handicapped persons to enter marriage and the witness they can give to the beauty of married love.'

(*All People Together*, a statement of the Roman Catholic Bishops of England and Wales 1981)

Of course there are matters of concern that need looking at. For instance, when one of the spouses suffers from an incurable genetic inherited disease which could be transmitted to the children of the marriage (e.g. Huntingdon's Chorea), should he or she be sterilized? Would the parents be able to look after any child born in the marriage? However, in considering these sorts of problems, it would be unfair to have higher expectations and tighter restrictions related to the marriage of disabled people than would be applied for couples for whom disability is not a consideration.

Jean Vanier has been called a 'modern day saint of the poor and servant of the handicapped'. In the reflection opposite he talks about the L'Arche Community that he founded.

REFLECTION

'Many things happen in our communities. There are crises of all sorts. Some people need good psychological help; some take a long time to find any peace of heart or healing. Some like to work; others hate it. There is joy, there is pain; it is the joy and the pain of living together.

Most of the people we welcome are called to be with us all their lives. A few leave and get married. But the majority are much too severely wounded. Assistants come for periods of one or two years, and more and more are putting their roots down in the community, making a life commitment into the family. This is essential. There are so many people in institutions who are yearning for a network of friendship and community. But there are few people in society willing to climb down the ladder of success and to become a brother or sister to a person with a mental handicap.

Our society sees the world in the form of a ladder: there is top and bottom. We are encouraged to climb that ladder, to seek success, promotion, wealth and power. At L'Arche, in living with our wounded brothers and sisters, we are discovering that to live humanly, it is not that ladder that we should take as a model, but rather to see the world as a body. In a body there are many different parts, each one is important, even the smallest and the weakest.

People with a mental handicap who come to our communities are called to rise up in hope and to discover the beauty of their beings. Those who come to help are called to see what is most beautiful in their own hearts. And thus the body is formed. We discover we are linked together.

And because we are linked together, we learn to forgive each other for we can so easily hurt one another when we live together. We learn to celebrate the fact that we have been called together. Little by little, we become people of joy because we are people of prayer, people of covenant relationship.'

FOR YOUR FOLDERS

▶ Try to explain the meaning of the following words: impairment; disability; handicap.

▶ What is the Roman Catholic view on the marriage of mentally handicapped people?

▶ What problems might face a handicapped married couple? How do you think these problems may be overcome?

▶ 'There are few people willing to climb down the ladder of success and become a brother or sister to a person with a mental handicap.' Explain what you think Jean Vanier is saying.

▶ What are the needs of the people at L'Arche?

▶ What is the inspiration behind L'Arche?

▶ What difficulties do you think people encounter in these communities?

▶ *'The world is a body not a ladder.'* Explain carefully after reading this reflection what this means.

ABORTION

Abortion – a definition

● premature expulsion of the foetus from the womb

● operation to cause this

The law

Following the 1990 Human Fertilization and Embryology Act, abortion is not allowed after the pregnancy has exceeded twenty-four weeks. Abortion is allowed if the physical or mental health of the pregnant woman, or of any existing children, is at risk, of if there is a substantial risk that if the child were born it would be seriously handicapped.

Christian viewpoints

Among and within the different Churches there are many different viewpoints. Abortion is a highly emotional issue as it touches on the key question, when does life begin? The Roman Catholic Church has particularly strong views on abortion, teaching that the human embryo must be treated as a human person from the moment of conception. Roman Catholic teaching therefore rejects all direct abortion. The view among Protestant Churches is that in certain cases direct abortion is morally justifiable. However, all Churches share the view of the sanctity and mystery of life, and the right to life of all human persons, and they all condemn the growing practice in many countries of abortion on grounds of mere convenience.

The Church of England view

The Church of England is against abortion in principle but generally accepts that each case is special. Therefore while abortion should not be generally accepted – certainly not as a method of birth control – it may be permitted in certain cases such as when there is a risk to a woman's life, when conception results from rape and when there is a risk that a baby would be born handicapped.

'We affirm that every human life, created in the divine image, is unique ... and that this holds for each of us, born or yet to be born. We therefore believe that abortion is an evil ... and that abortion on demand would be a very great evil. But we also believe that to withhold compassion is evil, and in circumstances of extreme distress or need, a very great evil ... Christians need to face frankly the fact that in an imperfect world the "right" choice is sometimes the acceptance of the lesser of two evils. '

(Church of England Board for Social Responsibility 1990)

The Roman Catholic view

The long tradition of the Roman Catholic Church has been to recognize the unborn child as a human, a gift of God and worthy of complete respect as a human being with the right to life. The Roman Catholic Church teaches that to kill an unborn child at whatever stage is wrong. Even while very tiny and hardly developed, the embryo or foetus is the beginning of human life, and life is God's gift.

There is a long tradition of condemnation of abortion within the Church, stretching back to a second-century document, *The Didache*, which says, *'You shall not kill by abortion the fruit of the womb.'*

Whatever the reasons advanced for abortion, the Roman Catholic Church teaches that the unborn child should be protected. Abortion should never be used as a means of birth control. In this context it should be noted that several birth control methods are in fact agents of abortion according to the Church, since they prevent the fertilized egg from implanting, or they prevent the growth and development of the fertilized egg in the mother's womb.

VOLUNTARY EUTHANASIA

Euthanasia – a definition

● a gentle and easy death; the bringing about of this especially in cases of incurable and painful disease

---

Voluntary euthanasia is carried out at the request of the person being killed. Despite great advances in medicine, dying can be a painful, long and distressing process. In fact, advanced medical techniques can keep a patient alive for much longer than in the past. Under present laws anyone (doctors included) who helps the sufferer to end their life risks the possibility of being charged with murder or manslaughter.

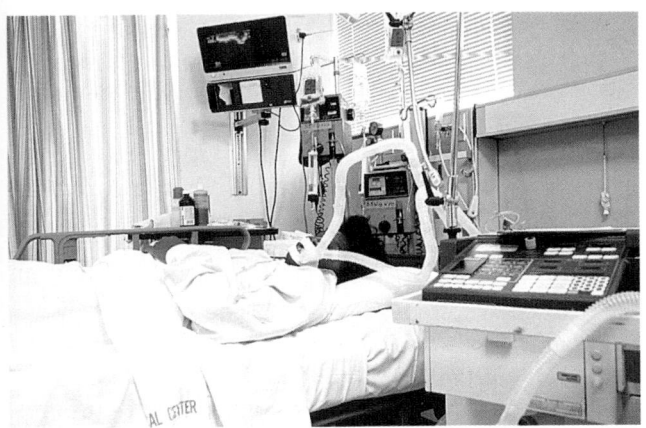

Hospital patient in intensive care

An organization called EXIT (the Voluntary Euthanasia Society) campaigns to change the present law. It believes that a person suffering from an incurable illness should be entitled by law to the mercy of painless death (if, *and only if*, this is their expressed wish). They also believe that doctors should be allowed to help incurable patients to die peacefully at their own request, provided the patient has signed, *at least thirty days previously*, a declaration making their request known.

Christian viewpoints

Generally most Christian Churches do not want to see a change in the law. They look to the teachings in the Bible which stress that human life is sacred and a gift from God. In Ecclesiastes 8:8 in the Old Testament, it says *'no one has power over the day of his death'.*

'Man does not have the right to end his own or another's life for the sake of avoiding possible suffering. We are stewards of our physical life, and God alone can determine when the power to take life shall be given to man.'

(Dr Huw Morgan – GP and Christian)

'The argument for euthanasia will be answered if better methods of caring for the dying are developed. Medical skill in terminal care must be improved, pre-death loneliness must be relieved, patient and family must be supported by the statutory services and by the community. The whole of the patient's need, including the spiritual, must be met.'

(Methodist Church statement 1974)

KEY QUESTION

Is there any difference between 'passive' euthanasia (withholding life-saving treatment and allowing death to occur) and 'active' euthanasia (giving a lethal dose of a drug)?

FOR YOUR FOLDERS

▶ Explain what the following words and phrases mean: abortion; conception; sanctity; euthanasia; voluntary euthanasia; incurable; passive euthanasia; active euthanasia.

▶ Explain in your own words what the law says about abortion and euthanasia.

▶ When does life begin according to the Roman Catholic Church? How does this affect the Church's view on abortion?

▶ What views on abortion do Roman Catholics and other Christians have that are similar?

▶ Explain in your own words the teachings of the Church of England and Roman Catholic Church on abortion. What are your views?

▶ How is EXIT trying to change present laws about euthanasia?

▶ Explain in your own words the viewpoints of Dr Morgan and the Methodist Church.

▶ How do you think some Christians might argue for euthanasia to be legalized? What reasons might they give?

INTRODUCTION

Over recent years astonishing advances have been made by medical science. With doctors and scientists achieving extraordinary power over matters of life and death, new moral dilemmas have been raised. Here are just some of these advances:

Artificial Insemination (husband) (AIH) – a husband's semen (seed) is put into his wife by means of an instrument.

Artificial Insemination (donor) (AID) – similar to AIH but the seed is provided by an anonymous donor and not the husband.

In vitro fertilization for husband and wife (IVF) or 'Test tube babies' – the ovum is withdrawn from the woman and fertilized with a man's semen under laboratory conditions. The embryo is then transferred to the woman's womb.

Egg donation – a woman donates an ovum, which is then fertilized by semen from a donor because both parties are infertile or both carry a genetic defect.

Surrogacy or 'womb-leasing' – a woman bears a child for a wife who cannot become pregnant, and hands the child over after birth.

Scientific research on human embryos – this ranges from the simple study of early embryos, to increasing knowledge of how human embryos develop (for infertility, etc.), to testing new drugs on embryos.

HUMAN FERTILIZATION AND EMBRYOLOGY ACT 1990

In 1990 laws were passed about human fertilization and embryology. These included the following:

- A statutory licensing authority, with substantial non-medical membership, should be set up to regulate those infertility services and research which the report regards as acceptable, including *in vitro* (test-tube) fertilization, semen or egg donation, embryo donation following *in vitro* fertilization, and the use of frozen embryos.
- There should be complete anonymity for donors of semen, eggs or embryos and for couples requiring their services. Both partners should give written consent to treatment. The number of children born to a donor should be limited to ten.

A woman giving birth as a result of egg or embryo donation should be regarded in law as the child's mother, and the donor should have no rights or duties relating to the child.

- Frozen embryos should be stored for a maximum of ten years. Up to ten years, an embryo's parents should have the right to decide on use or disposal; if both die or fail to agree, that right should go to the storage authority.
- Surrogate motherhood 'rent-a-womb' agencies should be outlawed.
- No human embryo should be kept alive outside the womb or used for research beyond fourteen days after fertilization. It should be illegal to transfer to a woman any embryo used for research, or to place a human embryo in the womb of another species.

The Churches' view

The Churches all have traditional teachings on the nature of human life. However, because of new advances in human fertilization, they have had to apply their teachings to modern science. Christians have had to think carefully about the connections – moral rather than scientific – between Christian marriage, sexual intercourse, conception, birth and the nurturing and parenting of children. Attitudes differ between different Churches, there are also different viewpoints *within* each Church.

A Roman Catholic view

'It is because of the concern of the Church to protect the embryo that caution has been expressed about some developments in in vitro fertilization. So that scientists can be sure of fertilizing an egg which will grow successfully when placed in the uterus, usually several eggs are fertilized, creating spare embryos which are either thrown away or used for experimentation. This is in effect killing off human life. While the Church does have sympathy with couples who are not able to have children, it does not consider it legitimate to treat the human embryo as experimental or as disposable material. Life is God's gift and we do not have a right to children. Means to aid birth between husband and wife are considered morally good. However, if this involves a third person (for example, artificial insemination by donor or a surrogate mother) this is not considered ethically acceptable.'

(Roman Catholic statement, 1990)

Anglican views

The quotations below are from *Human Fertilization and Embryology* (1984), the response by the Church of England Board for Social Responsibility to the Warnock report, but the views expressed are not necessarily representative of Anglican thinking.

'The majority of us agree with the [Warnock] Report that "those engaging in AID are, in their own view, involved in a positive affirmation of the family" and hence AID may be regarded as an acceptable practice.' However central records should be kept, no more than ten children should be fathered by one donor, donors should not be permitted to sell their sperm, and at 18 the child should have access to some information about the donor.

The Board said IVF is acceptable in cases of infertility and inheritable disorders.

On surrogate motherhood: *'it violates the dignity of motherhood that a woman should be paid for bearing a child. Strong bonding may take place between a woman and the child she bears in her womb, [with the result that] she is unwilling to give it up [at birth].'* The Board said it should be illegal. In 1988 the General Synod voted in support of *'the proposal to leave all surrogacy arrangements outside the protection of the law'.*

The Board stated: *'we support by a majority the recommendation [of the Warnock report] that research, under licence, be permitted on embryos up to 14 days old'.* General Synod rejected this recommendation.

Methodist view

'The Methodist Church believes that the important question is not how *the sperm fertilizes the egg, but* whose *egg is fertilized by* whose *sperm. On this basis, artificial insemination is acceptable provided the contributors of egg and sperm are the baby's long-term (or 'social') parents. Fertilization with the help of a third party (AID) is not considered desirable. It can provoke distrust between the parents, and severe identity problems for the child, who is unlikely to receive satisfactory answers to such questions as 'Where do I come from?' and 'Who do I really belong to?'*

Artificial insemination by husband (AIH) is acceptable, and has already enabled many couples to have children who would otherwise be childless.'

(Methodist Church statement 1990)

KEY QUESTIONS

When does life begin? Have embryos got rights? Could these modern techniques be exploited for the wrong reasons? Have the donors any rights? Who are the 'real' parents? Should humans interfere in God's creation? Is nature a 'material' given by God for us to experiment with? Do these techniques help family life? Have infertile couples the right to use any modern medical techniques to have children? Is sexual intercourse the only way humans should have children?

FOR YOUR FOLDERS

▶ Explain the following: genetic parents; procreation; AIH; AID; IVF; egg donation; embryo donation; surrogacy; infertility.

▶ Write an article called 'Babies in the front line of medical technology'. List some of the ways that the seven techniques could be misused.

▶ List some of the advantages of the techniques.

▶ Try to explain in your own words the Roman Catholic response. What techniques would the Roman Catholic Church find acceptable?

▶ List the techniques that the Anglican and Methodist Churches do and don't accept. Write a sentence about why each is acceptable or unacceptable to the Churches.

▶ What problems may face the surrogate mother and the parents who commission her?

▶ Discuss the key questions in groups. Write down some of your ideas and thoughts.

A mother in Guatemala mourns the disappearance of her daughter, torn from her by the state police

INTRODUCTION

We only have to look at the television or read the newspapers to find that human rights are being violated every minute of every day. Starving children, innocent victims of war, maimed refugees struggling to survive amidst disease and death, innocent prisoners locked up in filthy cells for doing nothing except speak out against injustice, hungry people living on dirty and dangerous streets, children forced into prostitution, young women raped and tortured by brutal guards, child slaves forced to work sixteen hours a day in terrible conditions – for these people, hell exists here on earth.

Many Christians are concerned about the modern world and about these living hells. In the reflection opposite Father Michael Evans, who works for Amnesty International, explains why Christians should be actively involved in defending, and promoting, justice and human rights.

WORKING FOR HUMAN RIGHTS

Amnesty International works to seek the release of all prisoners of conscience, to abolish the death penalty and obtain fair trials for all political prisoners. **Actions by Christians against Torture (ACT)** campaigns for the abolition of torture. If you want to live in a better world, you can **do something positive** by writing to these organisations and getting involved (see address section on p. 156).

FOR YOUR FOLDERS

▶ Why should Christians be involved in working for human rights according to Father Evans?

▶ What do you think his reflection tells us about Christian involvement in the world?

▶ What do you think he means by the statements and phrases that are in bold type? Explain them in your own words.

REFLECTION

'God created everything good, to exist in the God-centred harmony symbolized by the Garden of Eden. God's fingerprints can be found above all on every human being, and the fundamental dignity and therefore rights of every man, woman and child – no matter how weak, helpless and powerless – flow from humanity's special position as made in the image and likeness of God. Psalm 8 speaks of human beings as made "little less than a god", crowned with glory and honour.

But it is not simply a matter of individuals having dignity and rights. There is more to it than that. Human beings are all members of one single human family, bound up with each other and called together to share the life of their Creator. **The mystery of human solidarity and interdependence is such that whenever one human being is made to suffer, the rest of humanity suffers too and is weakened and threatened**. There is a real sense in which St Paul's image of the Christian community as a single living body is true also of the whole human race. We shed our own blood if we hurt others; torture and oppression are suicidal for humanity; **we allow our own freedom to be whittled away if we sit back while others are deprived of liberty. No one is an island**, and when the bell tolls for the victims of poverty, persecution, torture or oppression, it tolls for all of us. The deep invisible bonds between all human beings everywhere mean that wherever human rights are violated, we ourselves are violated. Because we believe in a God who created and is intimately bound up and involved with his people, there is a sense in which **the violation of human rights is a violation of God**.

In the history of humanity, God has revealed himself as the champion and liberator of the poor and oppressed. God is the One who does justice for the oppressed, the Lord who sets prisoners free, the Lord who lifts up those who are bowed down (Psalm 146).

God is also the One who demands justice, as we can see from the protests of the prophets against oppression. This is a challenge thrown down not only to the rulers of their day, but also to God's people now.

Such care for justice is the minimum requirement of love for one's neighbour, and **it is nonsense to talk of loving others if we do nothing practical to lift them out of their poverty, degradation and oppression**.

God does justice and demands justice. But he is also the One who promises justice. Gradually in the understanding of God's people there emerges the hope of the Anointed One, the Messiah, who will usher in the rule of God, the Kingdom. The coming of this Kingdom will be good news for the poor, the sad, the sick and the oppressed, because it will herald the end of their sufferings. The Messiah will be the one who, anointed with the Spirit, is sent to bring good news to the poor, to bind up hearts that are broken, to proclaim liberty to captives and freedom to those in prison (Isaiah 61).

The ultimate distinctive faith of mainstream Christianity is that Jesus was not only the promised Messiah but actually God in person, made flesh and living among us. This faith in Jesus as a man who is God personally sharing human life, suffering and death gives a new impetus to work for human rights. The Son of God has experienced arrest as a political agitator, and he has been beaten, tortured, humiliated and executed though he had done nothing wrong. **In the person of Jesus Christ, God has become a brother in the human family, the neighbour of every human being**. The Easter power of the Resurrection, breaking the limitations of Jesus' human availability, means that he is now present to everyone everywhere. He is so bound up with every human being that he takes personally whatever is done to anybody else! That is perhaps one meaning of those most disturbing and challenging words of Jesus, that whatever we do for the least of his brothers and sister, we do for Jesus himself, and that whatever we fail to do for them, we fail to do for him (Matthew 25:31ff). This applies in a special way to our commitment to the poor and oppressed with whom Jesus especially identified himself.

Jesus united in an indivisible way our relationship with God and our relationship with the rest of humanity. Our response to God's love will involve praise and worship, but also an active practical love for others, especially those in need. We cannot allow ourselves to "pass by on the other side" when we see human rights being violated, **but we have to be the Good Samaritan, stopping and giving practical help** – perhaps by writing a letter, sending a telegram or signing a petition.'

(Michael Evans – Amnesty International)

73 WORLD POVERTY

THE STATE OF THE WORLD

The richest people of the world (The North)	The poorest people of the world (The South)
● $573 spent on health per person	● Only $2 spent on health per person
● 79% of the population with toilet facilities	● Only 9% of the population with toilet facilities
● 98% of women and 99% of men able to read	● 29% of women and 55% of men able to read
● 18 in every 1000 children die before fifth birthday	● 176 in every 1000 children die before fifth birthday

Facts of death

- **35,000** people die every day as a result of hunger.

- More money is spent on armaments in one day than the world's two billion poorest people have to live on in one year.

- More people have died as a result of hunger in the past six years than have been killed in all wars, revolutions and murders in the past 150 years.

- **If the world's poor held hands they would form a line from the earth to the moon – and back – twice!**

World poverty has many causes, many of them linked – the arms trade, unfair trading conditions, overpopulation, big business interests, superpower struggles, racism, a history of exploitation by Europeans, the complacency of powerful governments, the cycle of debt. Poor countries need cash to develop their economies, so they borrow money from the World Bank and the International Monetary Fund (IMF), who charge huge amounts of interest, and in the long run make matters worse for the countries of the South.

Many Christians are concerned about the injustice and inequality in the world today. Two Christian organizations that work for the world's poor are Christian Aid and the Catholic Agency for Overseas Development (CAFOD). As well as these organizations, many Churches are increasingly speaking out about the evils of world poverty and trying to put pressure on the governments of the rich countries to change their present policies, which they see as self-centred and cruel.

CAFOD

CAFOD operates because it believes in the basic equality of all people in the sight of God. It believes that human dignity demands a reasonable standard of living. CAFOD works to make people aware of the plight of the world's poorest people. It raises money for a number of projects including food production, water supplies, preventive medicine, education, nutrition schemes, etc. It makes links between the continents of Africa, Asia and Latin America, and people in Britain. A CAFOD group in school or parish learns about the problems facing the poor, and they raise funds to support the self-help projects started by CAFOD.

CHRISTIAN AID

Christian Aid works to improve the quality of life of the poor and powerless by *giving them the power to help themselves*. It tries to work in partnership with the poor. It works in over seventy countries with more than 500 major partner organizations including Catholic agencies. As well as working in areas of poverty, Christian Aid also works in areas of emergency where it finances medical supplies, food and blankets, transport and building materials and tries to support, feed and resettle refugees.

Why do Christians become involved in the struggle for justice and equality?

- Christians believe that God loves the world and all that's in it. They believe that God became a human in Jesus and that in a real sense they *meet God in every human being*.
- Christian faith provides the *example of Jesus* and how he mixed with, and showed respect for, the poor and the despised.
- Christian faith provides *teaching on justice*, equality and treating people with compassion and respect.
- Christian faith provides a *vision* of what life could be like if people became less self-centred. They work towards this vision, by helping the world's poor.
- For many Christians, faith is not a private matter, means putting faith into action, in the real world.

Church that is in solidarity with the poor can never be a ealthy Church'

VERPOPULATION

n estimated 2.5 million human beings are born into e world every day. It took the human race 10,000 enerations to reach two billion members, but it is king one generation to explode from two billion to n billion.

Overpopulation will cause enormous problems r humanity. At the centre of the debate on what n be done is the Roman Catholic Church's refusal allow artificial methods of birth control. The hurch argues for a redistribution of wealth, not ntraception. Many other Christians disagree with e ban on contraception, arguing that unless people poor Catholic countries are allowed access to tificial methods of birth control the world is ading for disaster.

TALKING POINT

● *'What is needed is nothing less than a new international economic order so that the rich can no longer dictate to the poor countries the terms on which they will trade with them.'*

(Baptist Church statement)

THINKING POINT

● *'A Church that is in solidarity with the poor can never be a wealthy Church. It must sell all, in a sense, to follow its Master. It must use its wealth and resources for the sake of the least of Christ's brethren.'*

(Archbishop Desmond Tutu)

FOR YOUR FOLDERS

▶ Design a poster called 'The state of the world North and South'. Include in it some reference from the box, Facts of death.

▶ What do you think are the main causes of world poverty?

▶ Explain the work of CAFOD and Christian Aid. What beliefs inspire some Christians to work for justice?

▶ Design a poster called 'Overpopulation – the human race to disaster?' Why is the Roman Catholic Church's teaching on birth control at the centre of the controversy about what should be done? What do you think?

▶ Explain in your own words what Archbishop Desmond Tutu means. Do you think the Christian Churches could do more to rid the world of the evils of mass poverty?

▶ *'What is needed is nothing less than a new international economic order.'* What do you think this means? How do you think we, as individuals, can help make this dream become a reality?

THE 'JUST WAR'

Many Christians believe that there is such a thing as a 'just war'. This is a war which they believe is morally right to fight. For a war to be just, three conditions were laid down in the thirteenth century by St Thomas Aquinas (1225–74). They were:

1 The war must only be started and controlled by the authority of the state or the ruler.
2 There must be a just cause; those attacked are attacked because they deserve it.
3 The war must be fought to promote good or avoid evil. Peace and justice must be restored afterwards.

Later, two other conditions were added:

4 The war must be the last resort; all other possible ways of solving the problem must have been tried out.
5 There must be 'proportionality' in the way the war is fought, e.g. innocent civilians should not be killed. Only enough force to achieve your goals must be used. (It would not be 'proportionate', for example, to bomb a whole village because the enemy was hiding in one house.)

THE 'HOLY WAR'

'Declare a Holy War, call the troops to arms.'

(Joel 3:9)

Holy wars are fought by people who believe either that God is on their side or that they have righteousness on their side. The Crusades were holy wars. They were campaigns against the Turks, in the eleventh and twelfth centuries, to liberate the holy places of Palestine from the Muslims. The Christian Church identified the Muslims with Satan and the Crusades with God. However, from a Muslim point of view their wars were holy too. Often holy wars are very viciously fought wars and the people who fight them are stirred up by their religion.

Holy wars have been fought through the centuries but morally they pose many questions:

● Who really knows what is right?
● Is it right to kill for religion or a set of beliefs?
● How can anyone know that 'God is on their side'?

WAR AND PEACE

In Matthew 24:6,7, Jesus is recorded as saying, *'And you will hear of wars and rumours of wars... this must take place... For nation will rise against nation.'*

In the 2000 years since these words were spoken the history of humanity has all too often been the history of war. The twentieth century has seen the largest and bloodiest wars in history. Millions upon millions of men, women and children have died, and still die today, as a result of war. Millions more have been, and still are, maimed and tortured. As well as shattered bodies there are shattered minds.

In Matthew 5:9, Jesus, in the Beatitudes, says, *'Blessed are the peacemakers: for they shall be called the children of God.'* Peace is very much at the heart of the teachings of Jesus, yet Christians have long been divided about whether it is ever right to go to war, or use violence.

Some believe that there are times when a Christian has no choice but to go to war. This is because they believe that the result of not going to war will be much worse. For example, the German theologian **Dietrich Bonhoeffer** (1906–45), who lived in Nazi Germany, was prepared to take part in an assassination attempt on Adolf Hitler. Although Bonhoeffer was a **pacifist** (someone who is opposed to violence of any kind), he was prepared to sacrifice not only himself but also his principles to try to rid the world of the evils of Nazism. The assassination attempt failed and Bonhoeffer was executed.

WEAPONS OF MASS DESTRUCTION

In the world today there exist weapons of mass destruction: chemical, biological and nuclear. *These weapons are a symptom of a system which accepts violence as a way of attempting to resolve conflicts.* All the Churches condemn the use of such weapons, although some believe that having them acts as a deterrent in preventing war. The Churches also condemn the continued testing of these weapons.

The arms trade is one of the evils of our time

'Though the monstrous power of these weapons act as a deterrent, it is to be feared that the mere continuance of nuclear tests undertaken with war in mind, will have fatal consequences for life on earth. Justice, right reason and humanity therefore, urgently demand that the arms race should cease; that the stockpiles that exist in various countries should be reduced equally ... nuclear weapons should be banned.'

(Roman Catholic teaching, *Pacem in Terris*)

PACIFISM

Some Christians, throughout history, have been *conscientious objectors*, who, because of their Christian conscience refuse to bear arms in military service. Many of these people are *pacifists*: people who are totally opposed to war. Pacifism has been particularly strong amongst the Religious Society of Friends, who have been inspired by the *Peace Testimony*, which they first presented to Charles II in 1660:

'We utterly deny all outward wars and strife, and fighting with outward weapons, for any end, or under any pretence whatever; this is our testimony to the whole world. The Spirit of Christ by which we are guided is not changeable, so as once to command us from a thing as evil, and again to move unto it; and we certainly know, and testify to the world, that the Spirit of Christ, which leads us into all truth, will never move us to fight and war against any man with outward weapons, neither for the kingdom of Christ, nor for the kingdoms of the world.'

THE ARMS TRADE

The *arms trade* is the business in which countries such as the UK, France and the USA sell weapons to other countries and make enormous profits. Many Christians believe that it is evil. The world spends more on arms than anything else, and it is one of the major causes of world poverty. If the money spent on arms was redirected towards peace, world poverty could be eliminated. *When we consider that over the last two years, more people have died from hunger than were killed in both world wars, we begin to realize that peace is more than just the absence of war.* As Dr Martin Luther King wrote: 'True peace is not merely the absence of tension, it is the presence of justice.'

THINKING POINT

● *'We used to wonder where war lived, what it was that made it so vile. And now we realize that we know where it lives, that it is inside ourselves.'*

(Albert Camus, 1923–60 – writer)

REFLECTION

'Peace I leave with you, my peace I give unto you: not as the world giveth, give I unto you. Let not your heart be troubled, neither let it be afraid.'

(John 14:27)

FOR YOUR FOLDERS

▶ In your own words explain what you think the difference is between a 'just war' and a 'holy war'.

▶ Under what sorts of circumstances do you think a Christian would be prepared to go to war?

▶ What is the meaning of the phrase 'conscientious objector'? What do you think makes some Christians refuse to serve in the armed forces?

▶ Imagine you met Dietrich Bonhoeffer. What do you think he would say about war and justice?

▶ Write a paragraph on the beliefs of a pacifist (take into account the Peace Testimony of the Society of Friends).

▶ Why do Christians oppose the testing of nuclear weapons and the arms trade?

▶ What do you think can be done to bring peace in the world? According to Albert Camus where does this process begin? What do you think he means?

Christianity has been, and still is, a missionary religion (see unit 30). In particular it has tried to convert the first peoples of the world – the original inhabitants of the land. Often missionaries have been ignorant of the cultures of the first peoples whom they were trying to convert. The legacy of missionary activity lives on, particularly in Africa and South America as can be seen in the article 'The sword and the cross' below.

Many Christians today accept that in the past the Church has forced people to be baptized as Christians. However, many modern-thinking Christians believe that missionary work should not be about proselytizing (persuading people to join a religious group), but about witness. In the 'dialogue' opposite two monks, Brother David and Brother Thomas, talk to the physicist Fritjof Capra about mission in the modern world.

FOR YOUR FOLDERS

▶ Explain the meaning of the following words and phrases: proselytize; witness; dialogue.

▶ What was missionary work about in the past, according to Brother David?

▶ How do the Missionaries of Charity of Mother Teresa give witness to this faith?

▶ According to Brother David, what is the task of Christian Mission?

▶ What sort of work do the Little Sisters of Jesus do?

▶ After reading the article 'The sword and the cross', explain what you consider to be the legacies of missionary work in Peru.

The sword and the cross

Indian religion has been under attack in Peru for nearly 500 years. The first Indian bishop of the Peruvian Methodist Church, Pablo Mamani Mamani, says: 'The Spanish tried hard to destroy Inca culture and religion. The Church was not interested in anything but our gold and our land. For nearly 300 years the Catholic Church did nothing to help indigenous people. What's worse, they worked hand-in-hand with the conquerors who killed millions of people.'

A Catholic priest was put in charge of administering most Andean villages if a Spaniard could not be found. This allowed many priests and their congregations to acquire both wealth and power; the Church confiscated land from indigenous people and forced them to work the fields without pay.

When the Spanish began to lose power in the early 19th century and Latin American countries were on the verge of independence, church officials asked that land taken illegally from indigenous communities be turned over to the Church. Consequently when the country gained independence in 1824 the Catholic Church became the largest land-owner in Peru.

Today, in Lima, the Church owns most of the worst slums in the down-town area and large tracts of land in the poor *barrios* that ring the city. In Pamplona Alta *barrio*, priests from one Catholic order recently built a wall around their property to prevent poor peasants from the countryside invading. The Dominican Fathers, who own most of the slum housing behind the presidential palace, recently raised rents to $35 a month. (The minimum wage in Peru is $54 a month.)

'For nearly 500 years the churches have worked with governments to preserve the position of the white dominant class,' says Reverend Enrique Minaya, Secretary General of the Evangelical Church of Peru. The Colombus Quincentennial is a time to reflect on the meaning of the Gospel.

Peruvian liberation theologian Gustavo Gutierrez echoes Minaya. He stresses that we must honestly accept what the 'discovery' of the Americas meant for indigenous people.

'We must avoid the tendencies of those who want to hide the immense destruction of indigenous people, their cultures and their ties to the earth,' says Gutierrez.

Lucien Chauvin

Peruvian prayer: a blend of Christianity and tradition

DIALOGUE

David: Missionary work used to be almost about competition, expansion, domination, of masculine emphasis on quantity – how many can we baptize in a hurry?

Fritjof: And what is mission now?

David: It went through an enormous crisis in recent decades. There are very few missionaries today who would try to turn the clock back. Basically *witness* is the key word today, not proselytizing.

Thomas: Witness and dialogue. In other words, our presence among these people and their religions, especially in Asia, is a presence of dialogue.

Fritjof: So the aim of mission is no longer to convert people to Catholicism?

Thomas: No. In fact, it never was. The missionary's aim is to be a witness to the good news of God's universal plan of salvation. 'Conversion' is not something the missionary does; it is uniquely an action of God within the heart of one who realizes, 'This is good news for me!'

David: There are now whole missionary groups who go into places where they will not make converts.

Thomas: One religious order's mission explicitly excludes preaching, converting, baptizing, and that is the Missionaries of Charity of Mother Teresa. Her mission is exclusively the work of love. In other words, she wants her sisters to witness to their faith solely through prayer and the works of love.

Fritjof: What does that mean: 'to witness to their faith'?

Thomas: To make known their faith not only by preaching it, but above all by living it. You see, the difference between witnessing and preaching, with the slight negative overtones that preaching can have, is that witnessing is not projected through my ego. In other words, I am simply present in order to let a great truth shine through me. In the end, I disappear, and the truth shines forth in those to whom I am present.

David: Please know that this is not a cunning way of getting others to sign up as Christians. It is simply a witness to our common humanity. That witness is always needed. Today we are sensitive to the great mistakes missionaries have made in the past and to the great shortcomings of Western colonialism that went hand in hand with mission. But we are apt to close our eyes to the serious shortcomings of many societies to whom the missionaries went. I admire the cultural integrity of those societies. But they were often in bondage to fear, in bondage to systems that kept their human potential suppressed. These are not things one often speaks about today, but, in all fairness, they deserve to be mentioned. In this context, mission means that you give witness to human dignity as Jesus did. Jesus wasn't proselytizing, he was liberating. He gave witness to the dignity of every single human being in the particular setting of his time and place. To do this remains the task of Christian mission.

Fritjof: Now for somebody like Mother Teresa or any of these missionaries who do not preach and do not baptize, what is their purpose in witnessing in Asia or Africa? Why not do it right here?

David: They do it right here, too. They do it everywhere.

Fritjof: And they call themselves 'missionaries' also here?

David: Missionaries means simply 'people who are sent'. According to the Gospels, Jesus sends out his disciples because they are full of enthusiasm for the new life he opens up for them. When you are enthusiastic about some good film that you have seen, you become a sort of missionary among your friends and colleagues.

Fritjof: So why would you be sent to Thailand as a Catholic missionary?

David: You may be sent anyplace where there is oppression, exploitation, human misery. For example, members of a group called the Little Brothers of Jesus and the Little Sisters of Jesus live here in America and in many other parts of the world, in the slums, with the oppressed, the poor. They spread joy, but they have no permission to preach.

Fritjof: So here the idea is not to go to Thailand because they have never heard of Christianity but to go to Thailand if there is a particular oppressive situation and to insert oneself into that situation.

(Fritjof Capra, *Belonging to the Universe*, Penguin Books 1992)

Mother earth is dying

- In the last 25 years serious birth defects have doubled world wide.
- Tropical rainforests half the size of California are being destroyed every year.
- The United Kingdom has more motor vehicles today than it had people in 1871.
- 72 square miles of desert appear on earth every day.
- Nearly half of Britain's scientific research is devoted to war.
- Between 1988–91 British rain became 23 per cent more polluted.
- If today is a typical day we will lose 40 to 100 species – forever.
- One fifth of British power is used up by colour TV viewing and tonight the earth will be a little hotter.

FOR DISCUSSION

▶ 'The earth is at the same time mother. She is mother of all that is natural, mother of all that is human. She is the mother of all, for contained in her are the seeds of all.'

(Hildegard of Brigen)

▶ 'Already the human race has begun to feel the effects of the wounds that we have inflicted on mother earth. We have begun to put our hands in her lanced side and in her crucified hands and feet … Mother earth is dying. Is Mother earth not the most neglected of the suffering voiceless ones today? And along with her, the soil, forests, species, birds and waters are not being heard. Is the human race involved in a matricide that is also ecocide, genocide, suicide and even deicide? Are we being kept in the dark about it by our media, government officials, and educational and religious institutions?'

(Matthew Fox)

Through the work of pressure groups such as Greenpeace, concern for the environment has grown in recent years. Global warming, transport, CFCs, the destruction of forests by acid rain, nuclear accidents, the hole in the ozone layer and polluted seas are just some of the massive problems *we all face*.

CHRISTIAN RESPONSES

In principle the Christian religion has taught that God created the earth and human beings are the responsible *stewards* (or managers) of creation. Human beings should work wisely to protect what has been given to them, to work with nature and not against it. However, people have been – and still are – exploiting nature for greedy economic gain. Today enormous multinational companies make vast sums of money by exploiting the earth's natural resources and they show little concern for the environmental damage that they themselves cause.

Some Christians believe that some of the teaching of the Christian religion have been deliberately abused by greedy people in the pursuit of wealth and power. In particular, they point to the idea that nature only exists to serve humanity and that humanity has some sort of divine right to exploit nature. These ideas have come about by wrongly interpreting the account of creation as recorded in the Book of Genesis. Nowhere in this account is humankind told to *exploit* creation:

> '… and God said unto them, Be fruitful and multiply, and **replenish** the earth'

(Genesis 1:2)

Over recent years the Churches have begun to speak out about the environmental crisis we now find ourselves in.

> 'The universe is a showing faith in God's creative and imaginative will. Its variety of parts is **interdependent**. Men and women are to be stewards and curators, not exploiters, of its resources. Christians must support those working for conservation, and the development of more appropriate, sustainable lifestyles.'

(Methodist Conference statement 1991)

> 'The earth and all life on it is a gift from God given to us to share and develop not to dominate and exploit.'

(Roman Catholic statement 1991)

REFLECTION

'It may require courage to respond to the call to walk in harmony with the Spirit of Life which is present even in decay. We seem to be at the turning point in human history. We can choose life or watch the planet become uninhabitable for our species. Somehow I believe that we will pass through this dark night of our planetary soul to a new period of harmony with the God that is to be found within each of us and that S/He will inspire us to use our skills, our wisdom, our creativity, our love, our faith – even our doubts and fears – to make peace with the planet.'

(Pat Saunders, a Quaker)

KEY QUESTIONS

Shouldn't our increasing power over nature be used responsibly? How can we begin to see the difference between need and greed in our own lives? How can we individually stop Mother earth dying?

Canticle of the Sun

This prayer by St Francis of Assisi gives thanks to God for the beautiful world.

'O most high, almighty Lord God,
    to you belong praise, glory, honour,
    and all blessing!
Praised be my Lord God
    for all his creatures,
    especially for my brother the sun,
    who brings us the day and
    who brings us the light; fair is he
    and shines with a very great splendour;
    O Lord, he signifies you to us!

Praised be my Lord for our sister the moon,
    and for the stars, which he has set
    clear and lovely in heaven.
Praised be my Lord for our brother
    the wind, and for the air and clouds,
    calms and all weather by which you
    uphold life in all creatures.
Praised be my Lord for our sister water,
    who is very serviceable to us and
    humble and precious and clean.
Praised be my Lord for our brother fire,
    through whom you give us light in
    the darkness; and he is bright and
    pleasant and very mighty and strong.
Praised be my Lord for our mother the earth,
    who sustains us and keeps us and
    brings forth various fruits and flowers
    of many colours, and grass.'

FOR YOUR FOLDERS

▶ Design a poster entitled 'Mother earth is dying'.

▶ Explain the meaning of the word 'steward'. What does it mean in relation to the environment?

▶ Why do some people feel that the ideas about creation in the Christian religion have been deliberately abused?

▶ What do you think the Methodist Church means by 'more appropriate sustainable lifestyles'?

▶ Find out the meaning of: interdependent, matricide, ecocide, genocide, suicide and deicide.

▶ What does Pat Saunders mean when she talks about the 'turning point in human history'?

▶ What do you think it means to make 'peace with the planet'? Do you think we are at war with the planet? How do you think peace can be achieved?

SOME IMPORTANT ADDRESSES

Actions by Christians Against Torture
32 Wentworth Hills
Wembley
Middlesex HA9 9SG

Amnesty International
99–119 Rosebury Avenue
London EC1R 4RE

Baptist Union of Great Britain
Baptist House
PO Box 44
129 Broadway
Didcot
Oxon OX11 8RT

CAFOD (Catholic Fund for Overseas Development)
2 Romero Close,
Stockwell Road
London SW9 9TY

Catholic Housing Aid Society
209 Old Marylebone Road
London NW1 5QT

Catholic Truth Society
38/40 Eccleston Square
London SW1V 1PD

The Children's Society
Edward Rudolf House
Margery Street
London WC1X 0JL

Christian Aid
PO Box 100
London SE1 7RT

Christian CND (Campaign for Nuclear Disarmament)
22–24 Underwood Street
London SW9 9TY

Christian Consultative Council for the Welfare of Animals
23 Ravensbourne Road
London SE6 4UU

Christian Ecology Group
c/o Mrs Joan Hart
17 Burns Gardens
Lincoln LN2 4LJ

Church Action on Poverty
Central Buildings
Oldham Street
Manchester M1 1JJ

Community and Race Relations Unit
Council of Churches in Britain and Ireland
Inter-Church House
35–41 Lower Marsh
London SE1 7RL

Lesbian and Gay Christian Movement
Oxford House
Derbyshire Street
London E2 6HG

The Methodist Church
1 Central Buildings
Westminster
London SW1H 9NH

Peace Pledge Union
Dick Sheppard House
6 Endsleigh Street
London WC1H 0DX

Quakers (The Religious Society of Friends)
Friends House
173–177 Euston Road
London NW1 2BJ

The Salvation Army
Territorial Headquarters
101 Queen Victoria Street
London EC4P 4EP

Survival International
11–15 Emerald Street
London WC1N 3QL

The United Reformed Church
86 Tavistock Place
London WC1H 9RT

- State clearly what information you require and why you require it.
- Send one letter from your class, rather than lots of individual letters.
- Always send a stamped, self-addressed envelope.
- For local organizations, use your telephone directory or a reference library.

GLOSSARY

Absolution   pronouncement by a priest of the forgiveness of sins

Adoration   a combination of feeling and action expressing love for God

Advent   'coming'; four weeks before Christmas, observed by Christians as a time of preparation

Agape   Greek word for 'love'

Alb   a long white robe symbolizing purity worn by priests at the Eucharist

Altar   table on raised level surface where the celebration of the Eucharist takes place

Amen   literally 'let it be' said at the end of prayer

Anglican   a person whose church is in full communion with Canterbury

Annunciation   the time when the Angel announced to the Virgin Mary that she would give birth to the Messiah

Apocalypse   literature that describes the end of the world

Apocrypha   'hidden', non-canonical books of the Old Testament

Apostle   literally 'one who is sent'

Ascension   the last appearance of Jesus as he went up (ascended) into heaven

Assumption   taken up, some Christians believe that just as Jesus went to heaven, so they will too

Atonement   the belief that Jesus restored the relationship between God and humankind

Baptism   the rite or sacrament of initiation into the Church

Baptistry   a building or specially built pool for believers' baptism

Base Communities   meetings of ordinary people and priests in South America for study, prayer and planning social action

Beatitude   one of the nine blessings spoken by Jesus in the Sermon on the Mount (Matthew 5:1–12)

Bible   from a Greek word biblia, meaning books; the holy book of Christians

Canon   a list of books in the Bible that have the authority of a religious community

Canonization   process of making somebody a saint

Catechism   a series of questions and answers used for instruction by the Roman Catholic Church

Catholic   'universal'

Chalice   cup used for Holy Communion

Christ   'Anointed One', 'Chosen One', 'Messiah'

Christmas   the festival celebrating Christ's birth

Chrismation   ceremony in the Orthodox Church which takes place after baptism

Church   the whole Christian community; a place where Christians meet

Communion   literally means 'common sharing'

Confession   telling one's sins to a priest and asking for forgiveness

Confirmation   ceremony in which those baptized confirm their faith

Congregation   those who are present, audience or gathering

Consecration   the act of making something holy

Contemplation   the act of thinking deeply; a silent form of prayer or meditation

Creed   a statement of belief

Crucifixion   a form of capital punishment used by the Romans

Deacon/Deaconess   assistants to priests

Dedication   an act which makes a building or a person sacred to God

Denomination   a group of churches with their own individual tradition

Diocese   an administrative area of a Church, controlled by a Bishop

Disciple   someone who followed the teaching of Jesus

Easter   the central Christian festival, celebrating the rising of Jesus from the dead

Ecumenical   'worldwide'; a movement to bring the Churches together

Elder   senior member of the Free Churches

Epiphany   a season in the Christian calendar, celebrating the showings of Jesus as the Son of God (e.g. the worship of the Magi; the baptism of Jesus)

Epistles   letters to be found in the New Testament

Eucharist   service of thanksgiving (also called Holy Communion, Mass, Breaking of the Bread, the Lord's Supper), using bread and wine as the body and blood of Christ

Evangelism   spreading the Christian message

Faith   an inner attitude of belief and trust

Fall, the   the sinful state of humankind; the story of Adam and Eve

Font   a place reserved for the baptism of infants

Fundamentalist   someone who believes in the Bible word for word (literally)

Genuflection   going down on right knee a person enters the Church as a sign of respect to God

Glossolalia   speaking in tongues

Gospels   'good news'; first four books in the New Testament

Grace   the loving help of God

Heretic   somebody who holds a belief against what is accepted by the Church

Holy Spirit   the third person of the Trinity

Holy Week   the week before Easter

Hymn   religious song of the Christian Church which the congregation sings together

Icon   'image' – special picture of Christ, a saint which is used to assist worship

Immaculate conception   conceived without having had sexual intercourse

Incarnation   the act by which God became a human person in Jesus

Infallible   literally 'without error'; usually refers to the authority of the Pope

Inquisition   the brutal persecution of heretics by the Roman Catholic Church, which began in the thirteenth century

Lay/Laity   word used to describe ordinary Christians who are not ordained

Lectern   a stand from which the Bible is read at a religious service

Lent   a season of forty days before Easter

Litany   a series of short prayers to which the congregation responds

Liturgy   from a Greek word meaning 'service'; an act of worship according to rituals that have been laid down by the Church

Martyr   somebody put to death for remaining loyal to his/her faith

Mass   Roman Catholic name for the Eucharist

Matrimony   the sacred act of marriage

Messiah   the anointed or chosen one

Minister   the person in charge of a Free Church

Mission   the particular work for which one believes oneself to have been sent into the world

Moderator   one of the twelve overseers of the United Reformed Church

Monotheistic   belief in one God

Nave   main part of a church from the door to the chancel

Ordination   ceremony by which a person is accepted as a Church leader

Original sin   the sin of Adam (humankind), far deeper than any personal sin, which no one entering the world can escape

Orthodox   the Christian Churches which broke away from Rome

Pacifist   someone who rejects war and violence as a means to solve disputes

Parable   a story with an outer and an inner meaning

Paraclete   Greek word meaning comforter; referring to the Holy Spirit

Parousia   Greek word meaning the Presence or the Return of Christ – the Second Coming

Pater Noster   the Latin words for 'Our Father'

Patriarch   leader of the Orthodox Church

Penance   an act to demonstrate sorrow for one's sins

Pentecost   Jewish festival when the early Christians received the Holy Spirit

Pilgrim   somebody who goes on a religious journey

Pope   the 'Father', title given to the Bishop of Rome, the leader of the Roman Catholic Church

Presbyter   Greek word meaning 'Elder'

Priest   ordained minister authorized to perform religious ceremonies

Pulpit   an elevated stand from where sermons are given

Purgatory   a state between heaven and hell where people are prepared for heaven

Redemption   to obtain freedom; for most Christian salvation is obtained through the death and resurrection of Jesus and/or working to follow his teachings

Redeemer   a saviour, or liberator

Reformation   period in the sixteenth century when a wave of protests marked the beginning of the Protestant Churches, which split from Roman rule.

Resurrection   when Jesus is believed to have risen from the dead

Reverence   a deep love; an awareness of the sacred

Ritual   actions that carry deep meanings

Rosary   a set of prayers honouring the Virgin Mary using a string of beads

Sacrament   an outward visible sign of an inward invisible blessing, obtained through certain rituals

Sacred   the holy; places, people and things touched by the divine power

Salvation   wholeness; the healing of the broken relationship between God and humankind

Sanctification   the process of being made holy

Scripture   the sacred writings of a religion; for Christians this is the Bible

Sermon   talk or message given by a church leader

Shalom   the Hebrew word for peace

Sin   from the Greek *hamartia* – literally means to miss the mark; wrong attitude of self-centredness

Supplication   praying for help

Testament   a special agreement (also called a *covenant*) between God and his creation

Transcendent   a reality that is above, beyond, and yet also within this world

Transfiguration   the glorious change in the appearance of Christ as described in the New Testament

Transubstantiation   a traditional Roman Catholic belief that the bread and wine during the Eucharist mysteriously become the body and blood of Christ

Trinity   the doctrine of one God in three persons; three ways of being God

Vocation   a special call from, or choosing by, God, to do certain types of work

Whitsun   the day when early Christians received the gift of the Holy Spirit (also known as Pentecost)